# Cold Cash,
# Cool Climate

# Cold Cash, Cool Climate

## Science-based Advice for Ecological Entrepreneurs

### Jonathan Koomey, Ph.D.

Analytics Press
PO Box 1545
Burlingame, CA 94011-1545
http://www.analyticspress.com

Analytics Press
PO Box 1545
Burlingame, CA 94011-1545
SAN 253-5602
Internet: http://www.analyticspress.com
email: info@analyticspress.com

ISBN-13: 978-0-97060-193-3 (paperback)

Library of Congress Control Number: 2011961421

Production: BookMatters
Cover design: Chris Hall
Printer and binder: Sheridan Books, Inc.

Text credits:

Figures 2-4, 2-5, 2-6, 2-16, and 3-3 are adapted from graphs
developed by the University of New South Wales Climate Change
Research Centre for their publication titled *The Copenhagen
Diagnosis 2009: Updating the World on the Latest Climate Science*.
Reprinted with permission.

Figures 3-1 and 3-2 are adapted from graphs developed by the
Carbon Mitigation Initiative, Princeton University. Reprinted with
permission.

This book is printed on acid-free recycled paper (30% post-con-
sumer content) in the United States of America.
10   9   8   7   6   5   4   3   2   1

*For Stephen H. Schneider (1945-2010), my colleague, mentor, and friend, as well as one of the inspirations for this book.*

# TABLE OF CONTENTS

# FOREWORD

*Saul Griffith, Ph.D.,*
*Other Lab, San Francisco, CA*

Climate change, energy independence, and sustainability: all of these things are rightly getting more attention than ever before. They are complex global problems requiring not one, but thousands, of solutions. Some solutions require mandates, some rely on politics, some need technology, and some hinge on behavioral change. All of the solutions will require entrepreneurs – stubborn, fast-moving, single-minded, goal-oriented individuals, either in the private or public sector. Without these entrepreneurs pushing boundaries and the speed of deployment, uptake of these solutions will be too slow to avert the worst consequences of these global challenges. This book is a motivational treatise that pushes the green entrepreneur of the future to fulfill this important role.

More than that, this book is about the scientific knowledge that helps define the character and limitations of these solutions. If we are to leave a livable world (and hopefully a vital and vibrant world) for our children and grand-children, the scale of what needs to happen this century is daunting. Achieving even a mildly ambitious outcome of stabilizing the climate at 450 parts per million (ppm) of $CO_2$ equivalent will mean the world of our future will look very different from today. Our transportation systems, heating and cooling systems, built environment and architecture, food systems, and even health-care and education systems will all need to change – some a little, most a lot. Lots of people are scared of change, but the true entrepreneur embraces it. This is the green entrepreneur's century.

Back in 2007, I was bedridden with chicken pox. Like most entrepreneurs, I don't take to idleness very well, so I set myself a task: measure every measurable impact of my lifestyle in terms of energy. I was already a 'Green Entrepreneur' – the CEO of a venture-financed, utility-scale wind energy startup – and generally someone that people would look at as a model citizen when it comes to the environment and combating climate change. I was (mostly) a bicycle commuter; I was working on audacious new energy technologies.

What I learned shocked me. Although I thought I was a model citizen of the new cleaner world, I found that my lifestyle was consuming double or more the amount of energy that the average American was, and more than ten times that of the average Chinese citizen! Measuring everything that I did, quite literally down to my use of aluminum foil for cooking and the choice of textiles that I wore (as well as the more obvious things like miles travelled and electricity consumption), I realized that we now live in an age of consequence. It is possible to measure everything that you do – and its environmental impact. Whether you care about water, energy, carbon, or habitat destruction, we can now infer or estimate the impact of any purchasing decision on any of those outcomes. This exercise also made me furious with the often misleading reporting on new 'green' products and technologies. I became an angry young man again.

Being angry doesn't help much though, whereas being an entrepreneur does. It's been a few years since I had my wake-up call. People typically believe that the future for their children will be better, brighter, cleaner, and more wonderful than the past. That's our challenge right now. We have to figure out how to make the future better than the past, while meeting the implied demands of the science of climate change. I no longer get angry about poorly written press releases and green-washing. In fact, they're probably useful in that they socialize the idea of a cleaner and greener future, while the entrepreneurs who do the math and have the analytical rigor create the truly revolutionary products consumers are increasingly starting to demand.

I'm personally dedicated to creating these new products and services and bringing them to market. I have to acknowledge, however, that we need lots of entrepreneurs, working on lots of things, so that all of our contributions will add up to the kind of future that we want to live in – one that will be more wonderful than the past. It means that we'll need to develop new sources of energy, and that there are thousands of technologies, solutions, and great companies to be built in the trillion-dollar energy generation game. There are even more technologies, solutions and great companies to be built in the consumer space. Here's the trick: think of any product or service that you use today, whether it be how you get your milk, how you heat your home, or how you get your music. Figure out a way to deliver that product or service at one-half,

or even better, one-tenth the amount of energy/water/habitat destruction/tox-
icity, and you likely have yourself a multi-million or multi-billion dollar product or service. This is why this book will be a great guide for the entrepreneurs
of this century, and why Koomey's treatment of the subject matter provides a
great handle for the time-strapped entrepreneur.

There is a huge amount of science and engineering and math that the entrepreneur of the future would like to know, but in some sense we can reduce the
problem to a few handy pieces of technically grounded practical advice. In the
sections that follow, I include the equations for the technically minded reader,
but you can just jump straight to the summaries that immediately follow those
if you prefer.

## REGARDING TRAVEL OF ANY KIND

In high school, we learn mechanics in the Newtonian world, but in reality,
almost any time we move, we do so through a fluid, usually air or water. Thus,
for almost any transportation the power $P$ required to move an object is given
(roughly) by

$$P = \frac{1}{2}\rho A C_d v^2$$

where $\rho$ is the density of the fluid (usually air or water), $A$ is the frontal area
of the moving body, $C_d$ is drag coefficient, which is determined by the shape,
and $v$ is the velocity of movement. Colloquially speaking, this means to
design any product or service that has to move with a lower power or
energy requirement:

- *Decrease $A$.* Make it small and long.
- *Decrease $C_d$.* Make it aerodynamic, or 'fish-shaped'.
- *Decrease $v^2$.* Travel slowly.

This means that a really big, fast, low-energy super car is never going to
exist, despite the attractiveness of the idea. Beautiful designed cars that recognize the constraints of the physics above could be far more efficient, and more
of a pleasure to drive (or be robotically driven in). For short trips we will do
even better by not driving at all, and by utilizing modern electric drive trains
in lightweight personal vehicles.

## REGARDING THE HEATING OR COOLING OF ANYTHING

The power P required to heat or cool any object is given by

$$P = -kA\frac{\Delta T}{\Delta x}$$

where k is the object's thermal conductivity, A is the cross-sectional area between hot and cold, $\Delta T$ is the temperature difference, and $\Delta x$ is the distance between hot and cold. As above, this equation implies that to make more efficient transfers of heat, we must

- *Decrease k.* Insulate well.
- *Increase $\Delta x$.* Use thick walls.
- *Decrease A.* Small is beautiful.
- *Decrease $\Delta T$.* Heat or cool only as much as necessary.


## REGARDING THE MANUFACTURING OF ANYTHING

The average power requirement over the life of a product is given by

$$P_{lifetime} = \frac{E_{manufacture}}{T_{lifetime}}$$

where:

$$E_{manufacture} = M_{massofobject} \times E_{embodied}$$

And $E_{embodied}$ is the energy content of the material of which a device is constructed.

What this says is we must:

- *Decrease $M_{massofobject}$.* Make it weigh less.
- *Decrease $E_{embodied}$.* Use materials with lower embodied energy (e.g. substitute wood for aluminum).
- *Increase $T_{lifetime}$.* Making objects that last much longer, perhaps with service and repair-based business models, will have the biggest effect.

## REGARDING THE DESIGN OF ELECTRONICS

Power consumption in electronic devices is generally given by

$$P = I^2 \times R$$

where $I$ = current and $R$ = resistance.

This equation implies that lowering resistance, voltage, and current will reduce the power needed to accomplish a task. For electrical devices:

- reduce the current (I) by improving efficiency and redesigning the task
- make the wires bigger (reduces R)

## HARNESSING THE POWER OF INFORMATION

Of course, the most important new tool we have in our toolbox is information. Wherever possible, use information technology to eliminate wasteful energy use. Examples abound: Replacing flights or driving by teleconferencing is a huge win for the environment. Using information to match needs with wants, such as ZipCar or City CarShare, eliminates the need for ownership of energy-intensive items. Using information technology such as Netflix, the Kindle, or the Apple iPad eliminates the physical delivery of goods.

## A CALL FOR PROMPT ACTION

The battle is not over once we have pioneered newer, more ecological technologies. We must still overcome the political, cultural and economic barriers to get people to adopt the low-carbon options really fast. With these challenges, the imperative of this book is more apt than ever: we need entrepreneurs to lead the decarbonization of our lives now, and to make it happen pronto! I hope this book serves as a call to action for the next generation to capitalize on this age of consequence, building an awesome future harmonious with our understanding of how our home planet works.

# PREFACE

Books on climate solutions generally fall into one of two categories: hard-core technical books and readable but imprecise popular tomes. My goal for this book is a bit different: to summarize the knowledge and experience of a seasoned energy scientist in a way that will be useful and interesting to a mostly lay audience of entrepreneurs. That means I won't address all the nooks and crannies of the climate science debate, and I'll use my judgment as to which of the various solution areas to emphasize.

Of necessity, that implies that I'll surely offend somebody—that's the nature of giving advice to entrepreneurs, who don't have time for the niceties. If your pet technology is gored in the process, please forgive me in advance (or email me and try to convince me I'm wrong—I promise a fair hearing to well-reasoned arguments). I do, of course, give references galore (in endnotes so they don't get in the way of the narrative) and I will explain my reasoning along the way, but none of us have time to waste on technologies that won't result in rapid reductions in greenhouse gas (GHG) emissions soon.

We're already committed to some degree of warming from our past emissions of greenhouse gases, and as the current presidential science advisor John Holdren has said for years, our choices for response are threefold: mitigation, adaptation, and suffering. The world will do some of each of these in coming decades, but how much of each we do is up to us.

I focus on opportunities for mitigation because adaptation is hard to do well unless you know what's going to happen, and the current path we're on is likely to be so disruptive that we are going to have a hard time adapting fast enough. In addition, ecosystems can't adapt as rapidly as we're currently changing the climate, and there's little we can do for them except mitigate as rapidly as we can. Suffering, of course, is what remains if we fail.

The focus of this book is on the implications of the climate problem for entrepreneurs looking for opportunities, focusing on the essentials that (in my opinion) are what you need to know about this issue to be conversant and effective. In the process, I've systematically ignored the mostly manufactured controversies over the climate science, except where describing them can illustrate some important point about how we're going to get out of this mess. And I've focused exclusively on opportunities in mitigation (as opposed to adaptation), for the reasons listed above.

 I've also chosen to not go into great detail about uncertainties, as many technical studies of this problem do. I made this choice for two reasons:

1) While detailed uncertainty analysis is useful for sophisticated policy makers, it just confuses the issue and muddies the message for most folks. This may distress my technical colleagues, but it's really true, and for my audience clarity about the scientific community's best estimates is more important than detailed assessment of uncertainty. I bring up the issue when discussing climate sensitivity and elsewhere when it yields some business-relevant insight, but I don't dwell heavily on it. To paraphrase Andy Revkin: Scientists view uncertainty as data, but ordinary folks view it as a reason to doubt what someone is telling them.

2) Adopting the evolutionary approach I advocate makes the need for extensive up-front uncertainty analysis less pressing. Instead, the focus is on learning by doing, applying economics to assess cost-effectiveness of alternative options for reaching some warming limit, trying lots of options, failing fast, then doing more of what works and less of what doesn't. While uncertainty analysis would be useful for evaluating near-term technology, policy, and business choices, the need for it for the long term is less important than when using more conventional approaches.

If you are a climate scientist or technology researcher reading this book, please keep this explicit choice in mind and remember that the audience for this book is primarily not the scientific community or sophisticated policy-makers, but entrepreneurs looking for opportunities to start companies. They don't need to know all those details, although they can clearly benefit from some lessons of detailed uncertainty analysis, and I bring those into the narrative where I think it would be helpful.

One final point: this book is not about the mechanics of creating a successful startup company—if that's what you seek, check out Guy Kawasaki's *The Art of the Start* for an introduction.[1] You should also read Brenda Laurel's quirky but inspiring book titled *Utopian Entrepreneur*,[2] which deals with Laurel's experiences starting for-profit companies with a public goods component to their mission.

## HOW TO USE THIS BOOK

I've written this book for entrepreneurs, but recognize that others will find the narrative useful, as it distills many years of energy modeling and data analysis experience into a readable and concise form. I wrote it to be read straight through. I've included references as endnotes so they don't disrupt the narrative flow, but they are there for those who want to delve into more depth. In general, I've avoided citing popular treatments in favor of primary material (like refereed journal articles, books, and technical reports), although you will find the occasional blog post or newspaper article in the notes. This preference for primary sources makes the text helpful for students and others who really want to understand the supporting material. It is also consonant with my goal of making this book one that truly advances understanding of climate solutions, while also serving its main audience of entrepreneurs and investors.

## THE STRUCTURE OF THE BOOK

The book focuses on the concerns of entrepreneurs creating products that reduce emissions and also improve people's lives. In each of the chapters below I take the perspective of a scientific advisor to your company and describe the key information I think you need to know to be successful in this space. The focus is on advice for business, not on technical subtleties, but those interested in the technical issues can benefit by delving into the endnotes.

Chapter 1 describes the nature of the climate problem, explains why I think it's fertile ground for entrepreneurial innovation, and explores why it's not amenable to a simple technical fix.

Chapter 2 explains the climate consequences of current trends, based on a recent MIT projection that is extraordinarily comprehensive in its treatment of the problem. It describes the main contributors to warming, both historically and projected over the next century.

Chapter 3 presents an alternative way of thinking about the future, based on "working forward toward a goal", in this case a warming limit of no more than 2 Celsius degrees above preindustrial levels. It also defines greenhouse gas emissions for a "Safer Climate" case that meets that constraint.

Chapter 4 argues that the limitations of conventional forecasting models present a challenge to the use of benefit-cost analysis for the climate problem. These models are unable to accurately predict the future of technological and economic systems, and so researchers need to find ways to learn about the future that are less dependent on the accuracy of such models.

Chapter 5 assesses the scope of the challenge in terms of the rate of emissions reductions required in the Safer Climate case, and shows that we'll probably need to scrap some capital in the energy sector to keep global temperatures from warming more than 2 Celsius degrees. It also argues that entrepreneurs can accelerate the turnover of capital by making products that are simply better than what they replace, thus encouraging consumers to retire old capital earlier than expected.

Chapter 6 presents tools for identifying and evaluating opportunities for emissions reductions, combining the "working forward toward a goal" approach with the power of whole systems integrated design. It also lists important resources and insights relevant to that challenge.

Chapter 7 lists resources to help in addressing the concerns of investors skeptical about the climate issue, and delves into some of the reasons why people deny the reality of the climate problem. It also explores the importance of property rights and governance, as well as the appropriate role of government, topics that in my view are too often ignored in these discussions.

Chapter 8 explains why I think optimism is the right stance to adopt in the face of this daunting problem.

Chapter 9 summarizes in a compact form what I've learned in the process of writing this book.

## CONTACTING ME

I encourage readers to contact me with their comments, ideas, and thoughts about how the book could be improved. I'm also interested to hear more about specific examples that illustrate key points, as I'm already thinking ahead to the second edition. I'm particularly interested in applications of ultra-low-power mobile computing, sensing, control, and communication technologies, but anything that drastically reduces greenhouse gas emissions while reducing costs will no doubt pique my interest. You can contact me via my web site: http://www.koomey.com.

# ACKNOWLEDGEMENTS

In the course of writing this book, many friends and colleagues have aided my research.

I'm especially grateful to a handful of colleagues who shared their deep understanding of climate issues with me as part of their reviews of this book as it evolved. Danny Cullenward of Stanford, Stephen DeCanio of UC Santa Barbara, Rebecca Ghanadan of E3, Stacy Jackson of the Energy and Resources Group, and Jim McMahon of Lawrence Berkeley National Laboratory all gave helpful comments on drafts of the text at various stages of its creation. Frances Moore of Stanford dutifully answered more than her share of queries about adaptation and related literature, and she also has my gratitude.

Mort Webster and Andrei Sokolov at MIT endured my endless queries about their scenarios with remarkable patience. I hope I did their work justice.

My brother, Chris Koomey, encouraged me at an early stage to focus on identifying and evaluating entrepreneurial opportunities, and he was quite correct in that judgment. My dad, Richard Koomey, supported the idea for this book from the very beginning.

Greg Ness, Jim Trout, Jason Green, Jen Fraser, and Jeff Rose of Vantage Data Centers all helped me understand their collaborative model better, and for that they have my thanks.

Others supplied data, references, ideas, and explanations of key issues, including Hashem Ackbari, Sam Borgeson, Ken Brill, Kurt Brown, Rich Brown, Erik Brynjolfsson, Johanna Buurman, Ken Caldeira, Chris Calwell, Vicki Calwell, Ralph Cavanagh, Rob Collier, Napier Collyns, John Cook, Peter Crane, Mark Delucchi, Rick Diamond, Paul Ehrlich, Chris Ertel, Andrew Fanara, Jon Foley, David Fridley, Ashok Gadgil, Michel Gelobter, Brad Gentry, Nate Glasgow, Peter Gleick, Peter Goldmark, Hartmut Grassl, Steve Greenberg, Arnulf Grübler, James Handley, John Harte, Ephraim Heller, Tom

Heller, Peter Hennicke, John Holdren, Adrian Horotan, Holmes Hummel, Emily Humphreys, Roland Hwang, Mark Jacobson, Dan Kammen, Dina Kruger, Fred Krupp, Skip Laitner, Dan Lashof, Matt Lecar, Mark Levine, Marc O Litt, Tod Loofbourrow, Diane Loviglio, Amory Lovins, Chris Marnay, Eric Masanet, Gil Masters, Alan Meier, Malte Meishausen, Evan Mills, Amey Moot, Mark Morland, Nebojsa (Naki) Nakicenovic, Greg Nemet, Erica Newman, Brian O'Neill, Michael Oppenheimer, Rick Piltz, Lynn Price, Keywan Riahi, Andy Revkin, Hans-Holger Rogner, Joe Romm, Terry L. Root, Art Rosenfeld, Stephane de la Rue du Can, Jayant Sathaye, Irene Scher, (the late, great) Lee Schipper, Katja Schumacher, Geoff Sharples, Elton Sherwin, Jonathan Sinton, Lene Sorensen, Mary Starhill, Philip Starhill, Rob Swart, Jim Sweeney, Mike Ting, Michael Totten, Bill Weihl, John Weyant, Tom Wigley, Ernst Worrell, and Chris Yang.

I'm indebted to my friend and colleague Florentin Krause, who introduced me to much of what I now know about climate mitigation. I hope this book makes him proud.

I was delighted when Saul Griffith volunteered to write the foreword after a brief conversation about the book. He was immediately enthusiastic, and his foreword captures the spirit of what I tried to accomplish in the main text.

Zachary Schmidt at UC Berkeley diligently compiled the data on oil & gas, coal, and tobacco company revenues, and conducted analysis of comments on Paul Krugman's op-eds about climate issues, and for all that good data analysis he has my thanks.

Chris Hall deserves great credit for the classic cover, Dave Peattie and Bea Hartman of BookMatters are responsible for the lovely interior design and meticulous typesetting, and Heidi Fuchs did rapid and precise copyediting. All have my gratitude for their careful work.

Finally, my wonderful wife Melissa endured the creation of this book with patience and good humor, and for that (and many other reasons) she has my gratitude and love. My sons, Gregory and Nicholas, don't know what patience means yet, but they will appreciate having more time with Daddy now that the book is out in the wild.

I alone am of course responsible for the content of the book and any errors contained herein.

*–Jonathan Koomey, January 2012*

|

---

# INTRODUCTION

---

*"The problem of our time is how to preserve the familiar without destroying the future."* —MARC O LITT

Humans are no longer small compared to the earth. Because of our numbers, our wealth, and most importantly our technology, we are able to affect the earth's life-support systems in irreversible ways.

With the advent of nuclear weapons, this truth became crystal clear in the mid-twentieth century, but other evidence showed up as well. Population swelled fourfold from 1900 to 2000[1] (after only growing 60% in the preceding century), reaching about 7 billion by the end of 2010[2]. World gross domestic product (GDP) grew more than eighteen-fold in inflation-adjusted terms from 1900 to 2000,[3] and by 2009 totaled more than US$50 trillion (2009 $).[4] We're becoming more powerful, more numerous, and vastly more wealthy than at any time in human history.

These trends have caused measurable changes in global, regional, and local ecosystems.[5] By the year 2000, 90% of the big fish had disappeared from the oceans,[6] the result mostly of ever-more efficient fishing techniques. Widespread land-use changes and incipient climate change have led to a rate of species extinction that "far exceeds anything in the fossil record".[7] Ocean phytoplankton levels are 40% below where they were in the mid-twentieth century.[8] Global mercury deposition has increased roughly threefold since preindustrial times[9], about 90% of current mercury emissions come from either mining operations or combustion of fossil fuels (mainly coal) in power plants,[10] and methylmercury has spread throughout the food chain, with significant and unpleasant consequences for humans[11] and wildlife.[12] Hormone-disrupting chemicals have become widespread and are beginning to affect the fertility and development of organisms in a measurable way.[13] Plastics are now found throughout the food chain, wreaking havoc with marine wildlife and in some cases raising human health issues.[14] About one-third of the tropical rainforests and woodlands existing in 1700 have been converted to other uses.[15] And rates of change in some aggregate indicators appear to have accelerated in the 20th century, tracking the increasing growth in population, which took 125 years to double from 1800 to 1925, but only half a century to double again.[16]

In addition, the effects of burning billions of tons of fossil fuels have now become manifest in the increasing concentrations of greenhouse gases (GHGs) in the atmosphere. GHGs increase global temperatures, and any reasonable combination of growth trends in population, economic activity and energy use in the next century will move the earth well outside of the comfortable climatic range in which the human species evolved. The result of these trends, if unchecked, will be significant and irreversible damage to both the economy and the environment, putting millions of lives at risk and threatening the continued orderly development of human civilization.

This book presumes that you accept the results of increasing GHG emissions described in the last paragraph. If you don't believe those results then I refer you to the resources in Chapter 7, where I address the concerns of climate skeptics from the perspective of an entrepreneur trying to convince a skeptical investor. But this book isn't about defending climate science. That knowledge, developed over more than 150 years, is based on some of the most well-established principles in physical science, and others have done a superb job of describing what the peer-reviewed literature says on the topic.[17]

I and others have also written technical books and papers discussing and comparing climate *solutions* in minute detail, but this book really isn't mainly about such sophisticated comparisons either. Instead, it contains the advice I would give you if I were a scientific advisor to your startup company, summarizing my best judgments for those who have real money on the line. It is focused on finding opportunities and designing successful solutions, a process that can be daunting to the uninitiated and difficult even for trained analysts. Finally, it describes how our scientific knowledge about climate science and solutions can and should inform people who want to solve this problem and make a profit in the bargain. I hope my experience will be valuable for those who yearn to make a difference on one of humanity's biggest twenty-first century challenges.

## WHY FOCUS ON ENTREPRENEURS?

One week after I arrived at the Yale School of Forestry and Environmental Studies as a visiting professor in Fall 2009, I had the pleasure of chatting with Sir Peter Crane, the school's new dean. He had just arrived a few weeks before, so he, too, was getting acclimated to his new surroundings.

We talked about the difficulties in getting institutions (universities, large companies, government) to make fundamental changes, and he had a particularly nice way of framing the problem. "It's the burden of history," he said, by which I took him to mean that institutions evolve over time, but the path each institution takes constrains the rate and scope of change that is possible in the future. The characteristics and limitations of the people who populate these institutions is also in part a function of history. In other words, these systems are *path dependent*.

Institutions are fundamentally conservative places. Academia promotes individual and disciplinary research, a reward system that can be antithetical to team-based interdisciplinary problem-solving and integrated whole system design. Big business and government bureaucracies generally reward participants for small incremental changes (or no changes at all). Only in exceptional times of crisis or in special organizations do human institutions embrace rapid changes. But if we are to stabilize the earth's climate, it is rapid change that we need, and not just rapid technological change. We also need people and institutions to alter their behavior, and to do so in short order.

So where to turn for rapid innovation? In my experience, the people most comfortable with rapid change and least tolerant of fossilized thinking are those who carry the entrepreneurial spirit. Their whole purpose in life is to intensify and encourage what the economist Joseph Schumpeter called "creative destruction", and they are famously scornful of the phrase "it can't be done".

The entrepreneurial spirit can be found anywhere there are creative people: in startups and large companies, in non-profit organizations and government agencies, in foundations and research labs. I hope this book will encourage these innovators to turn their attention to facing the climate challenge, because we need them now more than ever.

## PROFITS ARE GOOD

A powerful lesson from both evolution and business is that self-replicating activities have to be rewarding. If we're to create a low-pollution economy, we'll need to make people's lives better in the bargain, offering new technologies that are simply better than what they replace. New products can't just be less polluting; they have to be fun, exciting, and profitable for business to produce.

Many in the environmental community do not yet understand this lesson and have an antipathy toward business that is at best counterproductive (I won't name names, but you know who you are). And business folks often caricature environmentalists as crazy tree huggers or worse (I won't name names here either, but you also know who you are).

In fact, both groups need each other. Business needs environmentalists to alert them when they stray too far toward activities that are bad for their customers and society as a whole. And environmentalists need business if they ever hope to have the wide acceptance of technologies, ideas and practices essential for building a sustainable world.

If we subvert all environmental concerns to promote economic growth, we will soon undermine the environmental foundations of that growth, making catastrophic disruption of human society increasingly likely. If, on the other hand, we resort to overly restrictive anti-pollution laws that stifle innovation, the result will be the opposite of what environmentalists intend—a backlash against those regulations and a halt to progress in reducing emissions.[18]

The world can afford neither of these outcomes. Instead, we need to find paths in between these two extremes that result in a smooth transition to a low-pollution world. And that's what I hope you, the entrepreneur, can help us do. It's my job to help you do that as effectively as I can.

## IT'S SPUTNIK, NOT APOLLO

I talked with Stephen Strauss, a science journalist for the Canadian Broadcasting Corporation, in September 2009. He told me about a conference he had recently attended about space-based solar power systems, which are orbiting satellites that collect solar power from massive arrays of photovoltaic cells and then beam it to earth.

"Why are so many people focused on this exotic and very expensive technology?" he wondered. I pondered this for a moment. This option couldn't really be ready to make a significant difference in global power production for at least a decade, probably longer, and would by the advocates' own studies cost ten times as much as conventional power sources. It occurred to me that the people arguing for this option are yearning for a simple, technically elegant, large-scale fix to the climate problem. The reasoning goes something like this: "If only there were some kind of Manhattan project (or Apollo project) where we could invest a lot of money, then we could fix this big problem without struggling with difficult social and institutional problems." It's the same impulse that leads people to advocate geoengineering[19] and other exotic climate "solutions".

Unfortunately, the climate crisis is so complex and so intertwined with human society that it is simply not amenable to an overarching quick-fix solution. We'll need coordination and innovation on an unprecedented scale, and significant changes in virtually every part of the economy. So we don't need another Manhattan project, we need something more akin to the broad societal mobilization in the US after the USSR launched Sputnik, with massive funding increases for science and engineering education as well as for research and development efforts of all types.[20]

The nature of the climate problem is such that we can't predict with precision what combination of solutions would allow us to stabilize long-term global temperatures, because many of the actions needed to achieve this goal will occur decades in the future. So it is ultimately futile to try to create an all-encompassing elegant solution because we really don't know and can't predict how the pieces will fit together—we'll need to try a lot of options, fail fast, and learn quickly. This is why calls for a new Apollo project will fail to bring the rate and scope of change we need, even if significant resources were made available for that effort.

Instead, we need to bias our immediate technology choices to those that allow us to learn quickly what works and what doesn't. Promising technologies that can't make a difference for decades should be the subject of extensive R&D efforts, but *the bulk of our resources should be focused on near-term emissions reductions, both because such reductions are urgent and because that experimentation will tell us which paths before us are likely to be the most promising ones.*

Opportunities for business ventures abound in such an experimental environment, which is one reason why entrepreneurial focus on this issue is so critical. This approach diversifies our investments and so is less risky to implement because it relies on many smaller actions, any one of which can fail and not imperil the whole enterprise. It's also the one that is appropriate for the evolutionary, path dependent world in which we live.

## PATH DEPENDENCE, VALUES, AND CHOICES

When I say that the world is "path dependent" I mean that our choices now affect our options later. We choose the paths we follow, and those choices create opportunities and foreclose other possibilities, just like in day-to-day life.

If you choose to go to college you'll have options for jobs that won't be possible if you don't. Same for grad school. And if you choose to start a business instead of pursuing further education, you'll have other options that won't be available to academics, because your experience and knowledge will be different than theirs.

The funny thing about choices, though, is that they inevitably involve values. We get to envision the world we want to create, but to imagine that world requires answering questions like "how we want our lives to be?" and "what kind of world do we want?" So creating a low-carbon world isn't just a technical question, although many folks mistakenly think it is.[21]

Those in business usually don't make that mistake, because successfully selling products means you know something about how your customers want their lives to be. The situation is a bit more complicated when thinking about outcomes for society, but a world that's economically vibrant but with far less pollution than today is a product that should be easy to sell. And that's one of the motivations for this book.

## SO YOU WANT TO SOLVE THE CLIMATE PROBLEM . . .

If you've read this far, you're either working on a new climate-related business venture or thinking about it. So why is this a fertile area for new ventures, anyhow? I boil it down to three things: it's big, it's urgent, and it's widely misunderstood.

### It's big

The changes needed to solve this problem are so pervasive that opportunities abound. To achieve climate stabilization, all parts of the economy will need to be examined, evaluated, and re-engineered to wring every last gram of emissions from the system. That doesn't just mean the energy system, it means every process by which we wrest value from the universe, which is why the opportunities are so vast.

### It's urgent

There's real urgency to this problem, but you'd never know it from the US public debate on the topic. As I'll discuss later in the book, climate change is driven by cumulative emissions of greenhouse gases. That means that it's not just annual emissions that matter—our actions up until now constrain the possibilities, and acting sooner is cheaper than "wait and see".

To keep the earth's average temperature within comfortable limits we'll need to turn emissions downwards this decade and rapidly reduce them in absolute terms over the next 40 years, in spite of increases in GDP, population, and other important economic drivers. That won't be easy, and waiting will increase the costs of taking action (according to the International Energy Agency, every year of delay will add another $500B to the costs of solving the problem from 2010 to 2030).[22]

Our competitors in Europe and Asia recognize the reality of the climate problem and are racing to invest in the industries of the future, by some measures outpacing us handily.[23] If we don't get with the program, we'll be left far behind as the world retools for a low carbon world. It need not work out that way, as the US still has many entrepreneurial advantages, but if we don't change our direction soon, our competitors will eat our collective lunch.

### It's misunderstood

Due in part to an extraordinary propaganda campaign funded by the fossil fuel industry,[24] misconceptions about climate abound. Most folks on the right think that this is all an elaborate hoax perpetuated by a cabal of scientists all in it for the money, that reducing emissions will be horrendously expensive, and that there are few options available to us (even if climate were a problem). Most folks in the political center have no idea just how many changes will be required if we're to preserve anything close to the world we grew up in. Many folks on the left think the climate problem can be solved by requiring industry to fix it or by simple personal actions like recycling. And the pessimists among us think this problem will be impossible to fix at all, so we're doomed to destroy the world (they always have been sourpusses, and there's nothing we can do to change *that*).

None of these views is remotely accurate, but that means opportunity. When people misperceive reality on a vast scale, it creates an opening for clear-minded entrepreneurs to change the world. The most important misconception relates to humanity's options for mitigation. They are many and varied, and not horrendously expensive. Current technology already gives us the ability to substantially reduce emissions at modest costs (or even at a profit), so it's not just a question of inventing our way out of the problem (although we will need new technologies and institutional innovations to keep the pace of emissions reductions continuing in the next few decades). And even if fixing the climate problem costs society a modest amount, there will be great profits to be made in the transition.

## CONCLUSIONS

As Amory Lovins has been saying for decades, "Our future is choice, not fate". With our every waking breath we create the future. That means we get to choose what kind of world we want to leave for our children and grandchildren. Let's make sure we choose wisely.

## CHAPTER 1: KEY TAKEAWAYS

• Humans are no longer small compared to the earth. Humans are more numerous, more wealthy, and more powerful than at any time in history, and we can now affect the natural life support systems on which we all depend.

• The climate problem is big, it's urgent, and it's misunderstood, which make it fertile ground for starting new ventures.

• Entrepreneurs are the key to effecting large and rapid societal changes—government and big business are far too slow.

• If we're to get out of this mess, we'll need business to help new technologies and institutional innovations spread rapidly throughout the society, and that means many will make fortunes along the way.

• The best analogy is Sputnik, not Apollo—for solving this problem the scope of change is so vast and the rate of change required so rapid that hoping for a simple technical fix will inevitably lead to disappointment. All parts of the economy need to change, and pronto.

*"Do you want to spend the rest of your life selling sugared water, or do you want a chance to change the world?"*

—The late **STEVE JOBS** of Apple to John Scully in 1982[25]

# 2

## WHERE WE'RE HEADED

*"Facts are stubborn things; and whatever may be our wishes, our inclinations, or the dictates of our passions, they cannot alter the state of facts and evidence."* — JOHN ADAMS

This chapter presents the key evidence on climate in a concise way, supporting my claim in the last chapter that this challenge is big, urgent, and misunderstood. Scientists worry about climate change because our current path will push the earth into uncharted and dangerous territory. So dangerous, in fact, that we risk destabilizing the very life support systems upon which we all depend.

That judgment is based on well-established physical principles, real measurements, and plausible extrapolations of current trends, so it can't just be dismissed as fear mongering. Reasonable people who understand the evidence should come to the same conclusion—we need to act, and act fast.

### HOW DO WE KNOW?

There's been plenty of noise in the popular press emphasizing the uncertainty in the climate science, but that's virtually all fossil-fuel-industry-funded nonsense.[1] Uncertainties always exist in science, but when we confirm scientific findings by multiple, independent lines of evidence, we call them "facts". That means there may still be uncertainty, but the preponderance of the evidence points toward these facts accurately describing how the physical world operates.

The US National Academy of Sciences, which is not known for its wild speculation, concluded in 2010:

> A strong, credible body of scientific evidence shows that climate change is occurring, is caused largely by human activities, and poses significant risks for a broad range of human and natural systems. . . .
>
> Some scientific conclusions or theories have been so thoroughly examined and tested, and supported by so many independent observations and results, that their likelihood of subsequently being found to be wrong is vanishingly small. Such conclusions and theories are then regarded as settled facts. This is the case for the conclusions that the Earth system is warming and that much of this warming is very likely due to human activities.[2]

The academies of science for 18 other countries (including China, India, Russia, Germany, Japan, Brazil, and the UK) have released comparable statements about the science of climate.[3] The Intergovernmental Panel on Climate Change, the global scientific body charged with investigating this issue, stated with uncharacteristic bluntness in 2007, that "warming of the climate system is unequivocal, as is now evident from observations of increases in global average air and ocean temperatures, widespread melting of snow and ice and rising global average sea level."[4]

This scientific assessment is backed up by actual measurements. The National Aeronautics and Space Administration (NASA) tracks global temperatures, and they post their constantly updated data online.[5] These data show clearly that the 2000s was the hottest decade on record. The 2000s were hotter than the 1990s, which were hotter than the 1980s, which were hotter than the 1970s. There was a period of comparative stability in global temperatures from the early 1930s through the 1970s, so the rise in temperatures since 1970 (totaling about 0.6 Celsius degrees) is particularly striking.

There are many contributors to this warming effect.[6] **Figure 2-1** summarizes the most important ones causing warming in 2005 since preindustrial times. You don't need to understand the units on the graph, just think of them as a measure of the warming power of each factor listed in the graph. Higher numbers mean more warming effect, and negative numbers mean that factor is causing cooling.

The main historical driver of greenhouse gas concentrations[7] in the atmo-

**FIGURE 2-1** Contributors to warming in 2005 compared to preindustrial times

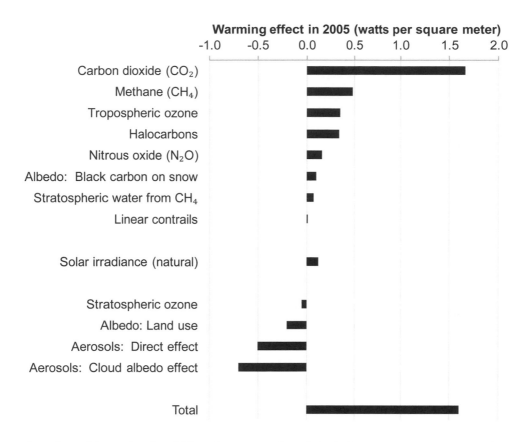

Best estimate of the warming effect of different factors expressed as radiative forcing (watts per square meter). For technical reasons, the total is not the simple sum of all the various components. There is uncertainty in each of these components, with the most consequential uncertainties associated with aerosols, tropospheric ozone, land use changes affecting albedo, and black carbon.

SOURCE: IPCC. 2007. *Climate Change 2007: The Physical Science Basis–Contribution of Working Group I to the Fourth Assessment Report of the Intergovernmental Panel on Climate Change* [Solomon, S., D. Qin, M. Manning, M. Marquis, K. Averyt, M. M. B. Tignor, H. L. Miller Jr, and Z. Chen (eds.)]. Cambridge, United Kingdom and New York, NY, USA: Cambridge University Press. [http://www.ipcc.ch/publications_and_data/publications_and_data_reports.shtml]. Figure SPM.2, p.4.

sphere has been carbon dioxide ($CO_2$), mostly from combustion of fossil fuels, with a significant additional contribution from changes in land-use patterns (like deforestation). Next is methane, driven by land-use changes and agriculture, followed by tropospheric ozone (which is also a local air pollutant that causes human health effects), halocarbons (like the chlorfluorocarbons being phased out under the Montreal Protocol for ozone depleting chemicals, plus some others), nitrous oxides (also mainly from agriculture), black carbon (soot), and water vapor that makes its way to the stratosphere because of

**FIGURE 2-2:** Historical global emissions of carbon dioxide, 1850 to 2008

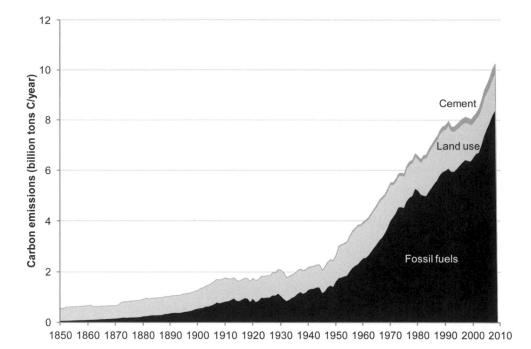

SOURCE. The Carbon Dioxide Information Analysis Center [http://cdiac.ornl.gov/]. Land-use emissions extrapolated from 2005 to 2008 at 0.8%/year (the growth rate from 2000 to 2005). Cement emissions data begin in 1928 but are too small before then to show up in the graph.

methane emissions. The cooling agents are aerosols (small particles that reflect sunlight) and contrails from airplane traffic. There's also a small increase in warming caused by modest changes in the brightness of the sun since preindustrial times, but it's a small effect.

The cooling effects just about cancel out the effect of everything but $CO_2$, but as I'll discuss later, that doesn't mean that we can ignore those other warming agents. As we start to phase out fossil fuels, the cooling effects from the aerosols will be reduced, so we'll need to compensate by also rapidly phasing out the shorter-lived agents like methane, tropospheric ozone, and black carbon.

**Figure 2-2** shows carbon emissions from 1850 to 2008, also including the process emissions associated with cement production (which are small compared to the other two factors). More than 90% of cumulative historical $CO_2$ emissions occurred after 1900, and almost three-quarters of cumulative emissions occurred after 1950. The twentieth century was clearly the fossil fuel century.

Those emissions have led $CO_2$ concentrations in the atmosphere to grow substantially, and to move well outside the earth's recent historical experience. Scientists have different methods to assess past concentrations of trace gases over time. One way is to drill for ice cores and extract air samples from bubbles in the ice. For more recent times (since 1959) we have very detailed direct measurements of atmospheric concentrations from the observatory on Mauna Loa in Hawaii. Over the last 650,000 years, the earth's atmosphere never held more than about 300 parts per million of $CO_2$,[8] but now we are closing in on 400 parts per million, an increase that has occurred in the span of about two centuries. **Figure 2-3** documents the trends for the past 400,000 years, and shows that we're moving rapidly into uncharted territory.[9]

One reason that we know that fossil fuels and land-use changes are the cause of the measured increases in $CO_2$ concentrations is because the total carbon emitted since the dawn of the industrial age is about twice as large as the total amount that remains in the atmosphere nowadays (the other half was absorbed by the oceans), and there are no other known sources of carbon that could account for such an increase in the atmosphere's $CO_2$ content. In addition, scientists can measure the prevalence of different isotopes of carbon in the atmosphere. It turns out that carbon that is derived from plant matter (like from fossil fuels and land use changes) contains a different mix of carbon isotopes than carbon that comes from geological sources, and scientists have measured changes in the concentrations of those isotopes in the atmosphere that are consistent with the additional carbon coming from these two sources.[10] So it's virtually certain that humans are the cause of these changes (as well as of similar increases in the past two centuries in concentrations of methane and nitrous oxides, which are two other important greenhouse gases).[11]

And these changes are warming the planet, as shown in **Figure 2-4**, and as predicted with surprising accuracy as early as 1975 in *Science*.[12] The best current estimates are that global average surface temperatures have increased about 0.8 Celsius degrees since 1900, and we're already committed to at least another 0.5 Celsius degrees once the climate fully equilibrates to current GHG concentrations (there are long time lags in the system).[13]

Concern about climate change from increases in these atmospheric trace gases is based on some of the most well-established principles in physical science. They go back at least a century to the Swedish scientist Svante Arrhenius,

**FIGURE 2-3** Earth's carbon dioxide concentrations (ppmv) for the past 400,000 years

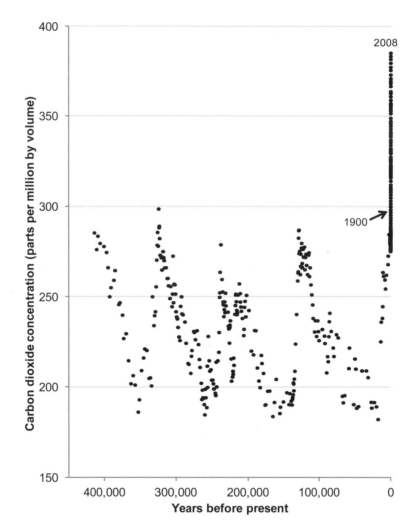

SOURCES: Data from before 0 AD taken from Vostok ice core research (Petit, J. R., J. Jouzel, D. Raynaud, N. I. Barkov, J. M. Barnola, I. Basile, M. Bender, J. Chappellaz, M. Davis, G. Delaygue, M. Delmotte, V. M. Kotlyakov, M. Legrand, V. Y. Lipenkov, C. Lorius, L. Pepin, C. Ritz, E. Saltzman, and M. Stievenard. 1999. "Climate and atmospheric history of the past 420,000 years from the Vostok ice core, Antarctica." *Nature*. vol. 399, no. 6735. pp. 429-436. [http://dx.doi.org/10.1038/20859), http://www.nature.com/nature/journal/v399/n6735/suppinfo/399429a0_S1.html]).

Data from about 1000 AD until 1975 AD taken from the smoothed 75 year Lawdome ice core data: D.M. Etheridge, L.P. Steele, R.L. Langenfelds, R.J. Francey, J.-M. Barnola and V.I. Morgan. 1998. *Historical CO$_2$ records from the Law Dome DE08, DE08-2, and DSS ice cores. In Trends: A Compendium of Data on Global Change.* Carbon Dioxide Information Analysis Center, Oak Ridge National Laboratory, US Department of Energy, Oak Ridge, Tenn., USA [http://cdiac.ornl.gov/trends/co2/lawdome.html].

Measured data from 1959 through 2008 taken from Keeling, R.F., S.C. Piper, A.F. Bollenbacher and J.S. Walker. 2009. *Atmospheric CO$_2$ records from sites in the SIO air sampling network. In Trends: A Compendium of Data on Global Change.* Carbon Dioxide Information Analysis Center, Oak Ridge National Laboratory, US Department of Energy, Oak Ridge, Tenn., USA doi: 10.3334/CDIAC/atg.035. [http://cdiac.ornl.gov/trends/co2/sio-mlo.html]

**FIGURE 2-4**   Global temperatures for the past 1500 years relative to the 1800 to 1900 period average

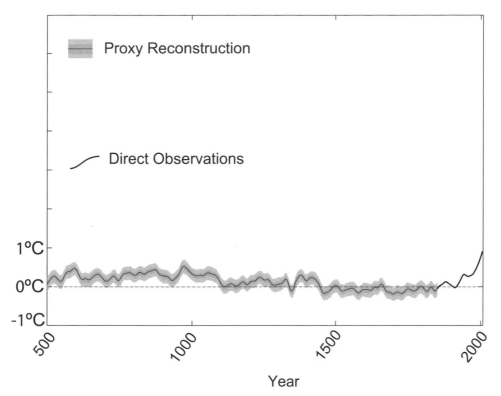

Taken from Allison et al. 2009 (The Copenhagen Diagnosis 2009, p.50), and adapted by deleting the forecasts shown below in Figure 2-12. For a detailed graph of the multiple temperature measurements after 1890, see [http://www.skepti-calscience.com/graphics.php]. Used with permission.

who calculated the first climate sensitivity of 4 to 5 Celsius degrees in 1896 (see below for discussion of the importance of climate sensitivity). Arrhenius's analysis was supported by earlier measurements made by John Tyndall that demonstrated the heat trapping abilities of $CO_2$. So the idea that greenhouse gases could warm the earth is not a new one, and in fact the first informed speculation about this topic was by the mathematician Joseph Fourier in the 1820s.[14]

These concerns are also validated by actual measurements of the climate system that corroborate theoretical predictions.[15] Satellite measurements show, for example, that as greenhouse gases have built up in the atmosphere, the heat emitted from the earth has been declining at wavelengths that exactly correspond to those absorbed by various GHGs.[16] Similar measurements show that thermal radiation back to the earth's surface from the atmosphere,

**FIGURE 2-5**   Actual sea ice extent in September compared to the mean and range from the IPCC Fourth Assessment Report (2007)

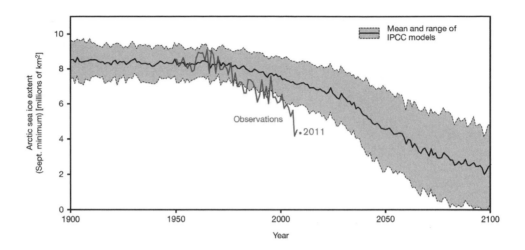

Taken from Allison et al. 2009 (The Copenhagen Diagnosis 2009, p.30), and adapted by adding the 2011 data from [http://nsidc.org/arcticseaicenews/]. Used with permission. Data from 2008 to 2011 fell between 4.33 and 5.1 million square kilometers, all well below the IPCC range. Used with permission.

which we'd expect to increase if greenhouse gases trap heat, has been increasing exactly as we thought it would.[17] And the amount of heat stored in the oceans over the past few decades has been rising rapidly, which is consistent with a warming planet.[18]

We can also examine data on some key indicators of warming, which by most accounts are changing at rates equaling or exceeding our worst-case predictions of just a few years ago.[19] These measurements are one of the main reasons why scientists are so alarmed about humanity's effect on the planet's temperature.

On a hot day ice in your drink melts rapidly, and the ice at earth's poles is no different. Consider **Figure 2-5**, which compares the observed trends for minimum sea ice extent at the North Pole to the range of predictions in the IPCC's Fourth Assessment Report (2007).[20] The minimum extent for the year (which typically happens in September) reached an all-time low in 2007, representing more than a 40% reduction compared to the 1979 to 2000 average. Later years have shown only slightly less melting, and sea ice extent in 2011 tracked the 2007 numbers for much of the year, with the minimum falling just above the 2007 figure (Figure 2-4). But the more important measurements are those of the *volume* of sea ice, not just the area of ocean covered, and arctic

**FIGURE 2-6**   Change in sea level 1970 to 2008 (relative to 1990 levels)

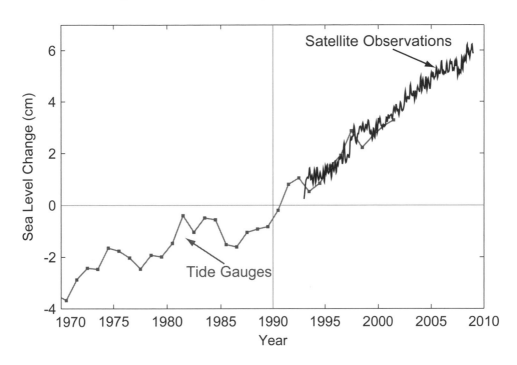

Data from tide gauges (1970 to 2002) are shown in the smoother line, while satellite data are shown in the more variable darker line. The grey band is the range from the IPCC Third Assessment Report (2001). Taken from Allison et al. 2009 (The Copenhagen Diagnosis 2009, p.37). Used with permission.

sea ice volume reached a record low in 2010 compared to the previous record in 2007.[21] These volume measurements show us on track for ice-free summers in the Arctic by the end of this decade, an event unprecedented in recorded human history.[22]

Glaciers and ice sheets on land only affect sea level when they melt. Measurements summarized in **Figure 2-6** show that sea levels have been rising at rates that are at the top end of the IPCC forecasts, in part because of melting land-based ice, and in part because warming oceans expand, so they take up more space. And the ocean is warming rapidly, as recent data show.[23]

As another example, consider rainfall extremes for the United States. Warmer oceans mean more evaporation and an overall increase in moisture content in the air. That means extreme rainfall becomes more common, and the data for the US show that effect (as do broader measurements for the Northern Hemisphere[24]). **Figure 2-7** shows the percent of US land area subject to extreme one-day rainfall totals, and that percentage has clearly increased

**FIGURE 2-7**   Percentage of US land area subject to extremes in US one day precipitation

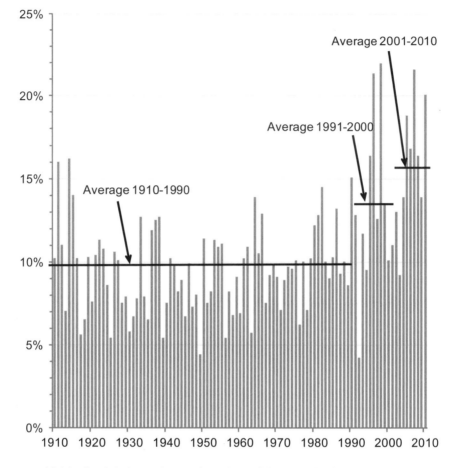

Extreme rainfall defined as the highest tenth percentile one-day rainfall events. Taken from [http://www.ncdc.noaa.gov/extremes/cei/], with graph captured on September 15, 2011.

since 1990 (and compared to the long-term average), a fact that will not be a surprise to US residents facing unprecedented flooding in 2011.

In summarizing these and other measurements, the IPCC concluded "observational evidence from all continents and most oceans shows that many natural systems are being affected by regional climate changes, particularly temperature increases."[25] The observations cited above are powerful evidence for a warming world, but they are not the only ones.[26] Glaciers are melting, growing seasons are lengthening, and insects and birds are changing their long-established patterns.[27] Something's clearly happening to the climate, and these indicators are consistent with what the last one and a half centuries of science has been saying about this problem all along.

## HOW ABOUT FUTURE WARMING?

The measurements described in the preceding section are independent of climate models, but to estimate how the climate will respond to future increases in greenhouse gas concentrations, we need models to keep track of the complexities. It's sensible to be skeptical of many computer models, but in this case that concern is misplaced. The models describing the climate are independently validated with real observations, multiple lines of independent evidence, and rigorous peer review, so you can have confidence that they represent our current understanding of reality (in spite of what you might hear in the media).[28]

The purpose of models is to assess the additional complexities and feedbacks, because the climate is not a simple system, and our intuition is not necessarily a good guide to how this system will respond to our actions. While models can't tell us with ten-decimal-place precision what will happen decades from now, they can help us determine which factors are big enough to matter and how we should choose where to focus our initial efforts. As I'll discuss later in the book, that's the best we can hope for (and it's exactly the same problem that businesses face when confronting unanticipated competition or big strategic challenges).

We need four things to estimate future human-induced climate change: a measure of how sensitive the climate is to changes in atmospheric concentrations of GHGs, knowledge about the warming power of each greenhouse gas (GHG), an estimate of how emissions of greenhouse gases will change over the next century, and an understanding of how long those emissions will stay in the atmosphere.

All of these factors are uncertain and are impossible to predict with precision. Nevertheless, we know enough to conclude that climate change will be a serious problem in the 21st century. That's because any reasonable combination of these factors will push the earth outside the comfortable temperature range in which humanity evolved.

### *How sensitive is the climate to changes in greenhouse gas concentrations?*
The results of climate models are typically expressed in terms of "climate sensitivity", which is the average long-term temperature change the earth's surface will exhibit for a doubling of $CO_2$ concentrations in the atmosphere.

Reviews of the various models produce a consensus climate sensitivity range of 2.0 to 4.5 Celsius degrees, with a "most probable" estimate of 3 Celsius degrees (5.4 degrees Fahrenheit).[29] This range hasn't changed much in the past three decades even though our analysis tools have gotten a lot more sophisticated and we've used many different methods to estimate it. That means that it's a reasonably well-known parameter, although some of the factors omitted in such models probably make the upper end of the range much higher than 4.5 Celsius degrees (see below).

Understanding what the range of climate sensitivity means isn't so hard. Consider a baseball player who over the course of several seasons achieves a 0.300 batting average but in occasional weeks hits as low as 0.200 or as high as 0.450. The best guess is around 0.300 for how he'll do on average next year, but in any given week the average could vary a lot. The most likely outcome for the climate (based on current knowledge) is 3 Celsius degrees for every doubling of greenhouse gas concentrations (a batting average of 0.300).

There are some good reasons for believing that we won't be able to reduce the uncertainty in that rather broad range for climate sensitivity, because it's difficult to pin down a complex system with many feedbacks.[30] We certainly won't be able to do it in time to make sensible decisions about future emissions, so we're going to need to factor that inherent uncertainty into our decisions.

There's also some probably unknowable chance that the climate sensitivity will be significantly higher than the upper end of that range, because of some feedback we haven't modeled well or don't understand yet. For example, Kiehl[31] argues, using paleoclimate data,[32] that "Earth's sensitivity to $CO_2$ radiative forcing may be much greater than that obtained from climate models." There are at least four possibilities we know of now: melting of the Arctic, Antarctic, and Greenland ice sheets (which is happening faster than anyone expected),[33] warming surface temperatures melting the permafrost,[34] drying and burning of northern peatlands,[35] and warming oceans releasing methane hydrates from the continental shelf.[36] None of these feedbacks has been adequately incorporated into current climate models. Such "known or unknown unknowns" argue strongly for caution, since climate sensitivities well above 4.5 Celsius degrees would surely spell catastrophe for humans and the earth's natural systems.

Using similar data, Hansen et al.[37] argue that including these feedbacks would raise the true climate sensitivity to 6 Celsius degrees for every doubling of greenhouse gas emissions. Hansen also argues that these feedbacks can occur rapidly, like over a century or two, which makes them dangerous for humanity. For example, melting ice sheets expose dirt and rocks that absorb more sunlight than ice does, accelerating the warming, and that feedback would hasten rapid warming as well as significant sea level rise (same for release of carbon or methane from hydrates in the tundra or under the ocean). An ice-free planet earth would have oceans that are tens of meters higher than today.[38] While that disastrous outcome would not occur for many centuries, even on our current path, it would be absurd not to plan to forestall it.

Even without the feedbacks considered by Hansen, our current path presents grave risks to the world in which our children and grandchildren will live, but these feedbacks are likely to be important. Even a small chance of real climate sensitivity of 6 Celsius degrees argues strongly for immediate restraints on our greenhouse gas emissions.[39]

## HOW FAST ARE GHG CONCENTRATIONS RISING?

OK, now that we have an idea of how much temperature change the earth will experience with every doubling of $CO_2$ concentrations, how many doublings are we in for? For that we need to know how long various GHGs stay in the atmosphere and how their emissions will change in the coming century. I will spare you the details by referring to a study completed by MIT in 2009, which did the math for us. That study tracks the important GHGs in what they call the "no-policy case" and carries the calculations through to atmospheric concentrations, and is unusually comprehensive in its treatment of this problem.

### *Drivers of emissions*

**Figure 2-8** shows some of the underlying factors that affect emissions in the MIT no-policy case, including population, wealth per capita (GDP per person), total wealth, and total primary energy use, expressed as a ratio of 2100 to 2000 values from the MIT no-policy case. Population increases by 60%, and GDP per person by almost a factor of six, leading total GDP to increase by a factor of 9.6 (about half as much as it did between 1900 and 2000).[40] Primary energy increases by almost a factor of four.

**FIGURE 2-8:** Ratio of year 2100 to year 2000 values for key drivers of emissions in the MIT no-policy case

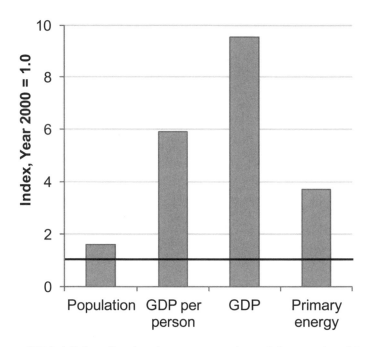

GDP is inflation adjusted, and so represents real growth in economic activity. Carbon intensity of primary energy supply is virtually constant over this period.

These factors reflect a world in which the richest countries continue to prosper, while the poorest make great strides toward modernity, with average wealth per person in 2100 comparable in inflation-adjusted terms to that in many developed countries today. These trends reflect typical expectations for growth in these parameters, with population peaking at almost 10 billion people, and primary energy use growing at about 1.3%/year. Inflation-adjusted (real) GDP grows at 2.3% per year, implying a change in the energy/GDP ratio of about -1%/year, which tracks historical trends from 1900 to 2000.[41]

The underlying assumption of this and all other such forecasts is that this business as usual world will actually be able to deliver the economic activity and ecological services needed to support a population of ten billion increasingly wealthy people. That is an open question, and it's not at all certain to be true by the end of the 21st century if we continue on our current path. Ronald Lee, writing in *Science*, states "nearly all population forecasts, including those by the UN, implicitly assume that population growth will occur in a neutral zone without negative economic or environmental feedback."[42] *If there are*

**FIGURE 2-9:** Historical and projected carbon emissions, in billions of metric tons of carbon per year (1900 to 2100)

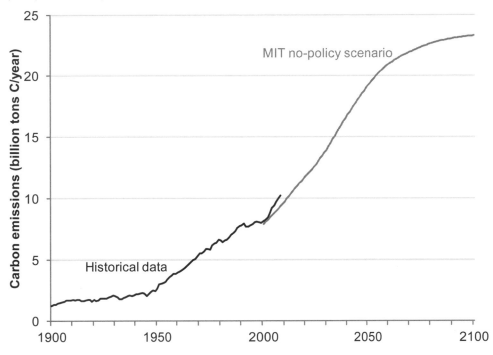

Historical carbon emissions include cement and land use, and are taken from CDIAC [http://cdiac.ornl.gov/by_new/bysub-jec.html]. Projected emissions are from the MIT no-policy case (mean run). Emissions expressed as billions of tons of carbon (Gigatons C or GtC). To convert to $CO_2$ multiply GtC by 3.667.

*significant negative consequences of climate change in a "current trends con-tinued" world (as there are almost certain to be, given our current understand-ing of the climate system), then our current forecasts are very likely to overes-timate human numbers and wealth at the end of the 21st century.*

### Emissions of GHGs

The main GHGs are carbon dioxide ($CO_2$), methane ($CH_4$), nitrous oxide ($N_2O$), and a variety of other gases including chlorofluorocarbons (CFCs). $CO_2$ is the most important of these gases, so I focus particularly on that one in this section.

I show in **Figure 2-9** historical global carbon emissions plotted with the MIT "no-policy case" projection, which looks a lot like the continuation of historical trends in emissions from the past half century. Historical emissions (which include both land-use and cement emissions, as in Figure 2-2) grew about 2%/year from 1900 to 2008, 2.3%/year from 1950 to 2008, and 1.6%

**FIGURE 2-10:** Historical and projected methane ($CH_4$) emissions, in millions of metric tons of $CH_4$ per year (1900 to 2100)

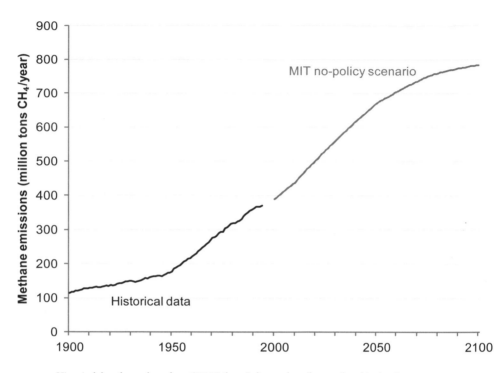

SOURCE: Historical data for methane from CDIAC [http://cdiac.ornl.gov/by_new/bysubjec.html].

per year from 1970 to 2008, while the MIT no-policy case grows at about 1.8% per year from 2000 to 2050, with much slower growth after that.

I find the emissions path described by the MIT "no-policy case" to be a plausible extrapolation of current trends in carbon emissions. **Figures 2-10** and **2-11** plot comparable graphs for methane ($CH_4$) and nitrous oxide ($N_2O$) emissions, respectively, and they tell a similar story.

Economic systems change relatively slowly without big shocks or changes in policy. In the absence of appropriate accounting for the true social cost of coal-fired power generation (which describes the situation virtually every-where in the world), coal is cheap to buy. Reserves of coal are huge (see Appendix A) and without changes in our current policies, lots of coal will be burned to generate electricity in coming decades. Natural gas will continue to be used in many applications for which it is often the most cost-effective choice for the user. And petroleum-based transport fuels will be dominant for

**FIGURE 2-11:** Historical and projected nitrous oxide ($N_2O$) emissions, in millions of metric tons of $N_2O$ per year (1900 to 2100)

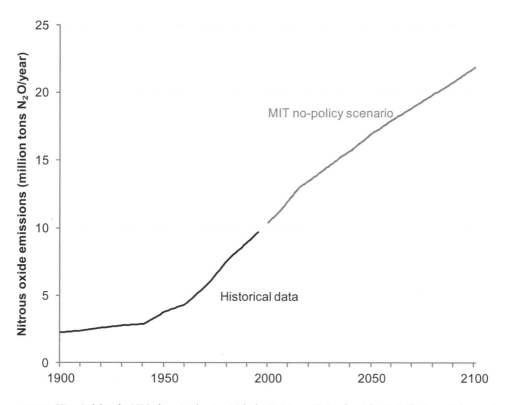

SOURCE: Historical data for N2O from Asadoorian, Malcolm O., Marcus C. Sarofim, John M. Reilly, Sergey Paltsev and Chris Forest. 2006. Historical Anthropogenic Emissions Inventories for Greenhouse Gases and Major Criteria Pollutants. Cambridge, MA: Massachusetts Institute of Technology (MIT) Joint Program on the Science and Policy of Climate Change. Technical Note No. 8. June (Revised July). [http://web.mit.edu/globalchange/www/MITJPSPGC_TechNote8.pdf]

at least a couple more decades, even if the shift to electric vehicles succeeds beyond anyone's wildest dreams. If that shift happens without a shift away from coal in the electricity sector, or if it doesn't happen at all, carbon emissions for transport will continue to grow.[43] That means continued increases in total GHG emissions if we don't change our current path.

As a test, we can compare the MIT forecast of carbon emissions to two more recent forecasts of global carbon emissions, from the International Energy Agency and the US Energy Information Administration.[44] To make them comparable to the MIT forecast, which includes cement and land use emissions, I added those emissions (derived from the MIT scenario) to the EIA and IEA forecasts. Those forecasts, completed after that nasty financial melt-

**FIGURE 2-12:** MIT no-policy case forecast for all carbon emissions compared to history and to EIA and IEA forecasts from 2010

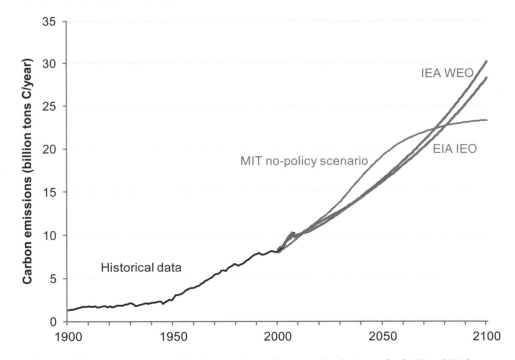

I added the MIT forecasts for cement and land-use emissions to the energy-related emissions for the EIA and IEA forecasts to make those time series consistent with the MIT forecast. I also extrapolated IEA's World Energy Outlook and EIA's International Energy Outlook past 2035 using average annual growth rates from 2008 to 2035.

down in 2008 and 2009, are plotted in **Figure 2-12,** and they show lower carbon emissions growth after 2008 (about 1.3%/year), mostly reflecting higher assumed rates of improvement in energy intensities over that period.

I've also taken the liberty of extrapolating the energy-related emissions from those two forecasts past their 2035 end dates using their annual average projected growth rates in emissions from 2008 to 2035, to see what I could learn. By 2050 the MIT scenario shows about 3 billion tons more carbon emitted every year than in the two later forecasts. The graph also shows that the date of reaching 15 billion tons per year of emissions is 11 to 14 years later for the two later forecasts. By about 2075, the IEA and EIA forecasts "catch up" to the MIT forecast, because MIT shows a leveling off of emissions by 2070 or so while the IEA and EIA lines represent simple extrapolations beyond 2035.

Those sound like big differences, but for carbon emissions it's cumulative emissions that really matter (I'll explore this issue more in the next chapter). If the lower forecasts are right (and who knows if they are?) then they only buy us a year or two in terms of reaching the cumulative emissions budget corresponding to the most aggressive policy scenario considered by the MIT analysts. That's not much of a difference, and the cumulative emissions from the simple extrapolations of these two scenarios are about equal to the MIT forecast by 2100. I'm going to stick with the MIT forecast because of its comprehensiveness (and because its carbon emissions growth rate matches recent history), with the understanding that there's some uncertainty in the cumulative emissions forecasts.[45]

One should always be skeptical about forecasts of economic and social systems. In the end, there's no way to predict the future with precision. But what the MIT "no-policy case" shows is that *continuation of current trends will lead to very substantial increases in GHG emissions and concentrations in coming decades.*

### Fossil fuel resources and the MIT no-policy case forecast

Is consumption of fossil fuels at the scale envisioned in the MIT no-policy case possible given existing global fossil fuel reserves? In Appendix A, I estimate *lower bounds* to global fossil fuel reserves and resources (which together make up what's called the "resource base", our best estimate of how many fossil fuel resources we have, not including exotic supplies like methane hydrates and other occurrences of hard-to-extract deposits). Reserves are well-known deposits that can be extracted at current prices and technologies, while resources are somewhat more speculative, but resources become reserves over time as exploration advances and technology improves.

I focus here on the lower bounds to make an important point: Even with estimates of the fossil fuel resource base at the low end of what the literature says, the amount of carbon embodied in *just the conventional sources of these fuels* is vastly larger than the amount of fuel assumed to be burned in the MIT no-policy case.

As shown in **Figure 2-13**, the lower bound estimate of the amount of carbon contained in all fossil fuels excluding exotic resources like methane hydrates is almost 10,000 billion metric tons of carbon, or roughly 6 times the amount that would be emitted from fossil fuel burning in the MIT no-policy case from 2000 to 2100. Just the resource base for conventional gas, oil, and coal would cover the fossil emissions in the no-policy case more than five times over. And

**FIGURE 2-13:** Comparison of lower bound estimates of fossil fuel resource base and proven fossil reserves to cumulative emissions in the MIT no-policy case

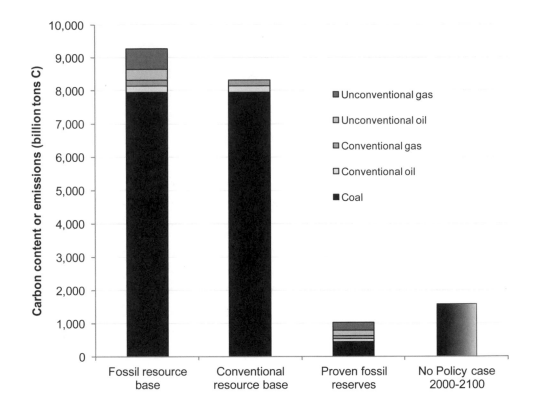

if we were to consume the conventional oil and gas resource base plus the coal reserves, we'd only need to use about 10% of the coal resources to reach the emissions in the no-policy case. And "peak oil" won't help much with this problem, as coal reserves are so vast.

I conclude from this comparison that *there's virtually no chance that resource constraints would provide a brake on carbon emissions in this century*, and the emissions in the MIT no-policy case are below what could be expected if we were to burn even a quarter of our entire conventional resource base in the next ninety years.

### Concentrations of GHGs

What does the MIT no-policy forecast imply for the *concentrations* of GHGs, which drive changes in the earth's temperature? **Figure 2-14** shows the result for $CO_2$ and the other categories of gases from the MIT study, expressed

**FIGURE 2-14:** Greenhouse gas concentrations in $CO_2$ equivalent, 2000 to 2100, from the MIT no-policy case

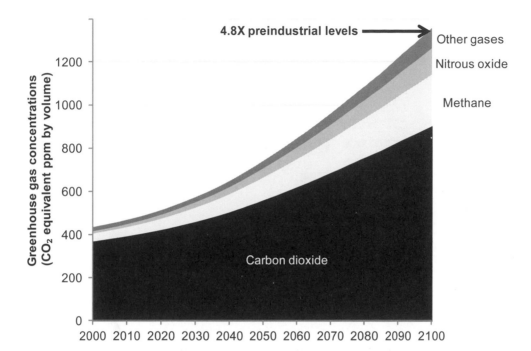

SOURCE: Adapted from data in Sokolov, A.P., P.H. Stone, C.E. Forest, R. Prinn, M.C. Sarofim, M. Webster, S. Paltsev, C.A. Schlosser, D. Kicklighter, S. Dutkiewicz, J. Reilly, C. Wang, B. Felzer, J. Melillo, and H.D. Jacoby. 2009. Probabilistic Forecast for 21st Century Climate Based on Uncertainties in Emissions (without Policy) and Climate Parameters. Cambridge, MA: Massachusetts Institute of Technology (MIT) Joint Program on the Science and Policy of Climate Change. 169. January. [http://globalchange.mit.edu/files/document/MITJPSPGC_Rpt169.pdf]

as $CO_2$ equivalent (the other gases are corrected for their varying warming power so that they can be accurately compared to the warming effect of $CO_2$). This forecast also accounts for the lifetime of each gas in the atmosphere when calculating GHG concentrations, which rise to about 1350 parts per million $CO_2$ equivalent by 2100. $CO_2$ alone contributes about 900 parts per million in 2100, and that total is still projected to grow at about 1%/year in the last decade of the 21st century, even though total carbon emissions start to level off in about 2070 or so. About two thirds of the total GHG concentration in 2100 is attributable to $CO_2$, with 18% for methane, 9% for nitrous oxide, and 7% for the other gases.

$CO_2$ concentration grows by a factor of two and a half by 2100 compared to the year 2000, while concentrations of the other gases roughly double over the same period. **Figure 2-15** breaks down the growth in GHG concentrations

**FIGURE 2-15:** Contribution of warming effects from different sources, 2000 to 2100, MIT no-policy case

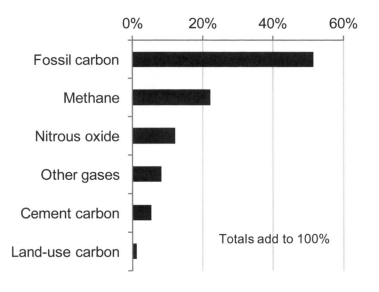

The MIT no-policy case assumes significant reductions in the current emissions from land use changes like deforestation, which accounts for that factor's very low percentage of the total.

from 2000 to 2100, so it's easy to see which components contribute most to the warming over that period. It shows that carbon emissions from burning fossil fuels is the largest single contributor to warming from 2000 to 2100 (contributing about half of the total), with methane emissions contributing about one fifth of the increase. Nitrous oxide and the other gases together contribute another fifth of the increase, and cement process and land-use emissions total 5% and 1%, respectively.[46]

One important conclusion from these results is that it's not just energy-related $CO_2$ that's an issue—*real solutions also need to address land-use changes, cement emissions, methane, nitrous oxide, and the other gases.* Fossil fuel emissions are about half of the problem over the next century, making them the single largest source for emissions reductions, but each of these different emissions sources needs to be targeted if we're to solve this problem in any meaningful sense of the term.

And in fact, it's even more complicated than that. There are some short-lived pollutants that cause near-term warming, and cutting those pollutants can have a rapid effect on warming. Methane is the most important of these, but black carbon (soot) and tropospheric ozone are also important, as are some others. Methane's warming impact is larger in the short term, which means that its effect in the next few decades is larger than the 25% net effect by the end of the century. We therefore need to think dynamically about this problem, focusing both on the short and long-term pollutants, and adjusting our mitigation actions as measured data indicate. It may in fact behoove us to undertake rapid mitigation on these short-lived pollutants in order to buy time as we ramp up to big long-term reductions in the longer-lived pollutants.[47]

## IMPLICATIONS FOR GLOBAL TEMPERATURES

What does that increase in GHG concentrations mean for global temperatures? The most common practice for assessing temperature changes is to measure them relative to preindustrial times (i.e. compared to 1750 or so). Concentrations of $CO_2$ at that time were about 280 parts per million, and the MIT no-policy case shows total GHG concentrations (including all gases) that are about 4.8 times higher than that by 2100. That means that *the MIT no-policy case forecast implies more than two doublings*[48] *of GHG concentrations by 2100 when all gases are included* (and more than that after 2100).

The consensus climate sensitivity range (i.e. the long-term temperature increase from a doubling of greenhouse gas concentrations) is from 2.0 to 4.5 Celsius degrees, with a 'most likely" estimate of 3 Celsius degrees (5.4 degrees F).[49] Two doublings is most likely therefore to increase average temperatures by 6 Celsius degrees or 10.8 degrees F compared to preindustrial times, after the climate system has fully equilibrated centuries from now. The MIT study calculates a slightly lower warming of 5.1 Celsius degrees by 2100 for the no-policy case because the climate sensitivity measures the long-term equilibrium for a doubling of greenhouse gas concentrations, and the full warming will take several centuries to show up in the data.

Let's consider the lower and upper bounds. Even in the very best case, we're in for at least a 4 Celsius degrees increase on average, but there's no guarantee of the best case. Our current path could also increase temperatures by 9 Celsius degrees on the high end, or even more if positive feedbacks turn out to be stronger than we expect in a rapidly warming world.

So what does all this mean? Consider past temperatures as one guide. Over the past 1500 years (the time over which modern society evolved), the temperature has been remarkably stable, as shown in **Figure 2-16**. It was only in the 1900s that temperatures started to increase. This figure also shows a range

**FIGURE 2-16:** Global temperatures relative to the 1800s, with projections to 2100

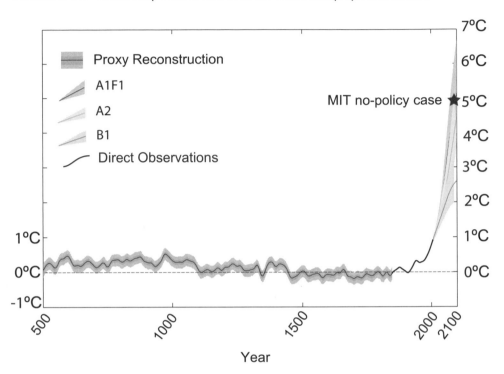

The climate has been remarkably stable over the past 1500 years, but the projections from the 2007 IPCC report would push the earth well outside the comfortable range in which modern human civilization was born. Adapted from Allison et al. 2009 (The Copenhagen Diagnosis 2009, p.50). Used with permission.

of forecasts, with the MIT forecast indicated with a "star" on the graph. The IPCC examined many different forecasts with a wide range of assumptions about population growth, GDP, energy intensity, and carbon intensity. The ones that look a lot like the past half-century extrapolated into the future are at the top of the range, right where the MIT scenario falls. That means that *if we follow the MIT no-policy case, we're in for a large change in average temperatures compared to modern humanity's historical experience.*

We can even look further back in time. What the historical record shows is that the warmest it's been over the past 2 million years was about 2 Celsius degrees more than the temperatures prevailing in preindustrial times,[50] which is one of the main reasons why the G8 countries adopted this upper temperature limit as their normative goal for climate in 2009.[51] *The path we're now on will push the world well outside the comfortable temperature range in which the human species evolved and in which industrial civilization was born, even if climate sensitivity is at the low end of the currently accepted range.*

**FIGURE 2-17:** Increasing average temperatures "load the dice" and make extreme temperatures more likely (and the extremes more extreme)

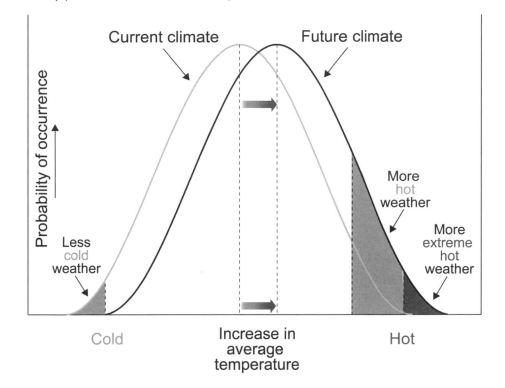

SOURCE: Adapted from a graph made by the University of Arizona, Southwest Climate Change Network [http://www.southwestclimatechange.org/figures/temperature-shift].

## HOW WILL THESE CHANGES AFFECT HUMAN AND NATURAL SYSTEMS?

The most important direct effect of increasing temperatures is stress on natural and human systems.[52] Greenhouse gases keep more energy in the climate system, and that energy has to go somewhere, as Naomi Oreskes points out. Where it goes is into extreme rainfall and temperature events, which will become increasingly difficult or impossible for humans to manage, and ever more devastating for natural systems (whose ability to adapt is even more limited).[53] **Figure 2-17** illustrates how a warming climate "loads the dice" and makes extreme temperature events more likely and the extremes more extreme, just as more moisture in the air makes high precipitation events more likely (and oddly enough, makes droughts in some places like the western US more likely and more intense).[54]

The global environment is accustomed to a relatively narrow temperature range, one that has prevailed for thousands of years. Species can sometimes migrate into areas that were historically too cold for them, but at different rates: birds and mammals can shift kilometers per decade, but trees and most other plants shift much more slowly. These movements are limited by geography and other constraints. For example, a stand of trees can gradually move up the mountainside as the climate warms (soil and geography permitting), but once it reaches the peak there's nowhere else to go, and extinction is the result. On our current path, a mass extinction event similar to the one that killed the dinosaurs could occur with plant and animal species that have existed for eons being driven to extinction over the span of 2-3 centuries. The IPCC, in its Fourth Assessment Report, stated bluntly "as global average temperature increase exceeds about 3.5°C, model projections suggest significant extinctions (40 to 70% of species assessed) around the globe."[55] More recent assessments have been even more pessimistic.[56]

Humans and their support systems (like agriculture) are also vulnerable to a warming climate. The path we're now on will make New York's summers like Georgia's summers now, and you don't even want to know how hot Georgia's summers will become.[57] Heat waves will become ever more frequent, and people in locations without air conditioning will either add it (which will worsen climate change), suffer, or even die (as tens of thousands of Europeans did during the heat wave of 2003). Our wastewater treatment plants and water supply systems are designed to handle current conditions, but will be difficult and expensive to adapt to a warming world's rapidly rising sea level and increasingly intense rainstorms. With even small increases in sea level, low-lying coastal areas will become increasingly vulnerable to storm surges, putting millions of lives at risk, particularly in the developing world. Those areas will also suffer from increased saltwater intrusion into groundwater supplies. The best current estimates for scenarios similar to the MIT no-policy case project a 1.4 meter (4.6 foot) rise in sea levels from current conditions by 2100,[58] which would represent significant challenges to human society.

There are also indirect effects. One of the most important is an increase in the acidity of the oceans, caused by more dissolved $CO_2$ (which creates carbonic acid). This development will make life increasingly difficult for many types of aquatic life, with rates of acidification proceeding more rapidly than at any time in the past 65 million years.[59] The acidification effect (plus the increase in ocean temperatures) means that coral reefs will likely be a thing of the past by the end of the twenty first century, and will pose increasing challenges to marine life of all types.[60] It also is one reason why schemes like those proposed to inject particles into the atmosphere to cool the earth are ultimately chimerical—as long as more $CO_2$ dissolves into the oceans, the acidification effect will intensify, and just reflecting more sunlight won't fix it.[61]

Remember also that the climate sensitivity measures the *average* temperature change. Changes at the earth's poles will be much larger (that's just how the system works). The most likely case for climate sensitivity combined with the MIT no-policy case emissions forecast would ultimately lead to an ice-free Planet Earth and sea level rises much bigger than even recent projections. It also means that large releases of carbon trapped in the permafrost and in methane hydrates beneath the ocean floor are much more likely, and that would amplify the warming effect.

## HOW LONG WILL GHGS PERSIST IN THE ATMOSPHERE?

Archer & Brovkin[62] show that much of the carbon emitted now will stay in the atmosphere for thousands of years, so the effects of these emissions are in some sense irreversible in the absence of active attempts to "scrub" them from the atmosphere (and except for improving land use patterns and reforestation, that's a thermodynamically difficult and expensive process at best). However, even if we are successful in removing carbon from the atmosphere, much of the warming effect is not reversible because of slower heat absorption by the oceans, which makes this problem even more urgent.[63] Methane and soot have relatively short lifetimes (and more potent short-term warming potentials), so immediate emissions reductions for those pollutants will have a large and rapid effect on warming. The other gases have lifetimes in the atmosphere comparable to or greater than $CO_2$ in many cases, [64] which is one of the reasons why "wait and see" is a dangerous approach to this problem—by the time all doubts are resolved about this issue, it will be too late for an effective response.

## CONCLUSIONS

Even the best-case climate sensitivity combined with the emissions of the MIT no-policy scenario would not be a pleasant place. The most likely outcome would be a disaster for the earth and for humanity, and the upper end of the range would be catastrophic. None of these are worlds in which I'd like my sons to live (although if we don't get our act together pronto they're going to have to deal with it).

So this is not a story with a happy ending, but this path is the one we're now on. As the old saying goes, "if we don't change our direction, we'll end up where we're headed." The next chapter describes where we might go instead.

WHERE WE'RE HEADED  •  39

**CHAPTER 2: KEY TAKEAWAYS**

• It's not just fossil fuel $CO_2$ that's an issue—solutions also need to address land-use changes, cement process emissions, methane, nitrous oxide, soot, tropospheric ozone, and other greenhouse gases.

• Current trends imply at least two doublings of equivalent $CO_2$ concentrations (all gases) by 2100 compared to preindustrial times, with no end in sight.

• Each doubling will most likely result in 5.4 deg F avg surface temp increase by 2100 (excluding some important positive feedbacks). Total temperature change by 2100 would therefore be 10.8 deg F under current trends

• Warming will be much higher at the poles, melting ice much faster than predicted.

• If feedbacks release carbon from permafrost, peat bogs, and undersea methane hydrates, temperature change could be much higher

• This is not a pretty picture.

*Ringer's Theory of Reality "emphasizes, first of all, that reality isn't the way you wish things to be, nor the way they appear to be, but the way they actually are. Secondly, the theory states that you either acknowledge reality and use it to your benefit or it will automatically work against you."* —ROBERT RINGER

# 3

---

## SO WHAT DO WE DO NOW?

---

*"The best way to predict the future is to invent it."* –ALAN KAY

As shown in the last chapter, the current trajectory for greenhouse gas emissions would increase substantially the risk of dangerous, irreversible, and, probably catastrophic changes in the global life support systems upon which we all depend.[1] As the White House Science Advisor John Holdren aptly puts it, we're "driving in a car with bad brakes toward a cliff in the fog."[2] If you're headed for a cliff, of course you steer your car away. Where should we steer instead?

To answer this question, we need to understand a bit more about how people have thought about this problem in the past. We'll then contrast the conventional approaches to this problem with one more akin to how businesses tackle big strategic challenges.

### CONVENTIONAL WAYS TO THINK ABOUT THE FUTURE

Most analyses of the climate problem project a business-as-usual (BAU) case, like the MIT no-policy case shown in Chapter 2, and then compile a list of policies and technologies that would reduce emissions, ranked based on costs and effectiveness. The simplest and most widely used example of this approach is that presented by Pacala and Socolow in *Science* back in 2004, which is often referred to as the stabilization wedges method.[3]

**FIGURE 3-1:** The stabilization triangle

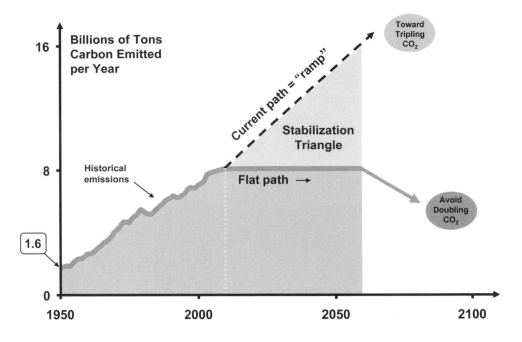

SOURCE: The Carbon Mitigation Initiative, Princeton University", [http://cmi.princeton.edu/wedges/]. Used with permission.

**Figure 3-1** summarizes what Pacala and Socolow call the stabilization triangle, which would keep emissions constant over 50 years.[4] The triangle is the area between the line representing constant emissions and the business-as-usual case. **Figure 3-2** shows that the stabilization triangle is made up of wedges, each of which avoids 25 billion tons of carbon emissions over 50 years. One wedge could be something like doubling the efficiency of all of the world's light duty vehicles from 30 to 60 miles per gallon, or increasing wind-generated electricity by 100 billion kWh per year each year for 50 years. Using the business-as-usual assumptions in their analysis (carbon emissions growth of 1.5% per year, which is slightly lower than that in the MIT no-policy case), it would take seven or eight wedges to keep emissions constant for 50 years, and more to actually make emissions decline.

The wedges approach has immense heuristic value because it allows people without much technical knowledge to increase their understanding of the problem and potential solutions. It also forces us to confront the enormity of the task ahead in a quantitative way, and was instrumental in convincing

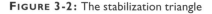

**FIGURE 3-2:** The stabilization triangle

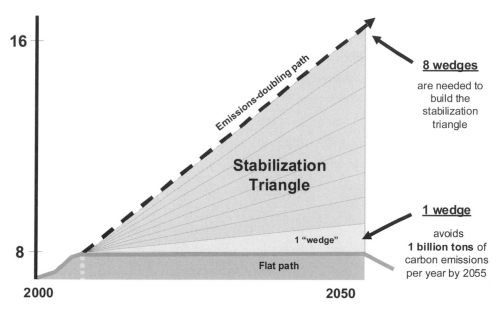

SOURCE: The Carbon Mitigation Initiative, Princeton University", [http://cmi.princeton.edu/wedges/]. Used with permission.

many that substantial strides toward a low-carbon world were possible with existing technologies.

However, one downside to this and all other conventional approaches is that the number of wedges we'll need to accomplish any specific goal is dependent on the baseline (i.e., the BAU case). If the underlying drivers of emissions are growing more rapidly than we first estimated, we'll need to implement more wedges than we initially expected to achieve any particular level of emissions reductions. So the focus on *savings* (or emissions reductions) instead of absolute emissions levels is a weakness of this type of analysis.

In addition, there are other issues with these conventional approaches. At least the wedges approach revels in its own simplicity and does not pretend to be something that it isn't. The same cannot be said about most other analyses of this problem, which rely on large computer models, big databases, and extensive analyses, usually conducted over years. These large studies have numerous problems, a topic to which I will now turn (and will expand upon even more in the next chapter).

In spite of the time and expense associated with such studies, they invariably rely on an incomplete and imperfect list of possible options, leading to overestimates of the costs of action.[5] Sometimes these omissions exist because an analyst wants to highlight a particular technology, like nuclear, wind generation, or carbon sequestration. Sometimes they exist because of ignorance, a lack of data, a lack of time, a model's structural limitations, or complexity in the systems being analyzed (combined generation of heat and power often falls into this latter category). And sometimes they exist because of ideological blinders: for example, economists typically assume that there can't be money-saving energy efficiency remaining because "if there were a 20-dollar bill on the sidewalk, someone would have picked it up already", in spite of empirical evidence to the contrary.

But whatever the reason, analyses of action on climate are biased toward higher costs by omitting options, and *every* analysis artificially constrains the options for the reasons listed above (and others). While most such reports will list the items they omit, the authors will still carry their analysis forward with those omissions and report their assessment of what the costs of emissions reductions will be, without reporting this systematic bias toward high costs of action. *In so doing they create an unintentional bias toward maintaining the status quo, because they make action seem more costly than it really is.*[6]

Back in the late 1990s I had a front-row seat to one way that such constraints are sometimes imposed on government-funded research studies. I was one of the senior scientists working on a project funded by the US Department of Energy to analyze the potential for reducing greenhouse gas emissions and solving other energy-related problems for the US.[7] This study became (and remains) the most detailed and comprehensive study of its type ever funded by the US government, but as we were starting the project, we received explicit instructions from the funders that we could not include a carbon tax as a policy option in the study. We were allowed to analyze carbon emissions trading, which was a more politically feasible option that had similarities to a carbon tax, but it struck me as odd that a policy option would be excluded from the beginning (especially when it had many advantages, especially lower verification/transaction costs, easier enforcement, and more predictable revenue).

There are also some deeper reasons to distrust analyses of this type. Analysts always impose their ideas of what is possible on which policies and technologies are analyzed, but as I'll argue in the next chapter, with few exceptions *it is very difficult to predict years in advance what is feasible and what isn't.* People

## PUTTING A PRICE ON GREENHOUSE GAS EMISSIONS

The US political system failed to institute an emissions trading system for GHGs in 2009, which was our best chance in history to get it done. A tax would be much simpler, cheaper to enforce, and less prone to gaming by the financial industry, so economists generally prefer taxes to tradable permits, but at this point we need a carbon price in any way we can get it.

What most folks don't understand is that the most important aspect of modest prices on carbon is *to influence fuel choices in industry, airline travel and the electricity supply side*, not to reduce consumer demand. Industry fuel prices are low compared to residential or commercial prices. A carbon tax is based on carbon content of the fuel, so the percentage change in price from the carbon tax on natural gas used in the residential sector (for example) is much lower than the percentage change in price for the same natural gas consumed in the utility sector. That makes the fuel choices for industry much more sensitive to any given carbon tax than those of residential or commercial consumers.

A carbon tax of $20/metric ton of $CO_2$ (which is roughly the price for the European emissions trading system in the past few years) adds about 2 cents/kWh to the price of coal fired electricity. Natural gas fired plants are much more efficient than coal plants and emit about half as much carbon per unit of electricity generated.* That leads to the carbon tax only being about 1 cent/kWh for a natural gas-fired combined-cycle plant, giving it a 1 cent advantage over coal fired generation compared to the case without a carbon tax. Non-fossil generation like wind or nuclear power would receive a 2 cent per kWh advantage. That result, combined with likely new constraints and regulations on coal emissions of all types, as well as very low prices for natural gas, makes it a challenging environment for coal-fired generation.

As long as fugitive emissions of natural gas are kept low, switching from coal to gas in the utility sector is a low-cost way to achieve carbon reductions quickly, given that so many existing coal plants were grandfathered under the Clean Air Act, are quite inefficient, and are comparatively dirty from the perspective of particulates and other criteria pollutants. Many gas plants, by contrast, are new, highly efficient, and relatively clean. They are also typically run at capacity factors that are much lower than their maximum capacity factors, so they have room to run more often to displace the output from retired coal plants.

*For more on the characteristics of coal vs. other kinds of plants, read Koomey et al. 2010. "Defining a standard metric for electricity savings." Environmental Research Letters. vol. 5 014017, no. 1 January-March. [http://iopscience.iop.org/1748-9326/5/1/014017].

also usually underestimate the rate and scope of change that can occur with determined effort, and this bias is reinforced by the use of models that ignore important effects (like increasing returns to scale and other sources of path dependence), and include rigidities that don't exist in the real economy (like assuming that individual and institutional decision-making will be just like it was in the past, even in a future that is drastically different).[8] For all these reasons, it is a mistake to rely too heavily on models of economic systems to constrain our thinking about the future.

And it is not just the creators of complex economic models who fall prey to this pitfall. Rob Socolow, one of the pioneers of the wedges method, was quoted in an article looking back on the contribution of his efforts as saying "I said hundreds of times the world should be very pleased with itself if the amount of emissions was the same in 50 years as it is today."[9] Now, I'm a big fan of Rob, we've been colleagues for years, and I have great admiration for what the wedges papers contributed to advancing the climate debate. But this statement has always rubbed me the wrong way, and I finally figured out why: it imposes his informal judgment about what is *feasible* on the analysis of the problem, and as I discuss in the next chapter, that is almost impossible to determine in advance.

Feasibility depends on context, and on what we are willing to pay to minimize risks. What if there's a big climate-related disaster and we finally decide that it's a real emergency (like World War II)? In that case we'd make every effort to fix the problem, and what would be possible then is far beyond what we could imagine today. It is therefore a mistake for analysts to impose an informal feasibility judgment when considering a problem like this one, and instead we should aim for what we think is the best outcome from a risk minimization perspective, and if we don't quite get there, then we'll have to deal with the consequences. But if we aim too low, we might miss possibilities that we'd otherwise be able to capture.

Judging feasibility without careful analysis really is a distraction—people obsessed with what is possible politically or practically kill innovative thinking because they miss the many degrees of freedom that we have to shape the future. They take the system as it is for granted, and we just can't do that anymore.

An archetypal example is the discussion about integrating variable renewable power generation (like wind generation or solar photovoltaics) into the grid. In the old days the grizzled utility guys would say things like "maybe you can have a few percent of those resources on the grid, but above that you'll destabilize the system". Now we know that's nonsense, and the "conventional wisdom percentage" of what's allowable has crept up over the years, but it always reflected a static (and incomplete) view of what the system could handle. Over time, we can even change the system to use smaller gas-fired power plants that respond more rapidly to changes in loads, install better grid controls, institute variable pricing using smart meters, use weather forecasting, diversify variable renewables (by type and location), and create better software for anticipating grid problems. All of those things together should allow us to handle much more variability than what a conventional utility operator might think is feasible. And as we become smarter about energy storage, things will get easier still.[10]

The same lesson applies to any attempts to envision a vastly different energy system than the one we have today. We need to take off our feasibility blinders and shoot for the lowest emissions systems we can create. That doesn't mean we can ignore real constraints, but we do need to throw off the illusory ones that are an artifact of our limited foresight. And if we don't quite make it, that's life, but at least it won't be for lack of trying.

I've described the problems with conventional approaches, which revolve around our inability to predict the future, either for the business-as-usual case or for alternative futures. These methods also result in a systematic bias against climate action, because they ignore important phenomena like increasing returns to scale, assume rigidities in the economy that are not actually evident, and omit technology and policy options from their calculus (these omissions all point toward overestimating the costs of altering the status quo, and I'll explore these issues more in the next chapter).

But is there another way? Why yes, there is.

## WORKING FORWARD TOWARD A GOAL

The most viable alternative to the conventional approach is to set a long-term goal and estimate what it would take to get there. In this way, *working toward our goals allows us to create the future.*

The most sophisticated businesses face strategic choices in this way. They know that forecasting accurately is impossible, so they develop a plan of action and modify it as developments dictate, taking account of relevant uncertainties. When I talk with my friends in business about this method they think I'm stating the obvious, but that's not how most folks have looked at the climate problem until recently. Instead, they've focused on assessing what Florentin Krause calls our "warming fate" if we adopt particular policies or technologies, using the conventional thinking I discussed in the previous section.

In the context of climate, the "working forward toward a goal" approach would involve setting a temperature target or *warming limit* (say 2 Celsius degrees above preindustrial levels) and then figuring out what emissions reductions, investments, behavioral changes, and institutional choices would need to happen to make that future a reality. This approach implies a certain greenhouse gas (GHG) budget, which is the cumulative amount of heat-trapping gases that we could emit over the next century while still staying under that warming target. It would also involve deciding on ways to measure progress toward the ultimate goal, so that if the world weren't on track to meet the goal, then we could change course to make it more likely that we'd get there on time and under (GHG) budget.

This way of thinking is diametrically opposed to the conventional approach I describe above, and changes the terms of the discussion. First, it puts the inevitable value choice front and center, in the choice of warming limit. This choice embodies our risk tolerance, and that involves an expression of our values. The more conventional approach hides value choices in ostensibly computational terms like the discount rate and other model parameters, but the value choices are there nonetheless (just hidden, as I'll discuss more in the next chapter).

Second, this approach turns the problem into an experimental and empirical one, with an emphasis on near-term actions from which we will learn by doing. No longer need we worry about whether we're calculating and following an optimal path for the next 50 years, because we've accepted up front that there isn't such a path, just lots of possible ones, many of which have broadly similar costs.[11] Then the focus becomes one of identifying near-term options about which we know a great deal and can implement rapidly, instead of speculating about unknowable things like the cost of a power plant in 2050. We'll need to try many things, fail fast, and do lots more of what works and less of what doesn't.

Third, this approach allows us to base our strategic decisions on the physical characteristics of the climate system, not on inherently less reliable models of economic and technological systems. It has always been ironic that many who argued against climate action because they said the climate models were unreliable are willing to put their faith in economic assessments of the problem that are demonstrably far less reliable than climate models. As I explained in the previous chapter, the climate models are validated based on measurements and designed based on physical principles, so they reflect our best understanding about how the climate system works. Economic models, on the other hand, are useful in certain contexts, but for reasons I explore in the next chapter, are incapable of accurate long-term forecasting in any meaningful sense of the term, ignore critical factors that govern real individual and institutional decision making in the real world, and impose rigidities on the economy that are not related to actual constraints on economic flexibility but are driven by modeling practice.[12]

Finally, this new approach uses economics to assess *cost effectiveness* of different near-term alternatives for reducing GHG emissions, but abandons the cost-benefit paradigm for this particular problem.[13] Cost-benefit analysis can work well for particular kinds of environmental problems (like those with shorter time constants and well-defined mitigation cost and damage functions) but once we admit that it's impossible to accurately calculate these functions for GHGs decades into the future, it becomes more hindrance than help.[14]

The operative phrase for this approach is "ready, fire, aim (adjust for continuous improvement)". It is, at its heart, an evolutionary approach to the problem, one that acknowledges that the world is path dependent and that learning-by-doing effects are dominant, not trivial (as all general equilibrium models assume). But learning by doing only happens if we *do*, and by not investing in different options we may very well preclude them.[15]

## WHAT WARMING LIMIT SHOULD WE CHOOSE?

There's no perfect answer to this quandary. When setting a warming limit, we'll need to balance the costs and difficulties of changing course with the potential risks to humanity and earth's natural systems of continuing on our current path. That means value judgments that inevitably will be based on imperfect information about the future. We will not know with certainty before we'll need to act and forestall the probable consequences—the climate problem is especially daunting for this reason.

The choice of warming limit is an explicit value judgment, but scientific knowledge can be brought to bear on the question. A review of the climate literature shows that 2 Celsius degrees above preindustrial levels is the highest the global temperature has been over the past two million years,[16] which is one reason why many scientists have argued for and many governments have adopted this warming limit as their target.[17] The history of the 2-degree limit goes back to the 1970s,[18] but the warming limit approach was not fully developed until the late 1980s.[19]

We know that the earth has been much hotter in the distant past, and there is a real concern that if we exceed the 2-degree limit we risk destabilizing the climate by initiating positive feedback loops (like the release of methane and carbon dioxide from the thawing tundra and methane hydrates in the undersea floor). We may still initiate these feedbacks even if we stay under 2 degrees, but we will almost certainly do so if we allow the earth to warm much past that limit. A case can be made for even lower temperature limits, but there's no strong argument for allowing the temperatures to exceed 2 Celsius degrees if we have a choice.

## WHAT CAN WE LEARN FROM THE WARMING LIMIT APPROACH?

The most important insight from this "working forward toward a goal" approach is that the choice of a warming limit implies a certain budget of greenhouse gas emissions that we cannot exceed if we want to stay below the limit. Because most GHGs stay in the atmosphere for a very long time, it is the cumulative emissions over the next century that matter, and scenarios with similar cumulative emissions will have comparable (though not necessarily exactly the same) warming impacts.

A related insight is that delaying emissions reductions makes our situation worse, not better, because we lock in carbon-intensive capital stocks and use up the budget. **Figure 3-3** shows what happens for a specific carbon budget if we delay. If we were to start reducing emissions in 2011, the maximum required rate of emissions reductions is about 3.7% per year for this particular

**FIGURE 3-3:** Wait and see doesn't work for climate change

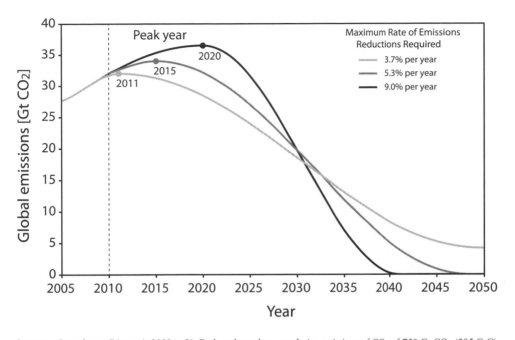

SOURCE: Copenhagen Diagnosis 2009, p.51. Each pathway has cumulative emissions of $CO_2$ of 750 Gt $CO_2$ (205 GtC) during the time period 2010-2050. At this level, there is a 67% probability of limiting global warming to a maximum of 2°C. The graph shows that the later the peak in emissions is reached, the steeper their subsequent reduction has to be. The figure shows variants of a global emissions scenario with different peak years: 2011 (light gray), 2015 (dark gray) and 2020 (black). In order to achieve compliance with these curves, maximum annual reduction rates of 3.7 % (light gray), 5.3 % (dark gray) or 9.0 % (black) would be required (relative to 2008). Used with permission.

budget. If we wait until 2015 to get serious, the maximum rate is 5.3% per year. And if we wait until 2020, the maximum rate is 9% per year, a daunting challenge. The budget strongly constrains what is possible, and once you acknowledge that the climate system depends on cumulative emissions, the argument for delaying action simply collapses.

**Figure 3-4** makes the same argument from a different perspective, that of turnover of capital stocks. Between half and 90% of major capital stocks that will exist in 2050 will have been built between now and then. The longer we wait to build low carbon infrastructure, the more obsolete high emissions capital we'll need to scrap to meet the emissions budgets described below, which is one reason why the International Energy Agency stated clearly in 2009 that each year of delay adds another $500B to the cost of achieving climate stabilization.[20] *Delay is simply foolish and irresponsible, and those arguing for it should be ashamed of their faulty logic.*

**FIGURE 3-4:** A significant fraction of equipment stocks existing in 2050 will be built between now and then

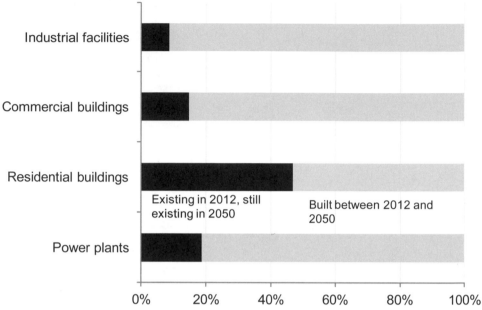

Between half and 90% of major capital stocks existing in 2050 will be installed between 2012 and 2050. These calculations assume that power plant capital stocks track the World Energy Outlook 2009 from 2012 to 2030 and continue at that rate to 2050, that residential buildings grow at the same rate as population, and that commercial/industrial facilities grow at the same rate as GDP growth over that period. Lifetimes for commercial buildings and power plants are assumed to be 50 years, residential buildings 100 years, and industrial facilities 30 years. Retirement rates are calculated from lifetimes assuming exponential retirements. These calculations ignore the possibility of retrofitting existing facilities, which can often result in significant emissions savings.

## WHAT'S OUR GHG BUDGET UNDER A 2-DEGREE LIMIT?

So what carbon budget is implied by a 2-degree warming limit for the next century, if we use the outputs from the MIT modeling framework? That study did not consider a "2 degree target" case, but it did have a scenario that came close (called "Level 1"), yielding a 2.4 Celsius degree temperature rise by 2100 (with another half a Celsius degree in the pipeline that would eventually manifest). That temperature increase corresponds to about one doubling over pre-industrial levels, when all gases are considered (see **Figure 3-5**).

The problem is that we've wasted more than two decades since it was clear climate change was going to be a problem, and we've allowed GHGs to accumulate in the atmosphere at an accelerating rate. To keep long-term temperatures from rising more than 2 Celsius degrees would mean (using our simple math from the last chapter and the calculations in Appendix B) keeping total

**FIGURE 3-5:** Greenhouse gas (GHG) equivalent concentrations from MIT's Level I case

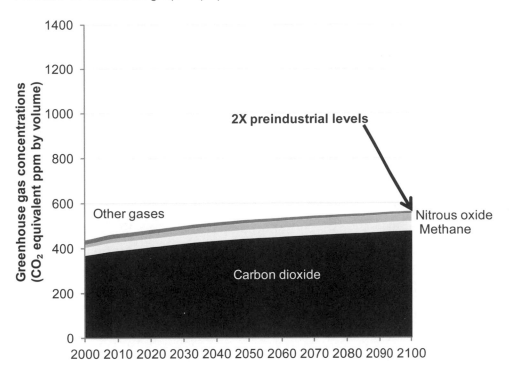

The Level 1 case keeps total GHG concentrations to about one doubling compared to preindustrial times by 2100.

GHG concentrations to about 444 ppm $CO_2$ equivalent, or about 1.587 times greater than preindustrial times (let's call it 450 ppm because that's a figure that is often cited in the literature on this topic). According to the output from the MIT study, $CO_2$ equivalent concentrations circa 2010 are about 471 ppm including all gases, so we seem on first blush to have already slightly exceeded the level needed to keep the temperature from rising more than two Celsius degrees from preindustrial times.[21]

But things are much more complicated than that. The simple calculation we did for the MIT no-policy case (number of doublings of GHGs times a climate sensitivity of 3 Celsius degrees) came very close to the actual results from MIT's complex model for 2100, but in a case where we rapidly reduce greenhouse gases, the dynamics are quite different. In this situation, we can exceed the GHG concentrations for hitting 2 Celsius degrees calculated using the simple approach as long as we don't do it for very long. This is what is known in the literature as an "overshoot" scenario,[22] and that appears to be our current situation.

That means that we need to rapidly reduce our current emissions (especially of short-lived warming agents like methane and soot) AND we need to figure out ways to sequester carbon from the atmosphere as rapidly as we can. The only currently feasible methods for large-scale sequestration of this type are those related to changing land-use patterns to encourage reforestation and better management of croplands under cultivation, but of course there are complexities in implementing such approaches on a broad scale.[23] And just stopping deforestation won't do it—the MIT no-policy case already includes very aggressive reductions in net carbon emissions from land use, so these other efforts would have to actually reverse the deforestation of previous decades, in spite of increasing populations and food demand.

There's a subtlety here that is important to understand. When we calculate $CO_2$-equivalent concentrations there are at least two conventions: one is to focus on all factors affecting the climate, the other is to exclude the cooling effect of small particles (aerosols released from coal and oil combustion and other human activities) as well as the effects of tropospheric ozone, soot, surface albedo, and a few other less important factors.[24] These aerosols affect the $CO_2$ equivalent calculations by preventing some of the sun's energy from reaching the surface and slowing the warming effect.[25] At this point, the aerosols just about cancel out the warming effect of the non-$CO_2$ gases, so the net warming effect in steady state will be similar to that induced by the $CO_2$-only concentration (or about 390 ppm in 2010). The MIT scenario data excludes the effect of aerosols from the $CO_2$ equivalent concentration, which is why the MIT calculations yield a $CO_2$ equivalent concentration of about 470 ppm.

This distinction sounds like a technical one, but it has real implications for people working on fixing the climate, since we're not actually in steady state. Any strategy that reduces use of high-sulfur fuels (like coal and heavy oil) will also reduce aerosols, so that beneficial effect of this pollutant will be reduced in any scenario where these fuels are phased out. But if we don't phase out fossil fuels the long-term effects of increased $CO_2$ concentrations will continue to warm the planet. So we're damned if we do and damned if we don't.

Fortunately, there is a simple way to think about this problem in the context of aggressive climate stabilization scenarios. The aerosol effect will eventually become less important because fuels that emit them will be phased out, so it's a temporary benefit, and the full warming effect in the long term is roughly represented by the $CO_2$ equivalent calculation from the MIT analysis. But that also means that our choices about how we implement that phaseout needs to be informed by that reality, and since aerosols have lifetimes of days to a few weeks, we can affect their concentrations relatively rapidly. There has been far too little work on these issues so far, but it's time to start thinking about them.[26]

This is yet another example of path dependence. The rate at which we phase out fossil fuels will affect the concentrations of aerosols, and so we need to think hard about the best way to implement that phaseout to minimize warming during that period. One strategy could involve phasing out shorter-lived GHGs rapidly in the near term so as to offset the loss of the beneficial effects of the aerosols, but this issue hasn't been studied in as much depth as some others. We don't have much time to figure this out, however, so we'd better get cracking.

## A BENCHMARK FOR ACTION

As we've discussed, the simple calculations we just did indicate that the MIT Level 1 case eventually stabilizes the climate at about 3 Celsius degrees above preindustrial levels. This isn't nearly good enough, if we take the 2 Celsius degree warming limit seriously (as well we should). But we can use the quantitative estimates from the Level 1 case as a benchmark to help us understand the rate and scope of emissions reductions that will be needed in a world that is rapidly phasing out fossil fuels. We can also use the results from more sophisticated analyses that explicitly ask the question "How many greenhouse gases can we emit and still stay under 2 Celsius degrees of warming?"

Let's start by examining **Figure 3-6**, which shows the emissions pathway for the MIT Level 1 case. This case assumed that emissions reductions started rapidly in 2005, slowed down a bit, but continued for the rest of the forecast. As I've discussed above, the most important thing about such a pathway is the cumulative emissions. From 2000 to 2100, the Level 1 case has carbon emissions of about 550 billion tons of carbon (or about 2000 billion tons of $CO_2$) including fossil fuel emissions, land-use changes, and cement production. I've also plotted on that figure an alternative pathway that has the same cumulative emissions from 2000 to 2050 and from 2000 to 2100, but that peaks in 2012 instead of 2005, to reflect a delay in taking action.

**FIGURE 3-6:** Global carbon emissions paths for MIT's Level I case, and the same case modified to reflect emissions peaking in 2012 instead of 2005

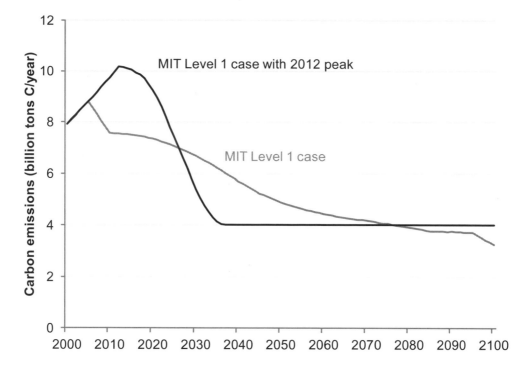

The cumulative emissions in the 2012 peaking case match those in the Level 1 case from 2000 to 2049 as well as those from 2000 to 2100.

The area under those two curves is equal, which is the same as saying that their cumulative emissions over that period are equal. And there are very few smooth curves that meet the joint constraints of cumulative emissions from 2000 to 2049 and cumulative emissions over the entire 21st century, so we don't have a lot of choice if we want to match the Level 1 emissions scenario (or even lower ones).

As I showed earlier, cumulative emissions constrain our choices and make delay costly. By waiting even seven years past 2005, we've made our required emissions reduction path more difficult, because the higher emissions in the interim ate up part of our carbon budget, and that has to be paid for with faster emissions reductions later so that the total budget comes out the same. If energy technologies improved as fast as computer technologies there might be an argument for waiting in some cases, but they don't, so it's a moot point.

That's why those who minimize the need for immediate action in preference for research and development (R&D) on new breakthrough technologies are making a grave error in logic. By all means let's do the R&D, but that does not absolve us of the responsibility to take immediate action (and as I'll show in Chapter 6, there are huge opportunities for emissions reductions using technologies now "on the shelf"). Cost reductions in new technologies generally result from learning effects that occur during deployment, not because of R&D breakthroughs, and these can drastically reduce the estimated costs of reducing emissions.[27] That's because individuals and institutions typically need time to reorganize their activities to better reflect the characteristics of new technology, but once they do, cost reductions occur rapidly as the use of that technology spreads throughout the society.

A comprehensive scenario analysis by Meinshausen et al.[28], which is based on the output of the most sophisticated climate models, relates the cumulative emissions of carbon and other greenhouse gases in a particular scenario to the probability of staying under the 2-degree warming limit. This tool gives a rough idea of our chances of staying under the 2-degree warming limit, but it is an approximation, albeit a reasonable one, which is all we can ask in facing such a complex problem.

The analysis of Meinshausen et al. puts the probability that the MIT Level 1 case would stay below 2 Celsius degrees from preindustrial times at about 60% by 2100.[29] To have a two-thirds (66%) chance of staying under the 2-degree warming limit we'd need to reduce cumulative carbon emissions from 2000 to 2049 by 9% compared to the Level 1 case. That scenario is plotted as the "Safer Climate" case in **Figure 3-7**. It also has about 30% lower total emissions over the 2000 to 2100 period compared to the Level 1 case. The reduced carbon budget for what I call the "Safer Climate" case implies very rapid reductions in carbon emissions, almost 7% per year (compounded) from 2012 to 2042 (the period of most rapid reductions).

To keep it simple, let's assume also that the cumulative methane and nitrous oxides are reduced by a comparable amount over the 2000 to 2100 period.[30] This assumption ignores complexities about the relative warming power of the various gases, but it's good enough to get started in the right direction (and as I'll argue in the next chapter, that's about the best we can hope for—we'll need to change course later as developments dictate). I've plotted the results of that assumption in **Figure 3-8**, showing the no-policy case, the Level 1 case, and the Safer Climate case as an index relative to the no-policy case for each gas. This

**FIGURE 3-7:** Global carbon emissions for the Safer Climate case compared to the MIT Level I cases

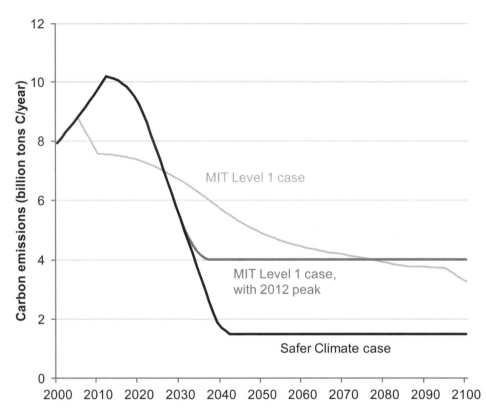

This graph shows global carbon emissions paths for MIT's Level 1 case, modified to reflect emissions peaking in 2012 instead of 2005 and constrained to either the same cumulative emissions as the Level 1 case or a 9% reduction in cumulative emissions from 2000 to 2049 (Safer Climate case). The Safer Climate case has a two-thirds chance of the world staying below 2 Celsius degrees warming, but it very tightly constrains our choices and represents very rapid emissions reductions.

graph shows that cumulative emissions from 2000 to 2100 will need to be reduced by about 80% for $CO_2$ and about 60% for $CH_4$ and $N_2O$ in the Safer Climate case.

Reducing emissions this much will be a big challenge, but the science is very clear and the logic of emissions budgets is inexorable. If we want even a decent chance of keeping global temperatures from rising more than 2 degrees above preindustrial levels, greenhouse gas emissions reductions need to start without delay.

*Our GHG budget is almost overspent. If the climate sensitivity is really 3 Celsius degrees (as multiple lines of evidence strongly indicate[31]), we will need to start aggressive emissions reductions immediately if want a strong chance*

**FIGURE 3-8:** Cumulative emissions (2000 to 2100) for the MIT no-policy case, the Level 1 case, and the Safer Climate case, expressed as an index (no-policy case = 1.0)

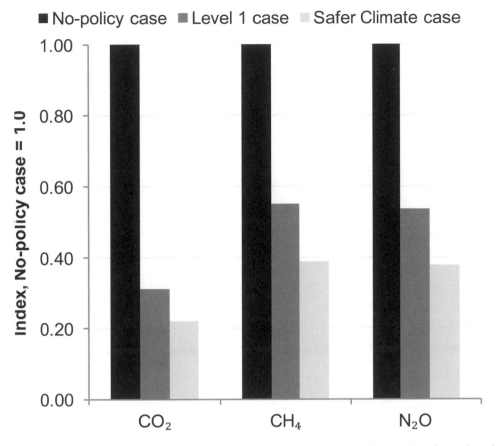

*of limiting warming to 2 Celsius degrees, focusing on both the short-lived GHGs like methane, black carbon, and tropospheric ozone as well as the longer-lived ones like $CO_2$ and $N_2O$. While there is uncertainty in this assessment, we will not be able to resolve the uncertainty before we'll need to decide what to do, so the uncertainty shouldn't interfere with prompt action.*

### SO WHAT NOW?

If we take the 2 Celsius degree warming limit seriously, we'll need to limit $CO_2$ emissions from all sources to no more than 315 billion tons of carbon (about 1150 billion tons of $CO_2$) from 2000 until 2049, which implies rapid phaseout of fossil fuels (as well as other sources of GHGs). That means we can't even

**FIGURE 3-9:** Climate stabilization at or near 2 Celsius degrees above preindustrial levels means either keeping some of our proved fossil reserves in the ground or sequestering the carbon from burning those fuels in a safe way

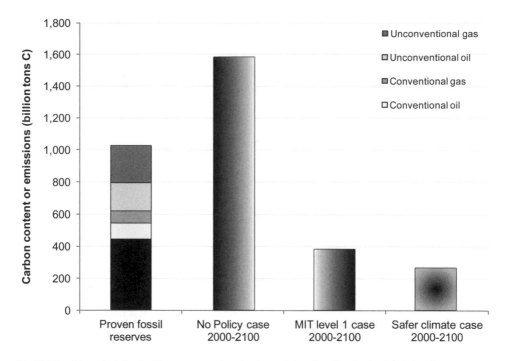

The MIT Level 1 case includes significant sequestration of carbon emissions from burning fossil fuels, but those sequestered emissions are not included in this figure, just the net emissions after sequestration.

burn the currently existing stock of proved reserves of fossil fuels and remain under the 2 Celsius degree warming limit (see **Figure 3-9**). Recall that the proved reserves data from Appendix A represents a lower bound, so the comparison is even more stark. We'll need to keep a significant fraction of our proved reserves from being burned, or we'll need to figure out a way to sequester carbon in a safe way (which is not currently feasible on the scales needed, though it has been successful in some applications).

## HOW DO WE MEASURE SUCCESS?

Another advantage of this approach is that we can set up easily measurable benchmarks to figure out if we are succeeding. We can calculate with reasonable precision emissions of carbon dioxide from fossil fuels and cement production, and can estimate emissions of methane, nitrous oxide, other GHGs, and $CO_2$ from land-use changes with a little more difficulty. We can compare the $CO_2$ emissions in any year with the Safer Climate pathway described in Figure 3-8 (and similar ones for the other gases). As we saw from the discussion above, a carbon budget that would keep temperatures from rising more than 2 Celsius degrees imposes very tight constraints on our actions—there is limited flexibility, which means that if we're not meeting the desired emissions pathway, we'll need to adapt rapidly to do more.

We can also estimate how fast we'd need to install low-pollution infrastructure to meet a given emissions budget, and compare those estimates to how much such infrastructure we're actually able to build in a given year. This type of calculation, first explored by Krause et al. in 1989[32] and then further developed by Caldeira et al. in 2003,[33] can help quantify the scope of the effort needed to displace fossil fuels. For example, we can estimate how many nonfossil power plants are needed to reduce the carbon intensity of electricity production by a specified amount, which can tell us whether we're on track to build enough this year and next. This kind of concrete planning information is one of the benefits of the warming limit approach.

### WHAT ABOUT 350 PPM?

I'm supportive of those (like NASA's James Hansen and 350.org) who advocate for a long-term atmospheric $CO_2$ concentration goal of 350 ppm.[34] We won't know if we can do it until we try, and having an aggressive goal that we fail to meet because it's actually beyond our reach is far better than setting our sights too low from the beginning.[35] I've already described why I think people underestimate the capacity for change, so better to aim high.

### CONCLUSIONS

Exploiting fossil fuels has brought extraordinary economic benefits since the industrial revolution, but it was only in the last century that emissions from burning those fuels were large enough to measurably affect the climate. The sheer mass of easily extractable fossil fuels in the earth's crust made this day of reckoning inevitable,[36] but our choices about how we structure our society have also influenced this outcome. And while the benefits have been large, so too have the problems, especially the mostly uncounted social costs of using those fuels.[37] There is, however, a silver lining: the technology we've developed over the past century will finally allow us to move past fossil fuels and ultimately to eliminate combustion itself in most applications. The only question will be if we can do it fast enough to forestall the worst of the consequences climate change has in store for us.

When I first started studying the Japanese martial art of Aikido more than two decades ago, a senior student told me that there were only two levels: introductory and beginner. That's exactly the kind of attitude we'll need to take for this challenge. We'll need to learn rapidly in coming years, because we've never faced anything like this before. Fixing the climate won't be easy, but fix it we must if we want to preserve a livable world for our descendents.

## CHAPTER 3: KEY TAKEAWAYS

• Most conventional analyses of the climate problem have attempted to assess our fate prospectively, assuming we take certain actions, but the models used for these assessments are limited in their applicability, constraining in their approach, and appalling in their inaccuracy.

• Working toward a specified warming limit is a more reliable way to think about the future, embracing Alan Kay's dictum that "the best way to predict the future is to invent it."

• Keeping earth's average temperature from rising more than 2 Celsius degrees from preindustrial levels will require immediate, rapid, and sustained greenhouse gas emissions reductions, with a goal of 450 ppm $CO_2$ equivalent. There's no more time to waste.

• Delaying action is foolish and irresponsible. The physics of the climate system and the logic of the warming limit approach impose strict constraints on the possible paths that keep the earth from warming more than 2 Celsius degrees.

# 4

---

## WHY WE CAN'T ACCURATELY
## FORECAST THE FUTURE

---

*"Prediction is very difficult, especially about the future."*

—NIELS BOHR

I've explained in previous chapters that I thought it was not possible to predict the future of economic, social, and technological systems, and that this limitation of our foresight has implications for how we should treat a long-term problem like climate change. This chapter explains why I believe it.

Those trying to assess the costs of fixing the climate problem often appeal to the results of economic models to argue their case. These models are flawed in many ways, but before getting to those flaws, let's talk about a more fundamental assumption of such attempts: that it is possible in principle to predict the future of economic and social systems.

Economic modelers try to find the "optimal" solution for the climate problem. They make estimates of the costs of reducing emissions and the avoided damages from increased emissions (as in **Figure 4-1**) and characterize the point where the two curves cross as the optimal one.[1] That point is where the marginal cost of reducing emissions is equal to the marginal benefits from reducing them. In this view, reducing emissions beyond that point would imply that we would have paid too much for emissions reductions—the costs for incremental emissions reductions would exceed the benefits. This particular model has worked reasonably well for short-term analyses of other kinds of pollution, like sulfur dioxide, which is why economists have tried to apply it to the climate problem.

If you talk with most economic and technological modelers they will tell

**FIGURE 4-1:** Standard application of benefit-cost analysis to the climate problem

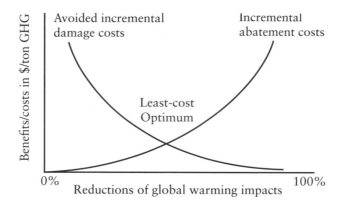

you that if only they had enough time, data, graduate students, coffee, and budget, they could accurately forecast the cost and benefits of fixing the climate, and do it before we need to make any decisions. In other words, they claim to be able to accurately estimate the costs and benefit curves in Figure 4-1 over the long term. But can this really be true? Is there such a thing as an accurate prediction for 2050 or 2100?

The optimism that modelers bring to this question is admirable, but it is quite misplaced. Accurate predictions are sometimes possible for certain kinds of physical phenomena (like the speed of light or the motions of the planets in our solar system), but economic and social systems are different, as the dismal record of accuracy for economic models quite clearly indicates. Economics is not physics, a caution that economic modelers continue to ignore at their peril.

In the mid-1970s and early 1980s, conventional wisdom held that modern societies could not reduce energy use without also reducing gross domestic product (GDP) and harming their economies. For example, Gordon Corey, vice-chairman of Chicago's Commonwealth Edison, stated in 1981 that "there is an unbreakable tie between economic prosperity and energy use." Similarly, the Chase Manhattan Bank stated, in its 1976 Energy Report, that:

> There is no documented evidence that indicates the long-lasting, consistent relationship between energy use and GDP will change in the future. There is no sound, proven basis for believing a billion dollars of GDP can be generated with less energy in the future.[2]

Believers in an unbreakable link between energy use and GDP assigned the immutability of a physical law to this historical relationship but found their belief shattered by events. From 1973 to 1986, US primary energy consumption stayed flat, but GDP rose 35% in real (inflation-adjusted) terms. These believers had forgotten that people and institutions can adapt to new realities, and historically derived relationships (like the apparent link between energy use and GDP that held up for more than two decades in the post-World-War-II period) can become invalid when events (like the 1973 oil embargo) overtake them. And this is not an isolated example, as explained by Ascher,[3] Craig et al.,[4] and DeCanio[5].

## THE IMPORTANCE OF STRUCTURE

The underlying reason for our inability to forecast economic systems accurately over the long term relates to what I call "structural constancy". If a system has an underlying structure that remains constant over time, then accurate predictions about that system are possible, barring unforeseen events. The laws of gravitation, for example, are constant. That means we can predict when the moon will rise and when Jupiter will be visible in the sky from any place on earth, even years in the future. Similarly, the speed of light in a vacuum is a physical constant that is the same when measured in the US, Tahiti, or Russia.

On the other hand, relationships between cause and effect for economic systems are dependent on institutional, social, and economic context. Furthermore, these relationships change over time. A market researcher attempting to assess consumer acceptance for a new toothpaste would find that a market test in San Francisco would likely yield quite different results than in Tahiti even though the speed of light remains the same in both places. In addition, if the same experiment had been conducted in the 1950s, the results would have presumably varied wildly from those of the current day.

It is for these reasons that I say that economic and social systems do not exhibit the same structural constancy as physical systems. Technology improves, institutional behavior evolves, and individual preferences change, so the underlying characteristics of the economic system are different month to month, year to year, or decade to decade. This inconstancy makes accurate long-term prediction impossible.

The rapidity of technological change exacerbates this effect. Consider what a forecaster in 1900 would have faced when trying to predict what life would be like in the year 2000. That forecaster might have had some notion of the potential for automobiles, electric motors and lights, telephones, and simple aircraft, but no inkling of relativity, widespread mass production, universal access to the electric grid and telephone networks, quantum mechanics, radio, television, antibiotics, atomic weapons, jet engines, transistors, integrated circuits, computers, software, the Internet, globalized trade, industrialized agriculture, the structure of DNA, and genetic engineering. It's hard to imagine how the entirety of these developments could have been accurately foreseen one hundred years ago.

Of course, all forecasted futures (even those for systems exhibiting structural constancy) can be influenced by pivotal events that affect outcomes in ways we cannot envision, making my argument even stronger. For example, if a large unknown comet slams into the moon, the accuracy of orbital predictions will surely be affected. Similarly, economic systems can be shaken by events like the 1970s oil shocks, the 1987 stock market crash, or the terrorist attacks of September 11, 2001. These events can be anticipated (as the scenario planners at Shell in the late 1960s anticipated the possibility of an oil supply shock) but the exact timing and character of these events is beyond our ability to foresee.

In the rare cases where long-run economic forecasting models actually try to account for structural changes, they generally assume that underlying structural relationships in the economy vary in a gradual fashion, and ignore the possibility of disruptive events (because they are impossible to model or predict). But the longer the time frame of the forecast, the more likely it is that these pivotal events will change the underlying economic and behavioral relationships that determine how the future actually unfolds. And disruptive events like these exacerbate the structural inconstancy of economic systems, making the argument stronger still.

So we can't expect accuracy from economic forecasting models, no matter how smart or hard-working the modelers are. But if I haven't yet convinced you of that, there are other reasons to view the results of these models with great skepticism.

## MODELING REFLECTS HUMAN FRAILTIES

Modeling is the result of a human process. That means that limitations on people's time, attention, and cognition affect the quality of the end-result. Models themselves always have buried assumptions and conceptual flaws, as any experienced computer programmer will tell you.

Data used by models are always limited and incomplete. Important characteristics of the energy/economy system may not be measured, or some critical measurements may not be published, making accurate characterization of the system difficult or impossible. There are also always time lags slowing the release of data, and there are time lags in modelers incorporating data into their models.

## MODELS OVERESTIMATE COSTS

Forecasting models are sometimes broken up into two categories: "top-down" and "bottom-up". The top-down models use aggregate statistical (econometric) relationships between things like prices and consumption to characterize how the economy works. The bottom-up engineering-based models start with the question "Who is using how much energy for what purposes?" and track energy use at the level of devices, which allows for detailed assessments of policies that affect the efficiency of energy-using equipment.

In my experience, both econometric and engineering-based models are almost invariably too pessimistic (i.e., they overestimate costs of action to mitigate climate change). The models

- *assume structural constancy*, implying that rigidities existing in the current economy (some real and some imagined) continue throughout the forecast, even for scenarios where policies and conditions shift significantly. For example, many modelers plug large carbon taxes into their models to assess the potential economic effects of changes in fuel prices induced by limitations on carbon emissions, but fail to adjust the parameters in the model characterizing personal and institutional behavior that would shift in response to such a policy.[6] Similarly, the models take the current structure of property rights as a given, but as I explain below and in Chapter 7, this structure can (and should) be modified to encourage more sustainable choices by market players. Assuming structural constancy is the equivalent of believing that energy and GDP would always march in lockstep, even after the 1970s oil shocks, and we know how well that assumption worked out. In bottom-up models, the assumption of structural constancy shows up in different ways, but it is just as common.

- *rely on incomplete technology and policy portfolios*, which always increases the apparent cost of action. Modelers focus on options they understand and can characterize in their models, and omit those that don't (each model is different in this regard). For example, cogeneration (the joint production of heat and power) is not simple to model, and many energy models omit this important resource because it's complicated to track its associated energy flows. The newer technologies are almost always the most interesting ones from the perspective of a long-term forecast, but they are also the ones about which we know the least. And most bottom-up analyses are unable to easily account for the effects of carbon taxes or other policies that affect fuel prices, so they generally ignore those effects or treat them in a simplified way.

- *ignore "no-regrets" options* that save money and reduce emissions. This is mainly an issue with the "top-down" models, which assume that markets are perfect and that any deviation from the current "optimum" will cost money. This approach ignores the three-plus decades of evidence that some policies (like minimum efficiency standards, utility incentive programs, and Energy Star labeling of efficient appliances) do indeed reduce total costs to society while also reducing emissions. The reason such options exist is because markets are not perfect in practice, and the retrospective analyses for these efficiency programs prove it. Few argue that there are no such options (and the few that do base the argument solely on economic theory, not data). The debate is now over just how many such options might exist, and that is ultimately an empirical question. When I describe the existence of market failures to folks in the business world they nod their heads and say "Of course! That's how we make our money."

- *use discount rates biased toward the present* – The discount rate accounts for the time value of money, but use of typical interest rates (like that for a credit card balance or home equity loan, for example) to conduct benefit-cost analysis makes the benefits of climate action (which occur decades or centuries hence) worth very little and makes the cost appear larger in the calculation. Unfortunately, this approach buries an *ethical* choice about what kind of world we want to leave for our grandchildren in what looks like a computational decision about the discount rate, sacrificing the interests of those not yet born.[7]

- *ignore increasing returns to scale*, which is one of the most powerful factors affecting how the future unfolds. The concept of increasing returns encompasses forces like learning by doing, economies of scale, zero marginal costs of reproduction for information, and network externalities. Virtually every economic model assumes constant or decreasing returns to scale, but they do this solely for computational convenience, to ensure that the model comes to a single unique equilibrium. Including increasing returns in a model introduces path dependence, technological "lock-in", and the possibility of multiple possible end-points for a given starting point, vastly complicating the analysis.[8] Increasing returns imply that our choices now affect the choices that will be available later. For example, investing now creates opportunities for cost reductions through learning by doing that would not occur without those investments. Increasing returns are pervasive in the economy, and ignoring them creates a clear bias toward overestimating costs. I'll have more to say about this concept in Chapter 6.

- *ignore the context-dependent nature of property rights*, the inclusion of which also implies multiple equilibria, as DeCanio points out.[9] The models typically take existing property rights as a given, but rarely consider modifications to the structure of such rights in their alternative scenarios (except in the obvious instance that property rights for the atmosphere *must* be defined in some way in order to solve the climate problem). The problem is deeper than just climate, however, because there are many different ways for property rights to be defined and enforced, and they depend on the context in which they are created. This context evolves over time, as it should, but that means that taking property rights as given is fundamentally misleading, given that redefining such rights can have a huge impact on how society develops.

In summary, the models, by assumption, ignore increasing returns as a force in creating the future. They embed rigidities in the models that do not exist in the real world. They bury ethical choices about intergenerational equity in ostensibly "scientific" concepts like the discount rate. They avoid the possibility of redefining property rights in ways that would alter market participants' behavior. And they omit real options for solving the climate problem from their calculations, thereby overestimating the costs of action.[10]

So even if you think accurate forecasting of economic systems is possible, there are many reasons to doubt the validity of the economic models assessing the costs of fixing the climate problem. Stephen DeCanio, an eminent economics professor (emeritus) at UC Santa Barbara, summarizes this view eloquently:

> The application of general equilibrium analysis to climate policy has produced a kind of specious precision, a situation in which the assumptions of the analysts masquerade as results that are solidly grounded in theory and the data. This leads to a tremendous amount of confusion and mischief, not least of which is the notion that although the physical science of the climate is plagued by uncertainties, it is possible to know with a high degree of certainty just what the *economic* consequences of alternative policy actions will be.

We must therefore reassess what we can expect from these models. They can be useful, but the ways they have been used to date have mostly caused what DeCanio would charitably characterize as "mischief" and I would less charitably call "analytical errors". And that is why I argued in the previous chapter for moving away from the benefit-cost framing of the climate problem to one based on comparing cost effectiveness of different near-term options for reducing emissions.

## CONCLUSIONS

In some sense this argument is about the nature of reality. If you believe that human systems are as constant as physical systems, then it is possible to maintain that with enough time and resources accurate forecasting is possible (at least until a discontinuity rears its ugly head). But if you believe, as I do, that human systems are different and that unforeseeable pivotal events are commonplace, then you need a different approach to assessing the future, one based on a more solid intellectual footing. Forecasting models can yield important insights, but they need to be used in the right way (to support cost-effectiveness analysis of working toward a normatively determined goal).

Finally, the very fact that economic systems can rapidly change their structures over time gives me hope that we can move much more rapidly to solve this problem than the models indicate. It also points to the most important areas where entrepreneurial innovation can make a difference: in changing institutional and personal behavior to make the profitable choices also the most environmentally beneficial choices.

**CHAPTER 4: KEY TAKEAWAYS**

• Economic models cannot make accurate long-term predictions, both because economic systems do not exhibit the same structural constancy as physical systems, and because the exact timing and nature of pivotal events cannot be predicted.

• Economic models

  –ignore important effects like increasing returns to scale

  –assume historical rigidities will continue into the future

  –omit relevant options from consideration, thus overestimating the cost of action

  –bury ethical judgments in ostensibly technical concepts like the discount rate

• The limitations of these models make calculations of the "optimal carbon tax" in traditional cost-benefit analysis an exercise in futility.

• Modelers need to accept these limitations of our foresight and develop new ways of learning about the future that are not dependent on the accuracy of forecasts.

*"It is fashionable today to assume that any figures about the future are better than none. To produce figures about the unknown, the current method is to make a guess about something or other—called an "assumption"—and to derive an estimate from it by subtle calculation. The estimate is then presented as the result of scientific reasoning, something far superior to mere guesswork. This is a pernicious practice that can only lead to the most colossal planning errors, because it offers a bogus answer where, in fact, an entrepreneurial judgment is required."* — *E.F. SCHUMACHER*

# 5

## THE SCOPE OF THE PROBLEM

*"No battle plan survives contact with the enemy."*

—HELMUTH VON MOLTKE THE ELDER

Climate change is probably the biggest challenge modern humanity has ever faced. It's bigger than World War II, because it will take decades to vanquish this foe. It's harder than ozone depletion, whose causes were far less intertwined with industrial civilization than fossil fuels and other sources of greenhouse gases. And it's more intractable than the Great Depression (or our current economic malaise) because financial crises eventually pass, assuming we learn from past mistakes and fix the financial system (again!).

Will we be able to avoid the worst effects of climate change? Nobody knows for sure, but in the face of an existential threat to human civilization, that's the wrong question. We must do whatever we can, as Winston Churchill said during World War II: "What is our aim? I can answer with one word: Victory—victory at all costs,[1] victory in spite of all terror, victory however long and hard the road may be; for without victory there is no survival."[2] We'll give it our best, and if it's not enough, we'll have to live with the consequences, but it shouldn't be because we lack understanding or fail to try. That's why I spent so much effort in the last few chapters explaining the details of the fix in which we now find ourselves: so we can face this challenge with clarity and full knowledge of how difficult it will be.

Let's try to put this problem in context. For about three decades, starting in 2012, we'll need to reduce global carbon emissions by on average almost 7% per year (compounded) to meet the constraints of the Safer Climate case, even as population and economic activity grow substantially, and poorer countries continue striving toward modernity. We'll also need comparable reductions in other greenhouse gases. This rate of emissions reductions is historically unprecedented, at least over decade-long time scales, but that doesn't mean it is impossible.

At the start of World War II, the US auto industry took *six months* to transition from building a few million autos a year to building planes and tanks for the war effort.[3] This shift wasn't easy or cheap, but it happened, and this example illustrates one important point about such rapid emissions reductions: they will likely result in some capital being scrapped before the end of its useful life. This is a problem from a political perspective, of course, but many modelers and analysts treat scenarios with premature capital retirements as infeasible. Based on the analysis below, I suspect strongly that we won't have that luxury, given the rapid reductions we'll need to achieve (and it will be particularly likely if we continue to build high-carbon infrastructure after 2012).

## EMISSIONS SCENARIOS
## AND ROUTINE EQUIPMENT RETIREMENTS

The Safer Climate case implies about 1.7% per year carbon emissions reductions for the first decade after 2012 (compounded), with reductions of about 6.1%/year for the following decade and 10.6% per year for the decade after that. This back-loading of emissions reductions makes sense—it will take some time to gear up manufacturing capability to the needed scale. This rate of emissions reductions is aggressive, but not as aggressive as these percentages might imply at first glance.

As emissions actually start declining, a given percentage reduction represents a smaller *absolute amount* of equipment to be retired or replaced each year (because the percentage is relative to a smaller base). That's why it's often helpful to express reduction rates as a percentage of some base year value, in our case 2012. This tells us what fraction of 2012 emissions would have to be eliminated in any year to meet the constraints of the safer climate case, and it is proportional to the amount of capital equipment associated with those emissions (as long as there isn't much change in the carbon intensity of energy supply, which is true in the MIT no-policy case). Using this metric, the reduction rate for total carbon emissions in the first decade after 2012 is about 1.6% of year 2012 emissions every year (comparable to the exponential rate calculated above). Between 2022 and 2032 it's about 4% of year 2012 emissions per year, and from 2032 to 2042, it's about 3% of year 2012 emissions every year.

**Figure 5-1** shows an illustrative calculation about energy-related carbon dioxide emissions to give you a feel for the magnitudes. I've taken the liberty of vastly simplifying the story to make a few key points. First, I've made a y-axis that shows carbon emissions as a fraction of 2012 emissions, so the lines on the graph are shown as an index with 2012 = 1.0. Next, I've plotted six lines. The topmost line is the MIT no-policy case emissions from 2012 to 2042 (which are the critical three decades in our Safer Climate scenario). That scenario shows average annual growth in emissions of 2.7% of year 2012 emissions.

Then I plotted a horizontal line to represent carbon emissions from the 2012 capital stock assuming there are no retirements of that equipment (or equivalently that it is replaced when retired with capital equipment that has exactly the same emissions characteristics as the 2012 stock). This line also corresponds to the emissions path that would prevail if all incremental energy service demand growth is met instead with energy technologies that emit no $CO_2$ starting in 2012, but equipment existing in 2012 continues to emit the same amount in perpetuity.

Finally, I plotted emissions pathways assuming different retirement rates for the 2012 capital stock, and assuming that all growth in emissions is met with zero emissions energy technologies, as is all energy service demand for retiring equipment that is displaced (retirement rates are expressed as a percentage of 2012 equipment stock). This thought experiment allows us to assess the rate of equipment retirement embodied in the Safer Climate emissions path, as shown below.

The retirement rates are related to the lifetimes of capital equipment. In the simplest case, a 1% per year absolute retirement rate means that the average lifetime of the capital stock is 100 years. Retirement rates of 2%, 3%, and 4% imply a lifetime of 50, 33, and 25 years, respectively, and are also expressed as a percentage of emissions in 2012 (this makes these retirement rates linear and absolute, as opposed to exponential, which is another simplification). In the real world there is great complexity in lifetimes and retirement rates of capital

**FIGURE 5-1:** Energy-related carbon dioxide emissions as a fraction of no-policy case emissions in 2012, assuming different retirement rates of 2012 capital stock and full replacement of retired stock and new growth with zero emission resources

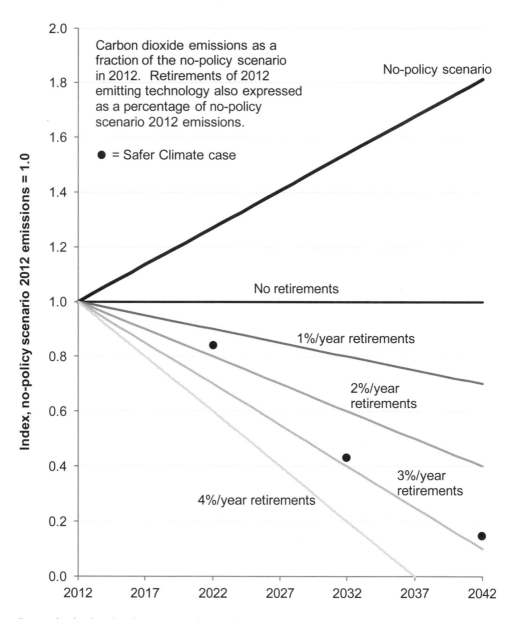

Energy-related carbon dioxide emissions in the no-policy case track energy-related capital stocks because the emissions intensity of primary energy supply doesn't vary much in this case. The no-policy case emissions grow at 2.7% of 2012 emissions every year over this period (that corresponds to about a 2% compounded annual growth rate). The "No Retirements" case represents emissions from the 2012 capital stock assuming there are no retirements of that equipment (or equivalently that it is replaced when retired with capital equipment that has exactly the same emissions characteristics as the 2012 stock). Finally, I plotted emissions pathways assuming different retirement rates and assuming that all growth in emissions is met with zero emissions technologies, as is all demand for replacement equipment (retirement rates also expressed as a percentage of 2012 equipment stock).

equipment, but for the high-level calculation here, this rough approximation is good enough.

It's important to distinguish between capital stocks on the supply and demand sides, because their lifetimes are so different. Supply-side equipment, like power plants and refineries, typically lasts 25 to 50 years, while most end-use equipment is replaced in 10 to 20 years. Building shells last longer, typically 100 years for houses and about 50 years for commercial buildings, but these usually undergo major retrofits every 20 to 30 years. A weighted average lifetime of 33 years corresponds to the 3%/year retirement case, which happens to roughly mimic the later years of the emissions path for the Safer Climate case.

This graph repays careful study. The required rate of emissions reductions in the last decade of the Safer Climate case is near the limit of what can be expected by taking maximum advantage of natural stock turnover when replacing the year 2012 infrastructure (assuming a 33-year average lifetime).[4] Even more troubling, the slope of the emissions reductions curve in the Safer Climate case from 2022 to 2032 (as represented by the slope of a line connecting the points on the graph for those two years) is comparable to that of the 4%/year retirements case, with an implied capital lifetime of 25 years (shorter than much energy supply infrastructure). That's why I suspect that some capital will need to be scrapped to meet the emissions goals of the Safer Climate case. It will take some time before we are able to build enough zero-emissions infrastructure to fully replace the high-emissions equipment that retires every year and offset emissions growth as well, so some high-emissions infrastructure will surely be built in the next few years (although we should keep such investments to a minimum).

Figure 5-1 indicates the scope of the challenge we face. On average, every year between 2012 and 2042 we'll need to build the equivalent of about 6% of year 2012 energy infrastructure, but do it using zero-emitting technologies.[5] Of course, we would have had to build that infrastructure anyway; we'll just need to do it with low emissions technologies instead of standard ones, which is likely to be somewhat more expensive in the beginning. In later years economies of scale will take hold and the net direct cost of the energy system is unlikely to cost more than a few percent of GDP relative to the business-as-usual case, and have significantly lower societal costs from pollution and other externalities.[6]

## IMPLICATIONS

This analysis has some important implications for our narrative, and for entrepreneurs confronting this challenge.

### Stop building pollution-intensive infrastructure

The more high-emissions infrastructure we build in the next few years, the more we'll have to scrap in the next few decades, so we need to stop as soon as we can. That means no more new coal plants, no new shipping terminals to move coal overseas, no more pipelines to unconventional oil supplies, and no drilling for oil in the soon-to-be ice-free Arctic. It will be politically difficult to stop these projects, but once built it will be even harder to shut them down, so it's better that they never get built in the first place.

### Some high-emissions infrastructure is already obsolete, so retire it!

About 15% of existing US coal plants (about 50 GW out of 300 GW total) are old, inefficient, polluting plants that were grandfathered under the Clean Air Act, so they have few or no pollution controls.[7] More than half of US coal plants are 35 years of age or older.[8] The total social cost of running many of these plants is higher than the cost of alternative ways of supplying that electricity (even without counting the damages from greenhouse gas emissions),[9] so they represent an obsolete capital stock from society's perspective. The most effective action we as a society can take would be to enforce existing environmental regulations, develop new ones (as the US EPA is now considering for mercury, mining, and other environmental issues), and charge these plants the full social cost of the damages they inflict upon us, which would double the cost per kWh of existing coal-fired plants even using low estimates of pollution costs. This will force lots of old polluting coal plants to retire, many others to reduce their hours of operation, generate lots of economic benefits in reduced health costs, give a boost to coal's competitors, and reduce greenhouse gas emissions, so it's a win all the way around.

### Retrofit existing capital

Given the constraints imposed by the natural rate of equipment retirements, it's natural to consider ways of retrofitting existing equipment. For buildings, that might mean upgrading the shell and the heating/cooling systems at the same time as the internal space is improved to meet modern standards.[10] It could also mean eliminating standard incandescent lighting in virtually all applications, which can be done very quickly (and cost effectively, given how inefficient such lighting is). For power plants, that might mean repowering coal plants with natural gas. For industrial plants, that might mean adding combined heat and power to replace an old boiler. When practical, renovations represent another way to accelerate the turnover of the capital stock and to repurpose existing capital toward a less-polluting use.

It's not just the capital equipment that needs retrofitting, of course. Reevaluating how capital equipment is *operated* can yield big savings as well, because we need to retrofit our procedures and institutions in the face of new developments in technology and operational needs. Such "commissioning" can result in very large and cheap savings in both dollars and emissions, and it's a different and very effective way of repurposing existing capital stocks. A 2009 study reviewed such efforts in 300 existing US commercial buildings and found savings averaging 16% with a simple payback time of 1.1 years, just by operating the buildings differently (and making the buildings more comfortable as well).[11]

### The entrepreneur's challenge

Since the constraints of the Safer Climate case will probably force us to scrap some capital stocks before the end of their useful lives, *it's your job to make existing capital stocks obsolete more quickly*. That means developing replacement products (and ways to retrofit existing buildings and equipment) that are so much better than current ways of delivering energy services that people are willing to scrap or repurpose that equipment to gain the advantages your product provides. That approach will allow us to minimize and sometimes sidestep the difficult political choices caused by premature retirements of existing capital.

As one example, consider light-emitting diode (LED) downlights that fit in those recessed ceiling cans that are so common in US homes. We installed almost 50 of these in our new house to replace our aging fixtures. We would have had to spend $20 to replace each fixture anyway, according to the contractor, and the LED fixtures we bought instead cost $50 each and fit right into the existing cans. Not only do they look better than what they replaced, they deliver bright and directional light, they come on instantly and dim just fine, their color rendition is so good that even my wife (who is a stickler in such matters) thinks they are great, and they will last 35,000 hours, which is probably 20 years at the rates that we use most of these fixtures.

The long lifetime (compared to at most a few thousand hours for incandescent bulbs and about ten thousand hours for compact fluorescents) was what put them over the top for us. We have relatively high ceilings throughout the house, so the prospect of climbing a tall ladder more than a dozen times a year was not an enticing one. The LEDs eliminate that hassle, and in fact are so good that they will surely encourage others to replace their fixtures before the end of their useful lives, because they are so much better than what they replace. And did I mention that they cut lighting electricity use by more than 80%?[12]

## SCALE OF ENERGY SECTOR INVESTMENTS

One advantage of the "working forward toward a goal" approach is that it invites an assessment, however imprecise, of the investments needed to achieve that goal, in the same way as businesses use a big strategic goal against which to plan their investments and cash flows over time. The closest recent analogue to such an analysis for my Safer Climate case is one created by the International Energy Agency in its 2009 and 2010 *World Energy Outlooks*.[13] In those analyses, the IEA explicitly adopted a greenhouse gas concentration goal of 450 ppm $CO_2$ equivalent and estimated the scale of investments needed to achieve that goal.

Now as Chapter 4 indicated, I'm the last person to take literally the exact numbers from an economic forecast, but I'm going to summarize the results so you have a sense of the magnitudes involved. The IEA is explicitly doing a cost-effectiveness analysis for meeting a warming target, not a more traditional benefit-cost analysis, so their approach is at least roughly consistent with the methods I advocate earlier in the book. They carefully tally energy sector investments at a detailed level, just like you'd do in a good business plan, so I have some faith that their numbers are in the ballpark.

The 2010 *World Energy Outlook* study gives estimates of additional energy sector investment spending in their climate stabilization case, which I express as a percentage of GDP in a given year in **Figure 5-2**. These numbers include both supply- and demand-side spending, but do not account for the energy

FIGURE 5-2: Global annual additional investment spending on low-carbon energy technologies in the International Energy Agency climate stabilization case compared to the Current Policies scenario

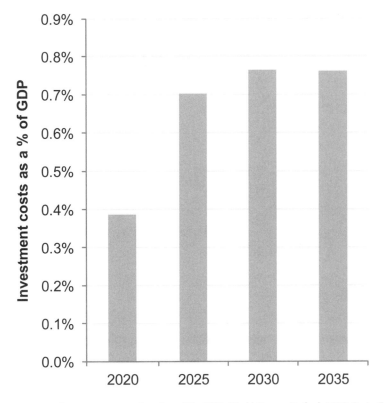

SOURCES: Investment costs taken from IEA. 2010. World Energy Outlook 2010. Paris, France: International Energy Agency, Organization for Economic Cooperation and Development (OECD). November 9. [http://www.worldenergyoutlook.org/]. GDP taken from US DOE. 2011. International Energy Outlook 2011. Washington, DC: Energy Information Administration, U.S. Department of Energy. DOE/EIA-0484(2011). April 26. [http://eia.doe.gov/oiaf/ieo/]

savings associated with many of the demand-side investments (those savings would reduce the net costs). The IEA stabilization case is not quite as aggressive as the Safer Climate case, but it's close enough, and it tells us that the increase in overall investment is less than 1% of GDP in the out years of the forecast. When all macroeconomic costs are tallied, this study finds costs of about 3.2% of GDP in 2035 (with significantly lower percentage impacts before that date), but it is not clear if the economic benefits of reduced emissions of particulates, sulfur, nitrogen oxides, and other pollutants are included in that figure.[14]

The key result is that the increase in costs for this scenario is a few percent of GDP in the later years of the forecast, which is comparable to other credible macroeconomic studies of achieving similar stabilization levels.[15] While the exact number is uncertain, it's clear that it's not 30% of GDP, which is the main point I'd like you to come away with (it is probably lower than 3% because of the various factors I discuss in Chapters 3 and 4). Reducing GDP by a few percent means delaying reaching a certain level of GDP by about a year at the expected growth rates in GDP for the *World Energy Outlook*, and this seems to me to be a small price to pay to avoid the serious effects of climate change I outline earlier in the book.

## UNDERLYING DRIVERS OF EMISSIONS GROWTH

Another way to think about the scope of the climate challenge is to examine the underlying drivers of emissions. For carbon dioxide, the main terms are land-use changes, cement production, and combustion of fossil fuels. For all three (as well as for many of the non-$CO_2$ warming agents), economic activity and population growth directly drive those emissions, but the way we choose to manage those drivers also plays a role. For example, cement can be produced in ways that significantly reduce $CO_2$ emissions,[16] and the productivity of agriculture can be improved in many ways,[17] making it less likely that additional forested land would need to be cleared for these purposes. Social and policy changes can also affect emissions growth, for example, by reducing population growth,[18] changing the composition of GDP toward less carbon-intensive development,[19] or changing the types of foods we eat.[20]

It is common to think about energy-related $CO_2$ emissions (which are by far the largest source of carbon emissions) as the product of 4 terms: population, wealth, energy intensity, and carbon intensity. I show these terms in **Equation 5-1**:

$$\text{Carbon emissions} = \text{Population} \times \frac{\text{GDP}}{\text{Person}} \times \frac{\text{Energy}}{\text{GDP}} \times \frac{\text{Carbon}}{\text{Energy}} \quad (5\text{-}1)$$

Where

- Carbon emissions = total energy-related carbon emissions (in billions of metric tons of carbon)

- Population = the number of people (in millions);
- GDP/Person = the average wealth of each person, expressed as Gross Domestic Product (in inflation adjusted dollars per person);
- Energy/GDP = the amount of total primary energy needed to generate one unit of wealth (in Exajoules or EJ [$10^{18}$ joules] per million dollars); and
- Carbon/Energy = the carbon intensity of primary energy supply (in billions of metric tons of carbon per EJ of primary energy).

This equation is known as the Kaya identity. There are more complicated forms of it[21] and there are complexities in applying it[22], but for our purposes here it's good enough. It shows that changes in population, wealth, energy intensity of economic activity, and carbon intensity of energy supply all influence total emissions.

You don't need to know much about the details to put it to use. For example, if you hold everything else constant but double wealth per person over some time period, you'd expect energy-related carbon emissions to also double. If you double wealth per person but halve energy use per GDP (by capturing more energy efficiency) then you'll keep carbon emissions constant.

You can break down annual average growth in energy-related carbon emissions into component parts that correspond to each term in the Kaya identity. **Figure 5-3** shows such an analysis for 1950 to 2000, using data for the world as a whole[23] (in principle, such calculations should be done by country or state, because specific circumstances vary so much). Population and wealth per person both grew around 2%/year, while the energy/GDP ratio fell a little more than 1%/year. Combined with about 0.5%/year decline in the carbon intensity of primary energy supply, growth in total global energy-related carbon emissions was about 2%/year over this period. The percentage growth terms add up to the total annual growth in emissions, which makes it easy to keep track of which terms are contributing most to the growth.

**Figure 5-4** shows the same calculations for energy-related carbon emissions in the MIT "no-policy case" from 2000 to 2050, also showing 2%/year growth. The main differences are that the historical data show much higher rates of growth in population (because the world hasn't yet gone through the demographic shifts anticipated by the UN population forecasts built into the MIT results) and the carbon intensity of energy supply decreases in the histori-

**FIGURE 5-3:** Average annual rate of change in the drivers of global energy-related carbon emissions, 1950 to 2000

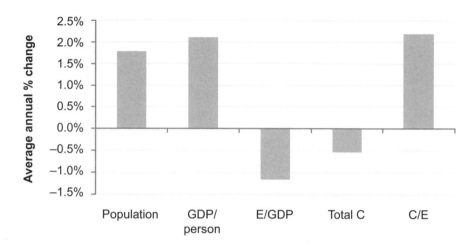

SOURCE: Data from Grubler, Arnulf. 2008. "Energy transitions." In Encyclopedia of Earth. Edited by C. J. Cleveland. Washington, D.C.: Environmental Information Coalition, National Council for Science and the Environment. [http://www.iiasa.ac.at/~gruebler/Data/EoE_Data.html]

**FIGURE 5-4:** Average annual rate of change in the drivers of global energy-related carbon emissions in the MIT no-policy case, 2000 to 2050

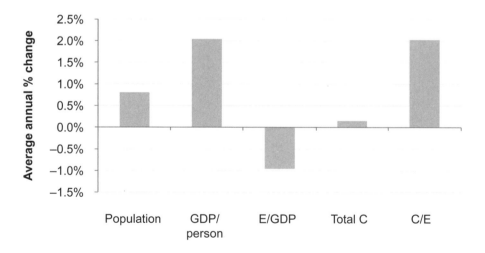

cal data while increasing in the forecast (probably because of the strong projected growth in energy demand in China, India, and other developing countries with significant coal reserves).

There are myriad opportunities for entrepreneurial innovation affecting each of the four terms of the Kaya identity, so don't limit your thinking to just improvements in energy efficiency or the carbon intensity of energy supply. New ventures can reduce population growth (by bringing vaccines, clean water, family planning, or education to those without them), change the nature of GDP growth (by affecting settlement patterns, eating habits, and other consumer choices), or affect several drivers all at once. To achieve the emissions path represented by the Safer Climate case, we'll need to reduce population growth and change the way we generate GDP, in addition to increasing rates of improvement in energy and carbon intensity severalfold over historical trends.

## AN EVOLUTIONARY APPROACH

We can't know exactly how much fixing this problem will cost or how much effort it will take, but we know it won't be easy. In the absence of perfect foresight, we can adopt an evolutionary and adaptive approach, and use indicators to see if we are on track to meet the demands of the Safer Climate case in each year.[24] One important indicator is actual emissions of greenhouse gases and other warming agents, which in most cases can be assessed a relatively short time after a calendar year has ended. Rates of change in average surface temperatures are another important indicator, as are glacial melting rates. For energy-related emissions, we can track the underlying drivers of emissions growth identified in the Kaya identity, to see how they are progressing compared to our initial expectations. That calibration too can yield important insights.

If we aren't meeting the Safer Climate emissions in any year (or if temperatures rise more rapidly than expected, given actual emissions), that means we'll need to increase the vigor of our efforts. If one of the Kaya identity components is changing in ways different than we expected, we'll need to focus more attention on that one or make up for it in activities affecting the other terms.

This approach places greater burdens on our ability to respond dynamically to events as they unfold, a skill that is not always manifest in governments and other large institutions. We will, however, need these institutions (and the people in them) to learn how to adapt, and to do so in short order.

## CONCLUSIONS

The climate challenge is unlike any other humanity has ever faced. We'll need every trick we've got to meet it in a way that will make our descendents proud, and there's simply no more time to waste. Entrepreneurs can help by making low-emitting products that are so good that people are happy to retire their existing equipment, thereby increasing the rate at which existing capital becomes obsolete. They can also affect the key drivers of emissions growth, like population and the structure of economic activity, in ways that can make the achievement of climate stabilization goals easier. And of course, they can create new ways of meeting human needs that emit many times fewer pollutants by aggressive use of whole system integrated design. I'll explore how to find and evaluate opportunities like these in the next chapter.

**CHAPTER 5: KEY TAKEAWAYS**

• The cost to society of meeting the constraints of the Safer Climate case is at most a few percent of world GDP, but that cost increases sharply with each year of delay.

• It is likely that some capital in the energy sector will have to be scrapped in the next few decades, given the rate of emissions reductions required for the Safer Climate case.

• One important role for the entrepreneur is to accelerate obsolescence of existing capital by making products that are so much better than what they replace that people will happily scrap their existing equipment to have it. That means higher quality, better services, lower emissions, and lower costs, all in one package.

• There will be opportunities in building new products and services but also in retrofitting old equipment as well as modifying our behaviors and institutions. All of these are fruitful areas for entrepreneurial innovation.

*"It is not the critic who counts, not the man who points out how the strong man stumbled, or where the doer of deeds could have done them better. The credit belongs to the man who is actually in the arena; whose face is marred by dust and sweat and blood; who strives valiantly; who errs and comes short again and again; who knows the great enthusiasms, the great devotions, and spends himself in a worthy cause; who, at the best, knows in the end the triumph of high achievement; and who, at worst, if he fails, at least fails while daring greatly, so that his place shall never be with those cold and timid souls who know neither victory nor defeat."*

— THEODORE ROOSEVELT

# 6

## LOOKING FOR OPPORTUNITIES

*"The future is already here — it's just not very evenly distributed."*

—WILLIAM GIBSON

Chapter 4 described my view that accurate forecasting of technological and economic systems for the long term is impossible. Should we then throw up our hands and flip a coin to decide what to do? Of course not! There are things we can know about these systems that can tell us something about how flexible they might be.

For example, I can't predict with certainty how many power plants will exist in 2050, but I know that power plants typically last 30-50 years once built. This means that waiting to take action on climate will saddle us mid-century with carbon-intensive plants that will last for decades, or we'll need to scrap a lot of plants we just built. As Amory Lovins says, if we can't afford to build it right the first time, how come we can afford to build it twice?

In this chapter, I combine the power of the warming limit approach (where we "work forward toward a goal", namely the 2 Celsius degree warming limit or supporting goals) with the concept of "whole systems integrated design". Together they yield real insight into this problem and its potential solutions. The big question is how to find the right project. By "right" I mean profitable and successful in reducing emissions, of course, but also *right for you*, given your skills, interests, and passions. Starting a new venture is an all-consuming endeavor, and it should fit you like a well-tailored suit. Otherwise you're at a disadvantage from the beginning.

What this chapter does *not* do is lay out a comprehensive tally of possible options for reducing emissions. I chose not to create that list because others have already done it, and there was no point in me recreating their work. So I decided instead to present a set of tools, high-level ideas, and concrete advice that can help identify and evaluate opportunities. I focus on practical aspects of finding emissions reduction opportunities and summarize what I believe to be the most promising areas of entrepreneurial endeavor in this space. I also list some of the sources with what I consider to be the best previous expositions of the range of solutions, so you can explore them on your own (most of these are written for government decision makers, not for businesses, but you can still learn a lot from them).

## WHERE TO LOOK FOR EMISSION REDUCTIONS

I've written much of this chapter in a way that will be useful to someone focusing on any kind of emissions reduction opportunity. My own particular preferences will sometimes come out in the discussion, but I think you'll still find it helpful no matter which opportunities you are pursuing. I base the choices I describe here on more than two and a half decades of experience in working on climate mitigation, plus the lessons I learned in writing this book.

So where would I look to find the biggest opportunities for entrepreneurial innovation in a world devoted to meeting the constraints of the Safer Climate case? I'd start by examining ways to better accomplish human goals, and redesigning those processes to minimize energy use. So energy efficiency comes first, because it is generally the cheapest and fastest way to meet energy service demands (this approach also allows us to eliminate the upstream losses in the energy supply system, which can be substantial).[1] I'd focus my efforts on technologies and services that scale, and that take advantage of information technology's transformational power.

My interests would then turn to energy supply technologies that are mass-produced (as opposed to site-built), that are in relatively small units of capacity, and that rely on renewable energy flows rather than depletable energy stocks. My preference is generally for electricity over direct use of fuels, because we have a plethora of options for decarbonizing the electricity system, and the high quality of that energy source makes it more efficient in supplying motive power, delivering energy to the actual point of use, and accomplishing other tasks. The electricity infrastructure is also already built, but of course it will need to be substantially improved and modernized to meet the demands of a system that uses many more variable generation resources like solar and wind.

These resources are at the highest level not constrained by availability but by our own cleverness in exploiting them and in managing the variability of their energy flows (of course there may be regional constraints related to the power density of large cities, and those may require moving power some distance from where it is generated). That means that energy storage is a critical area of innovation, which may take the form of better batteries, flywheels, thermal storage, or super-capacitors, or it could mean innovation in the relatively prosaic technology of pumped storage, where water is pumped up the hill to a big reservoir when power is available and then run through turbines to generate power when needed.[2]

We'll need to use natural gas as a bridge fuel, but that does not necessarily mean a huge expansion of natural gas supply. Improving efficiency of natural gas use in buildings and industry will allow us to reduce gas use there so that it can be shifted to the electricity supply side (where it can be used in industrial cogeneration plants, district heating facilities, fuel cells and high-efficiency gas combined cycle plants). This strategy is consistent with reducing the warming effects from methane leakage—gas leakage rates are generally lower and easier to control in utility applications than in small end-uses. Independent efforts to find and stop methane leaks will also need to be given high priority.

Of course, there may be interesting entrepreneurial possibilities in nuclear power, carbon capture and storage, or other large-scale emissions reduction technologies, but generally these require much deeper pockets than typical entrepreneurs have available to them. I'm also cognizant of the less-rapid learning that is likely for technologies that take many years to build (compared to a year or less for the smaller-scale generation technologies). I'm convinced that there are enough opportunities in the mass-produced technologies to keep me quite busy for the next few decades, so I leave commercialization of those other technologies for people with stronger interests in those areas.

## THE RATE OF INNOVATION IS ACCELERATING

Innovation in modern industrial societies has been driven in the past two centuries by a series of what economists call "general purpose technologies" or GPTs, which have far-ranging effects on the way the economy produces value. The most important of these were the steam engine, the telegraph, the electric power grid, the internal combustion engine, and most recently, computers and related communications technologies.[3] Brynjolfsson and McAfee write

> GPTs . . . not only get better themselves over time (and as Moore's Law shows, this is certainly true of computers), they also lead to complementary innovations in the processes, companies, and industries that make use of them. They lead, in short, to a cascade of benefits that is both broad and deep . . .
>
> Digitization . . . is not a single project providing one-time benefits. Instead, it's an ongoing process of creative destruction; innovators use both new and established technologies to make deep changes at the level of the task, the job, the process, even the organization itself. And these changes build and feed on each other so that the possibilities offered really are constantly expanding.[4]

The result is that the pace of innovation across virtually all industries is accelerating, which is a direct result of the use of information and communications technology (ICT) to improve production and business processes. And it's not just computers that are improving, it's all businesses that use computers to increase efficiency, improve organizational effectiveness, and reduce costs of manufactured products.

The implication of this development for our narrative is that in many cases, products introduced today could be made obsolete in a few months or years by innovators starting with a clean slate and taking advantage of the accelerating abilities of ICT to accomplish business tasks ever more effectively. It's also true of institutions, which are rarely optimized to start with and usually remain static until there's a shock to the system.

And the opportunities associated with such radically improved designs are resources that are constantly renewed and expanded by technological change. That's why, when I asked my friend Tim Desmond at Dupont whether his Six Sigma team (which is responsible for ferreting out new cost-saving opportunities across some of Dupont's divisions) would ever run out of opportunities, he said "No way!" Changes in technology, prices, and institutional arrangements create opportunities for cost, energy, and emissions savings that just keep on coming.

So how can you tap into this endless fount of innovation? You start by breaking out of old ways of thinking, using the "working forward toward a goal" approach. You'll then explore the complete design space available to you at any point using the concept of "whole systems integrated design", so you leave no stone unturned in your pursuit of revolutionary products that deliver large emission reductions combined with other compelling benefits.

## WORKING FORWARD TOWARD A GOAL

In Chapter 3, I described the warming limit approach, which is one example of the more general way businesses approach big strategic challenges. Business people know that they can't predict the future, so they do their best to create it. And to do that, they set a goal and then determine what they would need to do to achieve it, adjusting dynamically as reality dictates.

It's not as simple as that, of course. The process of making strategic choices is an iterative one that usually proceeds in a nonlinear and unpredictable fashion. It starts with simple thought experiments, followed by more detailed analysis, prototyping of key components, and exploration of alternative pathways, with lots of feedback, false starts, and reevaluation of initial assumptions.

The most sophisticated thinkers in this space use what's called "scenario analysis", which is a structured way of exploring the future.[5] While it's impossible to predict the exact time and place of pivotal events, it is possible to anticipate them, as the scenario planners at Shell demonstrated a few years before the oil crisis in 1973. They developed a formal process (still used by the Global Business Network[6]) that allows organizations to illustrate the possible effects of the most important and most uncertain factors shaping their future. They then think through responses to possible scenarios, so however the future actually does unfold, they have "on the shelf" a set of well-considered responses to those developments. As Randall and Ertel explain, the scenario approach "allows leaders to explore and exploit the unknown, and . . . enable[s] action in the face of uncertainty."[7]

### Other applications of this approach

I explained in Chapter 3 how we can use the "working forward toward a goal" approach to address the climate issue, but there I focused only at the very highest level, that of the aggregate emissions path of the Safer Climate case. In that context, we would analyze actual emissions in any year, current rates of temperature change, new developments in the components of the Kaya identity, and any other indicators to determine if we are on track to meet the demands of the Safer Climate case. If not, we'd then have to modify our behavior and adapt to the new reality. This approach takes away the urgency to do accurate forecasts, but places greater emphasis on our ability to track our progress and modify our direction as needed.

This same approach can be used for individual parts of the overall solution to the climate problem. For example, the use of renewable resources like solar photovoltaics (PVs) and wind generation is increasing rapidly (with associated cost reductions), and these sources of electricity will almost certainly play a large role in any low-emissions future. They are not resource-limited at the global level, though they generate power at times and places that don't always match how we currently use electricity.

We can use the "working forward toward a goal" approach to teach us something about what would have to happen for these kinds of resources to contribute substantially to meeting our climate goals. For example, let's assume that the price of PV modules drops from its current level of around $3/ peak watt for small purchasers to a price of $1/watt for small purchasers and $0.5/watt for large purchasers (which could well happen in the next decade or two, given the rapid price declines in recent years and the learning effects from continuing rapid increases in manufacturing scale for this technology). In this scenario, what other things would have to change in the system for PVs to become a widely used source of electricity in the US?

I can think of a few immediate answers (below), but I'll bet you'll come up with ones I didn't think of. For an insightful exploration of the issues surrounding scale-up of PV, wind, and other low-carbon technologies, see the report from the Gigaton Throwdown project.[8]

1) *Standardization of PV installations to reduce the balance of systems and installation costs* (which are nowadays comparable to the module costs in the aggregate for small installations).[9] This could involve, for example, requirements that new homes be "PV-ready", so that modules and inverters can just be "clicked in" to the house. One big cost in installing solar is that of having an electrician on-site to retrofit the wiring and make sure it all works. When building a new house, the incremental cost of adding such wiring is relatively low, so the balance of systems costs (labor plus materials) could be significantly reduced in this case (reducing cost from such standardization is one example of the power of "increasing returns to scale"). I'd also expect to see increasing integration of PV technologies with building materials (like roof tiles that also generate electricity), because such innovations deliver multiple benefits and thus lower the incremental cost of solar PVs.

2) *Improved and integrated power electronics.* Inverters are used to convert DC power from the PV panels to AC power to feed back into the electric grid. These systems are now often separate from the PV panels, but there can be cost advantages to small inverters integrated into each panel. This would simplify installation and would allow these components to benefit from manufacturing scale economies, just like the panels have.

3) *Massive scale-up of silicon manufacturing plants.* Most PV panels require silicon, and while it's not as pure as what's needed for computer chips, it still needs to be manufactured at enough scale to meet the demands that such low-priced PV panels would create. There are some methods for making panels (notably thin films) that reduce substantially the amount of material needed, but even in the case where thin films dominate (which is far from assured) there will still be a need for more silicon manufacturing capacity.

4) *Real-time pricing of electricity.* Because of the way we've traditionally operated the utility system, we've always thought of demand as something over which we don't have any control, but soon that will no longer be true. Once we introduce real-time pricing on a wide scale (which is possible with new smart-metering technology now being installed all over the US), all of that changes. That means that if there is a shortage of

electricity at any point, the price will go up and demand will respond dynamically to the higher price. We're still a ways off from implementing this for homes on a large scale, but it already exists for industrial and large commercial facilities (my friend and colleague Art Rosenfeld has been talking about this possibility since the 1980s, and it's finally close to widespread reality). In a utility grid with a lot of variable power generators, like wind and solar, this development could be a game changer.

5) *Widespread use of ultra-low power computers, sensors, and controls.* These technologies will deliver data and help consumers respond dynamically to real time pricing. They use batteries that last decades, or in the most interesting case, scavenge electricity from light, heat, motion, or even stray radio and television signals.[10] I explore this example more below because it's driven by predictable long-term trends and it's an especially fruitful area for brainstorming about opportunities.

6) *Storage on the electricity grid.* With the advent of real-time pricing and the need to balance out loads and supply resources dynamically, we'll see an explosion of research and implementation of electricity storage at utility scale, including batteries, flywheels, compressed air storage, phase-change heat storage, ice storage (for shifting cooling loads), and traditional pumped hydroelectric storage.

7) *Building more transmission lines.* There are significant solar and wind resources that are far from cities: wind in the Midwest plains, solar in the southwestern deserts. To move that power to the big cities will require transmission lines, and lots of them. Building them won't be easy, but to achieve the scale of renewable resources needed for a very low-carbon electricity grid, we'll probably need to do so. There's plenty of roof space to install solar in many places, but the power densities of big cities will still require that power be brought to them from outside, in addition to whatever can be generated near electricity loads.

Each of these ideas is a jumping-off point for exploring possible opportunities, depending on your interests and skills. They all flowed naturally from asking that simple but audacious question in the beginning: What would have to happen if PVs become *really* cheap?

Other questions of this type include:

- What would we have to do to allow the US to phase out all existing coal plants in the next fifteen years?

- How could we reduce carbon emissions from US electricity generation by 90% in 30 years? How many wind/solar/cogeneration/nuclear/geothermal/other low-emissions power plants would we have to build to accomplish this goal?

- If half of all US light vehicles were powered by electricity, by how much would that increase electricity demand?

- What would the US have to do to run the electric power grid if half (or more) of all electricity generation came from solar and wind?

Such thought experiments can yield real insight, and will help create the supporting actions and endeavors that will eventually enable the world to move beyond combustion. They prompt us next to assess the investments and innovations needed to achieve the audacious goal that prompted the initial question, and to summarize that assessment in a formal business plan, so others can review and critique it.

### *Freedom from self-imposed constraints*

So what makes this technique so useful in exploring the future? The main reason is that it frees you from the constraints embodied in your underlying assumptions and worldview. By making a hypothetical statement ("assume PV modules get cheap; what would need to happen in other parts of the value chain in that case?") we then focus not on all the reasons why something won't happen (which is most people's initial inclination), but on how we could make something happen that goes well beyond what those trapped by conventional thinking would find feasible. It places us squarely in the business of anticipating likely developments and shaping future events in a more promising direction than they might otherwise go (by inventing the future, as Alan Kay so aptly stated). And this is exactly the kind of thinking we'll need to pull us through the complex and difficult problem of climate change.

There are many examples of the power of this technique, but one of my favorites is in the recently released biography of the late Steve Jobs. In the 1960s, Corning Glass had developed a very durable type of glass they called "gorilla glass", because it was so tough. They had stopped making it, but in

2005 the CEO of Corning (Wendell Weeks) explained the material to Jobs, who immediately wanted to use gorilla glass for the first iPhone.

> [Jobs] said he wanted as much gorilla glass as Corning could make within six months. 'We don't have the capacity,' Weeks replied. 'None of our plants make the glass now.'
>
> 'Don't be afraid,' Jobs replied. This stunned Weeks, who was good-humored and confident but not used to Jobs' reality distortion field. He tried to explain that a false sense of confidence would not overcome engineering challenges, but that was a premise that Jobs had repeatedly shown he didn't accept. He stared at Weeks unblinking. 'Yes, you can do it,' he said. 'Get your mind around it. You can do it."
>
> As Weeks retold this story, he shook his head in astonishment. 'We did it in under six months,' he said. 'We produced a glass that had never been made.' Corning's facility in Harrisburg, Kentucky, which had been making LCD displays, was converted almost overnight to make gorilla glass full-time. 'We put our best scientists and engineers on it, and we just made it work.' In his airy office, Weeks has just one framed memento on display. It's a message Jobs sent the day the iPhone came out: 'We couldn't have done it without you.'[11]

Weeks is a brilliant businessman who knows how to make glass, but his initial inclination was "it can't be done". It was only by confronting Jobs' challenge (and I mean *really* confronting it) that he and his company were able to make it happen (to his own surprise). *Of course, we can't just ignore real physical constraints, but most of the time constraints are self-imposed and say more about us than they say about actual limitations on our actions.*

Another advantage of this technique is that it meshes well with the rapid pace of recent technological progress. Designing ahead of what's possible allows you to be ready when technology finally moves your way.

> Design is like a rubber band: if you stretch it too far from where you're starting, you experience more and more resistance, and ultimately it'll break. Thus, if you want to get to a new design space, you must jump straight to it, then stretch the rubber band back toward where you are now to accommodate technologies not yet ready for prime time: then as they mature, they'll relax back toward your goal.[12]

So "working forward toward a goal" is a way to sidestep the natural tendency to underestimate what is feasible, and to take advantage of advances in technical capabilities as they develop.

## A COMPANION TECHNIQUE:
## WHOLE SYSTEMS INTEGRATED DESIGN

The second key to unleashing the power of game-changing innovation is *whole systems integrated design*, the modern champion of which is Amory Lovins of Rocky Mountain Institute (RMI). Most engineering students are taught to focus on optimizing parts of systems, but rarely encouraged to look at the system as a whole.

For example, RMI commissioned a Ph.D. engineer to review how the main engineering textbooks in the US treated the economic analysis of pipe design (for transfer of fluids in an industrial plant) and insulation (in the design of a house). In the first case, every textbook had students optimize the size of the pipe against reduced friction, ignoring the capital cost of the pumping equipment. In the second case, the textbooks had students optimize insulation levels against saved heating costs, but ignored the capital costs of the heating system. In both cases, the focus on optimizing parts of the system leads designers to (as Lovins says) "pessimize the system".

RMI has created a set of 17 principles for doing whole systems integrated design,[13] from which I've abstracted some key points below. In this section I've also drawn upon the excellent book by Stasinopoulos et al. titled *Whole System Design*, where you can find many detailed examples combined with a nicely organized set of steps for organizing the design process. This approach is the best way I've found to generate game-changing innovations, and it's the perfect companion to "working forward toward a goal".

### *Start with goals and tasks*

The most important big-picture lesson about seeking opportunities is tracing greenhouse gas emissions back to *tasks*: people don't care about energy use, they want hot water, cold beer, and comfortable rooms.[14] Similarly, people really don't require greenhouse-gas-emitting processes, they want the *services* that those processes deliver. So identify people's goals and the tasks they undertake to accomplish those goals, and you'll be off to a running start.[15]

The focus on tasks is also important because you can then often eliminate system losses upstream. For example, if you think of the job of an electric utility to generate electricity as efficiently as possible, you will be limited by the thermodynamic constraints on particular power plants, which result in throwing away half to two thirds of the fuel entering a plant as waste heat, and then you lose an additional 7% in delivering the electricity to the end-user to run her refrigerator. But if you focus on tasks, you can figure out ways to reduce the electricity needed to keep the food cool (by putting in better insulation, for example), thus avoiding upstream losses as well. And if you focus on the whole system, you might even figure out ways to reduce the need for refrigeration, like using aseptic packaging for important perishable foods.[16]

Another benefit of focusing on tasks is that you can estimate the minimum energy theoretically needed to accomplish that task, and compare your efforts to that limit, to see how well you're doing. This can be done using the second law of thermodynamics, which allows us to define the second law efficiency as follows:

$$\text{Second law efficiency} = \frac{\text{Minimum energy needed to accomplish a task}}{\text{Actual energy needed to accomplish that task}} \quad (6\text{-}1)$$

This formulation indicates *the importance of how the task is defined*.[17] Redefining it can change the way you look at the problem. For example, if you need a structurally strong version of calcium carbonate with reduced environmental impacts of production, you could define the task as improving current production processes for Portland cement, which use high temperatures and pressures. Or you could mimic the room-temperature process of feeding a chicken (or the cold-water process of growing oysters), which produce harder materials in a more thermodynamically elegant and less resource-intensive process. The design space for improvements is clearly much greater than what would be indicated by a conventional incremental engineering analysis of a current cement factory.[18]

As part of defining the task, you'll need to correctly define the system you are analyzing, or you won't get it right. For example, the US Pentagon for many years used a design assumption of about one dollar per gallon for the value of fuel saved in military vehicles, which was the long-term average price of purchasing that fuel until half a dozen years ago.[19] The problem is that this price excluded the logistics cost of delivering the fuel to its end-users, and those costs are many times higher. For the fuel delivered in the US war in Afghanistan, total costs are between \$25 and \$45/gallon, with remote outposts sometimes costing ten times more than that to supply in harsh conditions. That led the military to build vehicles that were vastly less efficient than was economically justified. In addition, that choice had a cost in military effectiveness and human lives: more than one thousand US service members were killed defending fuel convoys, mainly hauling fuel, over the past decade.[20]

### Define shared and aggressive goals

Instead of 10 or 20% improvements, focus on big wins like factors of 3 to 100 in important product attributes. Be an insurgent—incremental changes aren't enough. To get people to adopt your new technology it will need to be vastly better than what it replaces. Without it, your new venture probably won't fly. In addition, it's only by facing truly big challenges that we are forced to confront our underlying assumptions and achieve game-changing resource savings. Fortunately, the rapid pace of technological change makes those opportunities vast and constantly expanding.

Consider the problem of fuel-based lighting in the developing world, which uses about 1.3 million barrels of oil a day, mostly for kerosene burned in horribly inefficient lanterns. The light produced is feeble and of poor quality, the lamps pose a fire risk, and the associated indoor air pollution is a major health hazard for those exposed.[21] In the past decade, a new technology has come onto the market that is 1000 times more efficient, costs less than \$25 without subsidy, and will pay back in reduced kerosene costs in less than a year. A book-sized photovoltaic array charges a small battery pack and lights a white LED for several hours a night, improving quality of life, reducing time spent obtaining fuel, and avoiding health impacts from indoor air pollution.[22] It's that kind of path-breaking innovation that can be a game-changer, and that's exactly what you should seek.

For climate, I showed in Chapter 3 how keeping global temperatures below the 2 Celsius degree warming limit implies aggressive action to limit greenhouse gas emissions. I also showed earlier in this chapter that this high-level goal translates naturally to a series of sub-goals and leading questions about parts of the energy system that can yield real insight. From these come the goals to be tackled in the whole systems design process, depending on the skills, interests, and expertise of your team.

### Create an interdisciplinary team

Your team needs a diversity of skills to truly explore almost any design space. That's because few people have the breadth and depth of knowledge across all relevant disciplines to assess what's possible. In addition, the process of brainstorming, if properly fostered, generates new ideas and acceptance by the team of the resulting design path (by virtue of their shared experience of brainstorming).

### Reward the team for substantially improved designs

The goal is radical improvement, not incremental changes, and the best way to achieve this result is to pay for what you want. This sounds like a common-sense notion, but that's often not how things are done. For example, engineers designing the heating and cooling systems in commercial buildings are usually paid as *a percentage of the capital cost of the system they install*, so it's no wonder they don't undertake whole system redesigns that would reduce capital costs.[23] So reward the team for game-changing innovation in whatever ways your pocketbook allows.

### Start with a clean sheet

While learning from past efforts is helpful, radically improved designs always start with a clean sheet. That's partly because rapid technology change has opened up previously unknown opportunities, but also because old designs embody old assumptions, and those often no longer hold. We also saw above how even talented people create artificial obstacles to accomplishing big goals, and starting fresh can allow you to sidestep that tendency.

### Rely on measured data

Baseline values for current products as well as for accomplishing the defined task need to be based on measured data, not on assumptions or rules of thumb. That's because only measured data conveys the *current* reality, while rules of thumb are based on history, and because of the rapid pace of change discussed earlier in this chapter, history is becoming less and less relevant to what is possible today.

### Go for multiple benefits

When designing a product, each component should (to the extent possible) serve multiple benefits, to minimize costs and maximize reliability. This lesson is also true for the product itself. Efficiency or low emissions *by themselves* won't sell products to the vast majority of consumers, but pairing those improvements with other benefits is the best way to ensure that low-carbon innovations are widely adopted. That means that products need to reduce emissions, save money, and make people's lives better all at the same time. That often means *saving time*, which turns out to be one of the most valuable scarce resources we have in our busy modern lives (I explore this idea more below).

### Incorporate feedback into the design

That means use of smart controls to make equipment operation more effective and data collection to improve both current operations and future products. With the advent of ever more efficient computing technologies, we'll be better able to incorporate such innovations into most future products, with corresponding increases in efficiency, reductions in emissions, and improvements in meeting human needs.

### Accept and foster a non-linear design process

Another important feature of true integrated design is that it is anything but linear, and that's all to the good. It's almost impossible to anticipate everything in advance, and the process of design creates new insights that would never arise without the inevitable false starts. For example, until you actually see a working prototype you can't really know whether it's what you want, as the team creating the first iPhone discovered as they neared the product launch.[24]

## BRINGING IT ALL TOGETHER

I hope by now I've convinced you that setting aggressive goals and using whole systems design to reach them is a promising way to identify opportunities. What do you do next? As usual, the first step begins with data, first on emissions, then on ways to reduce them. I follow in this section with some other important lessons I've learned about finding and evaluating opportunities for reducing greenhouse gas emissions.

### Locate or create an emissions inventory

If you're a big-company entrepreneur, your company may already have compiled the various internal sources of greenhouse gas emissions, breaking it down by business tasks. If not, that's the first step (that lesson is also true for policy makers in state and national government for both their internal operations and for broader use by others). Independent entrepreneurs will want to locate already existing emissions inventories at the city, state, and national level so they can begin their market research.

I've summarized the most important warming agents in **Table 6-1**, which shows the average lifetimes and warming power of each agent compared to $CO_2$. For a complete list of important greenhouse gases and their characteristics, consult Table 2.14 in the IPCC Working Group I report.[25] For detailed research on the non-$CO_2$ warming agents, see the special issue of the *Energy Journal* from 2006.[26] Finally, the US EPA compiles data on sources, characteristics, and mitigation options for most of the important greenhouse gases.[27]

These inventories can be used to show emissions by greenhouse gas type, by fuel source, by country or region, and by sector (with electricity sector emissions either split out separately or included in each end-use sector). They can also help in decomposing the underlying drivers of emissions growth, like population, primary energy use, economic activity, and the carbon intensity of energy production. Finally, the national or global emissions inventories can be used to create what is called a "life-cycle assessment" of the total emissions for delivering a product or service, including all parts of the value chain.[28]

One of the main sources for global emissions is the Emission Database for Global Atmospheric Research (EDGAR),[29] which was created for the use of climate modelers. It tracks emissions of the main greenhouse gases and has historical data going back for many decades. It is supported and supplemented by the databases at the Carbon Dioxide Information Analysis Center (CDIAC),[30] which also has emissions data for some other greenhouse gases, in addition to unparalleled detail on carbon dioxide emissions. For global carbon emissions from the electricity sector, check out the Carbon Monitoring for Action (CARMA) database.[31]

There are two main sources of global emissions projections from the energy sector, one from the International Energy Agency called the *World Energy Outlook*,[32] and one from the US Department of Energy's Energy Information Administration (EIA) called the *International Energy Outlook*.[33] These normally don't include the other gases or warming agents, though these agencies

**TABLE 6-1:**  Important GHGs and their characteristics

| | Chemical formula | Lifetime (years) | Global warming potentials (1) | |
| --- | --- | --- | --- | --- |
| | | | Over 20 years | Over 100 years |
| Carbon dioxide | $CO_2$ | Hundreds (2) | 1 | 1 |
| Methane | $CH_4$ | 12 | 72 | 25 |
| Nitrous Oxide | $N_2O$ | 114 | 289 | 298 |
| Chlorofluorocarbons (CFCs) | various | 45 to 1700 | 5310 to 11,000 | 4750 to 14,400 |
| Halons | various | 16 to 65 | 3680 to 8480 | 1640 to 7140 |
| Carbon tetrachloride | $CCl_4$ | 26 | 2700 | 1400 |
| Methyl bromide | $CH_3Br$ | 0.7 | 17 | 5 |
| Methyl chloroform | $CH_3CCl_3$ | 5 | 506 | 146 |
| Hydrochlorofluorocarbons (HCFCs) | various | 1.3 to 17.9 | 273 to 5490 | 77 to 2310 |
| Hydrofluorocarbons (HFCs) | various | 1.4 to 270 | 437 to 12,000 | 124 to 14,800 |
| Perfluorinated compounds | various | 740 to 50,000 | 5210 to 16,300 | 7390 to 22,800 |
| Fluorinated ethers | various | 0.33 to 136 | 207 to 13,800 | 59 to 14,900 |
| Perfluoropolyethers | various | 800 | 7620 | 10,300 |
| Hydrocarbons and others | various | 0.015 to 1.0 | 1 to 45 | 1 to 13 |
| Tropospheric ozone | $O_3$ | Hours to days | (3) | (3) |
| Black carbon | C | 2.4 to 8.4 days | 2200 | 680 |

Source (except where noted): IPCC Working Group I Report (2007), *Climate Change 2007: The Physical Science Basis*, Table TS.2, p.33.
(1) Global warming potentials defined relative to $CO_2$.
(2) Estimating the lifetime of CO2 is complicated, but David Archer summarizes as follows: "$CO_2$ sticks around for hundreds of years, plus 25% that sticks around forever." This formulation captures the fact that a quarter of $CO_2$ emitted stays in the atmosphere for thousands of years, so it has a very large warming effect over the long term. [http://www.realclimate.org/index.php/archives/2005/03/how-long-will-global-warming-last/].
(3) The very short lifetime of tropospheric ozone makes calculating a global warming potential difficult, but the current global warming effect (radiative forcing) of this pollutant relative to preindustrial levels is about twice that of nitrous oxide and 30% less than methane, so it is an important source of warming [http://cdiac.ornl.gov/pns/current_ghg.html]
(4) Black carbon lifetime and global warming potential from Bond, Tami C., and Haolin Sun. 2005. "Can Reducing Black Carbon Emissions Counteract Global Warming?" *Environmental Science & Technology*. vol. 39, no. 16. 2011/10/16. pp. 5921-5926. [http://dx.doi.org/10.1021/es0480421]

sometimes assess them in related reports. The most sophisticated climate modelers track all warming agents, of course (that's one major reason why I used the data from the MIT scenarios in the earlier chapters, because they cover all the major warming agents in an internally consistent framework).

For the US, the two main sources of information on current greenhouse gas emissions are EIA and the US EPA. The EIA report is titled *Emissions of Greenhouse Gases in the US*.[34] The EPA report is titled *Inventory of US*

*Greenhouse Gas Emissions and Sinks.*[35] Each report has its strengths and weaknesses—you'll need to look at both to see which one works best for your application. For California, the Air Resources Board has compiled a detailed inventory as well.[36]

The EIA also creates a detailed energy forecast for the US called *The Annual Energy Outlook*, which comes out every year.[37] It's often the best place to get aggregate data on energy and carbon emissions that can be mapped directly onto certain kinds of tasks (like water heating or refrigeration in buildings). It also gives you a "business-as-usual" scenario against which you can calculate the effects of your company's innovations, but as with all such forecasts, you need to take it with a grain of salt (as I discuss in Chapter 4).

For understanding the underlying drivers of emissions, you'll need EIA's more detailed surveys at the sector level. These are available for residential,[38] commercial,[39] manufacturing,[40] and transportation[41] sectors. You may also find the *Transportation Energy Databook* from Oak Ridge National Laboratory a useful resource.[42]

The most important benefit of these surveys is that they allow you to do analysis at a very detailed level of disaggregation. For example, the Residential Energy Consumption Survey (RECS) gives statistically representative survey responses on the energy-using characteristics, demographics, and measured consumption of more than 5000 households, and you can obtain the data down to that level of detail.[43] Why use simple averages for your market assessments when you can do them at the household level in order to much more accurately characterize the uncertainty in your results? You can supplement this information with detailed data from the US Census Bureau, namely the American Housing Survey and the decennial census.[44]

Once you've created your emissions inventory, you next need to determine which emissions are most important. You can slice that problem in different ways, depending on what business problem you're trying to solve. You could focus on end-uses with big emissions, fast-growing emissions, or easy to reduce emissions. In every case, you'll map business or consumer tasks onto emissions to figure out where to best apply your efforts.

### Assess mitigation options

There have been dozens of different assessments of ways to reduce greenhouse gases in the past two decades, and many of them still hold important lessons. The best non-technical introduction I've found is Al Gore's book *Our Choice*, which is also available in a wonderful e-book for the iPad.[45] It gives accurate high-level information about solutions in an easy-to-read format, full of photos and illustrations. If you are just getting started, that's the place to begin your reading.

Next, you should look at the work done on climate solutions in the past few years by the management-consulting firm McKinsey & Company. McKinsey is clearly betting that reason will prevail and that companies will need to take aggressive climate action in the near term. They've created public analyses of costs and potentials of mitigation options for many different countries and for the world as a whole.[46] They use these studies to market their services to companies within each country, for whom they create proprietary greenhouse gas reduction plans.

Not all of the assumptions of the McKinsey studies are transparent to the user (as they would be in an academic or government study), so you should use care in citing their results. I prefer to use the studies as a jumping-off point for further research, in which I can then accurately verify and reproduce their claims. In fact, all of the resources listed in this section will require you to do your own due diligence, because your particular business context may be quite different from the ones explored in these sources. And of course, all the limitations of modeling studies I explored in Chapter 4 also apply.

Lawrence Berkeley National Laboratory (LBNL) has been a hotbed of activity on climate mitigation for many years. They have groups devoted to China, energy efficiency standards, energy forecasting, electricity markets, windows, lighting, batteries, and other important topics.[47] The most important study on climate in which LBNL has been involved in the past couple of decades is colloquially known as the Clean Energy Futures study.[48] This report and supporting appendices are all freely downloadable, and are a treasure trove of data and results on ways to reduce carbon emissions in buildings, industry, transportation, and the electricity sector. I was in charge of the building sector analysis, the integrating modeling (where we combined the results from all sectors), and the economic calculations, so I know the work was done well. Even though the analysis is more than a decade old, the extensive documentation (on which I insisted for all sectors) still makes this study useful for serious students of greenhouse gas emissions reductions.

The International Institute for Applied Systems Analysis (IIASA) has an interactive scenario calculator posted online.[49] This tool allows you to choose from many different scenarios and download greenhouse gas emissions and warming results. You'll need to get some background on what's contained in the different scenarios to really understand the results, but it's a terrific resource, and one on which I rely heavily when I'm doing scoping calculations for global and regional scenarios.

Another source that focuses on the physical aspects of reducing emissions is David MacKay's book *Sustainable Energy*, which is freely downloadable.[50] His goal, he says in the Preface, is to "cut UK emissions of twaddle . . . about sustainable energy". He doesn't say much about economics, but he does bring quantitative physical insights to bear on different energy uses and sources. The book helps you develop your physical intuition about what's possible, and does so in a readable and entertaining way.

The comprehensive textbooks by Danny Harvey titled *Energy and the New Reality* (2-volume set) are a wonderful resource.[51] In about 1200 pages you get a remarkably detailed investigation of various mitigation options on the supply and demand side, and the book ties everything up nicely in a discussion of emissions scenarios and the warming limit approach. When purchased new these are a bit expensive (about $150), but if you borrow them from the library or buy them used the price will be more manageable.

Elton Sherwin's book *Addicted to Energy* lists dozens of options for addressing climate from the perspective of a governor or other high-level government official, written in the pragmatic style of a successful businessman (Sherwin is a venture capitalist who invests in clean energy and information technology). It is a concise and readable compendium of specific and practical ideas that will no doubt prompt you to think of others as you browse through it.[52]

Because of California's aggressive action on climate, there have been many reports studying options there. A recent one by the California Council on Science and Technology is of particular interest because it shows great potential for emissions reductions, even though California represents a difficult case.[53] The state is already quite energy efficient and the carbon intensity of its electricity sector is much lower than the US average. In spite of those disadvantages, the study found that reductions of 60% compared to 1990 emissions levels were possible by 2050 with aggressive implementation of existing technologies. To do better than that, we'll need new technologies, but we've got a decade or so to develop those while we're working hard to implement existing technologies.

In addition to the fine work Rocky Mountain Institute (RMI) has done on whole systems integrated design, there are three RMI books that I regard as "must reads" for entrepreneurs thinking seriously about how to move beyond combustion. The first is *Small is Profitable*, which describes the benefits of properly sized electricity technologies on both the supply and demand sides.[54] *Winning the Oil Endgame* (on which I am a coauthor) analyzes how the US could transition off oil over the next few decades, and how to do so profitably.[55] And *Reinventing Fire* (just released in October 2011) describes how to move beyond fossil fuels in the next four decades, reducing carbon emissions, eliminating oil dependence, and saving money at the same time.[56] The first two books are freely available online, while *Reinventing Fire* is available as an e-book.

As should be clear from the discussion earlier in this chapter, I regard energy efficiency as one of the most critical areas for entrepreneurial innovation, both because the potential is vast and because information technology is particularly good at solving the problems that lead to untapped energy efficiency in the first place. That means better measurement systems so we can track what's really happening, better real-time analysis so we can respond more quickly, and innovative business models to help us replace badly functioning institutions with new ways of organization that just work better (and also reduce emissions significantly).

The most complete short summary of cutting-edge issues on energy efficiency is the freely downloadable 2005 article by Lovins titled *Energy End-Use Efficiency*.[57] For a thought-provoking treatment by another one of the pioneers in this field, see the 2010 book by David Goldstein called *Invisible Energy*.[58] Together with the three RMI books I mentioned, these resources give an excellent overview of how to foster game-changing innovation in the way we use energy.

For a wide-ranging look at the issue of sustainability from the designer's perspective, nothing beats Ann Thorpe's *Designer's Atlas of Sustainability*.[59] Read this book after you've internalized the process for whole systems design and started to explore opportunities. It ties together many of the themes I summarize above in a way that will stimulate your imagination.

### Don't forget the other warming agents

As described in Chapters 2 and 3, most folks focus on carbon dioxide because it's the single biggest contributor to the climate problem, but we'll need similar or more rapid reductions in other warming agents in the Safer Climate case. Phasing out fossil fuels will result in a reduction in the cooling effects of aerosols (mainly from reduced coal combustion). To offset this effect, we'll need to rapidly reduce methane leakage, emissions of soot (black carbon), and other emissions that cause the formation of ozone in the lower atmosphere (troposphere). We'll also need to reduce emissions of dozens of other chemicals and change land-use patterns to increase the reflectivity of the earth and the carbon-sequestering abilities of soils and forests.

Both soot and tropospheric ozone have direct human health impacts, so the case for rapid reductions is clear, and the case for reductions of methane emissions is even stronger. Tom Wigley's recent work stated bluntly "unless leakage rates for new methane can be kept below 2%, substituting gas for coal is not an effective means for reducing the magnitude of future climate change".[60] Methane is a commodity with value, so there's direct economic benefit in reducing these emissions (as well as a warming reduction benefit) and it should be an easy sell. It also makes sense to minimize expanded use of natural gas for small end users in preference to using natural gas in power plants (where losses are lower).

For data on mitigation options for the non-$CO_2$ warming agents, check out the 2006 special issue of the *Energy Journal*. It's freely downloadable and is a terrific source for ideas and options.[61] Other resources on this critically important area include the US Environmental Protection Agency,[62] IIASA,[63] MIT,[64] University of Maryland,[65] and the US Clean Air Task Force.[66]

### Share the wealth

A key advantage of creating game-changing innovations is that you can share their benefits in ways that will make your customers happy and keep your business wildly profitable. The key is to develop the right business model.[67] If you are an experienced entrepreneur, you already know that. You also know that it's much harder when consumer benefits and profit margins are modest. So that's yet another argument for using whole systems integrated design to create game-changing products and services.

### Time is money

For a long time I was an avid recycler, drove a super-efficient Honda Civic VX, and *always* turned the lights out when I left the room. Then I had kids, and my diligence was tested, then abandoned, in the face of the demands of parenthood. I still do the best I can, but there's no way I can possibly do everything right and also be a good father (and the twins come first).

Fortunately, my decline in environmental virtue had a silver lining: it helped me understand what it will take to create a low-carbon society. Most folks don't have time in their busy lives to worry about environmental issues, so we need to make it easy for them to make the right choices.

A lot of environmentalists think of pollution as a moral problem, but changing people's morals is hard. Helping them make their lives better while also reducing pollution? That's a much easier sell, and that's the goal for which we need to strive.

I replaced my VX with a Toyota Prius in 2004, and that car exemplifies this lesson. Not only is it efficient, it's a *great* car, with Bluetooth, voice recognition, automatic unlock for the doors, adequate acceleration, lots of legroom, and a state-of-the-art navigation system. Soon after I bought it the Prius was named the Motor Trend car of the year—I finally owned a cool car! And the best part was that it was also the most efficient car on the road.

Time has value and good solutions embrace that fact; otherwise they won't become pervasive. It's hard to value time in our personal lives, but we all know it is limited, in the near term by life's complexity and ultimately by our finite lifespan. That's true for businesses, too, whose biggest cost is usually payroll. That means solutions that save time and reduce pollution will sell like gangbusters.

### Time is energy

Another truth that follows from basic physics is that speeding up physical processes usually requires more energy. So if you want to push a vehicle through a fluid more rapidly, the power needed goes up as the square of the velocity (as Saul Griffith points out in the Foreword). If you want to ship a package overnight, it will use substantially more energy than if you ship by ground. And if you travel by air instead of train, you'll use much more fuel.

One way out of this bind is to use information technology. You can use it to ship information directly (moving bits instead of atoms), in which case trans-mission is almost instantaneous, or you can use it to better plan your activities, so you reduce your need for physical travel. An example of the latter is the solar powered Big Belly trash compactor for outdoor applications, which not only compacts the waste five times, but also sends a text message when full, so the truck knows when to pick it up. These combined innovations reduce truck travel more than 80%! Information technology allows us to redefine the task to require less physical energy even though we are accomplishing that ultimate goal more efficiently and quickly.

### Harness information technology

Information and Communication Technology (ICT) speeds up our ability to collect data, manage complexity, and more rapidly learn and adapt. My incomplete list of new capabilities enabled by these technologies (taken mostly from *Turning Numbers into Knowledge*, which expands on most of these points[68]) is as follows:

> Near-zero marginal cost of reproduction and distribution, quicker pub-lishing, easier sharing of data, quicker review of technical material, easier ordering and distribution, direct feedback from suppliers to consumers (and vice versa), indirect feedback from consumers to suppliers (through data collection), collaboration among users, access to information 24 hours per day, universal searching, easier and more widespread public access to technical information, dematerializing products and services, improving measurement and verification of processes, improving the speed and accuracy of analysis, and enabling more rapid institutional change.

The last five ideas bear further examination because of their direct relevance to climate-related entrepreneurial innovation.

*Easier and more widespread public access to technical information*: Interactive links between the Internet and relational database management systems help those who possess detailed technical knowledge to make it useful to a wider audience (this information is often buried in impenetrable and obscure reports). Lawrence Berkeley National Laboratory (LBNL), for example, has for decades been the preeminent center on energy use in homes, but much of the information LBNL generated never reached the general public until the advent of the World Wide Web. LBNL's Home Energy Saver (HES) web site[69] was the first Internet-based home energy analysis tool; it embodies the technical expertise of dozens of LBNL scientists and has had more than 4 million users since it was created.

A user of this site has confidence that the tool accurately characterizes energy use in her home because of the expertise and credibility of those who created it. Even better, the HES has an API, so you can incorporate the technical knowledge of those who created it into your own software and avoid having to recreate all that detailed technical work yourself.[70] Think of it as your tax dollars at work.

*Dematerializing products and services*: My flip name for this category is "replacing parts with smarts" but it's actually even broader than that. It is usually possible to make products simpler in design using software and controls in the device itself, but we can also save energy and materials by avoiding the need to move physical objects and people from place to place. The three archetypal examples of this effect are telecommuting,[71] replacement of physical compact discs with downloadable music,[72] and video conferencing.[73] It is not always true that moving bits instead of atoms reduces emissions, but it is often true.

*Improving measurement and verification of processes*: Because of the rapid decline in the costs of monitoring technology (driven by improvements in computing and communications), our ability to understand the effects of our actions in real time is increasing at a furious pace. This means better control of processes, less waste, and better matching of energy services demanded with those supplied. The most sophisticated data center operators, for example, have sensors that measure temperature, humidity, power flows, and other key data tens or hundreds of times per second, so their control systems won't miss anything.

*Improving the speed and accuracy of analysis*: Fortunately, the inrush of data from monitoring technologies has been accompanied by improvements in our ability to analyze and understand those data. Without new tools we'd have a hard time keeping up, which is why new data centers and industrial operations are increasingly demanding more powerful tracking software.

These developments are important because the data starting to become available on energy use will be at increasingly fine levels of geographic and temporal disaggregation. With the proliferation of "Smart Meters" that allow real-time metering of electricity use, our ability to understand electricity use in buildings will rapidly improve. In the early days of energy efficiency analysis (in the 1970s), we conducted market assessments using simple averages of costs and savings for a single refrigerator model for the US as a whole (for example). Soon we'll be able to monitor the response of millions of households to electricity price in real time, and to disaggregate household electricity into its component parts with unparalleled accuracy. That will allow much more precise assessments of efficiency potentials and will give businesses the opportunity to target the biggest electricity users with energy-saving innovations.

*Enabling more rapid institutional change*: When companies first started buying computers on a large scale, economists were puzzled by the apparent lack of effect on productivity (this puzzle eventually became known as "the productivity paradox").[74] This delay actually had historical precedent. With electric motors, for example, the real benefits of that technology didn't arrive until production processes were modified to take full advantage of the new technology's benefits, and the same was true for computers.[75] Once companies reorganized themselves to capture those benefits, productivity improvements started on an upward march that continues today.[76]

But it's not just that ICT requires that companies reorganize themselves to take full advantage of its benefits, it also makes such reorganization easier because it improves communication, coordination, and process controls, and creates the conditions under which complementary cost-reducing innovations can more rapidly be brought to market.[77] It is in this deep sense that ICT is a transformational technology. As I'll discuss more below, institutional innovation is one of the beneficiaries of that transformational power, and it's one of the areas where entrepreneurs can generate the most rapid and pervasive changes in the emissions intensity of the economy.

### The Power of Mobile ICT

The performance of electronic computers has shown remarkable and steady growth over the past 60 years, a finding that is not surprising to anyone with even a passing familiarity with computing technology. What most folks don't

**BRAINSTORMING EXERCISE**

I've done this exercise with several groups of young entrepreneurs, and it's always been a fruitful one:

If computing efficiency continues its historical rate of change, it will increase by a factor of 100 over the next decade, with consequent improvements in mobile computing, sensors, and controls. What new applications and products could become possible with such rapid efficiency improvements ten years hence? What other innovations would need to be created in order to enable the more effective use of such computing technologies in the years ahead?

know, however, is that the *electrical efficiency* of computing (the number of computations that can be completed per kilowatt-hour of electricity) has doubled about every one and a half years since the dawn of the computer age (See **Figure 6-1**).[78] The existence of laptop computers, cellular phones, and personal digital assistants was enabled by these trends, which presage continuing rapid reductions in the power consumed by battery-powered computing devices, accompanied by new and varied applications for mobile computing, sensors, wireless communications and controls.

The most important future effect of these trends is that the power needed to perform a task requiring a fixed number of computations will fall by half every 1.5 years, enabling mobile devices performing such tasks to become smaller and less power-consuming, and making many more mobile computing applications feasible. Alternatively, the performance of some mobile devices will continue to double every 1.5 years while maintaining the same battery life (assuming battery capacity doesn't improve). These two scenarios define the range of possibilities. Some applications (like laptop computers) will likely tend toward the latter scenario, while others (like mobile sensors and controls) will take advantage of increased efficiency to become less power-hungry and more ubiquitous.

These technologies will allow us to better match energy services demanded with energy services supplied, and vastly increase our ability to collect and use

**FIGURE 6-1:** Long-term historical trends in the efficiency of computing

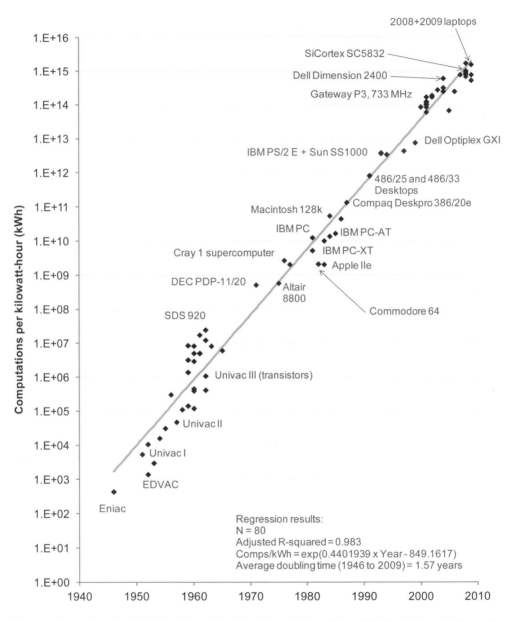

SOURCE: Koomey, Jonathan G., Stephen Berard, Marla Sanchez, and Henry Wong. 2011. "Implications of Historical Trends in the Electrical Efficiency of Computing." IEEE Annals of the History of Computing. vol. 33, no. 3. July-September. pp. 46-54. [http://doi.ieeecomputersociety.org/10.1109/MAHC.2010.28]

data in real time. They will also help us minimize the energy use and emissions from accomplishing human goals, a technical capability that we sorely need if we are to combat climate change in any serious way. The future environmental implications of these trends are profound and only just now beginning to be understood.[79]

As one of many examples of what is becoming possible using ultra-low-power computing, consider the wireless no-battery sensors created by Joshua R. Smith of Intel and the University of Washington.[80] These sensors scavenge energy from stray television and radio signals, and they use so little power (60 microwatts in this example) that they don't need any other power source. Stray light, motion, or heat can also be converted to meet slightly higher power needs, perhaps measured in milliwatts.

The contours of this exciting design space are only beginning to be explored. Imagine wireless temperature, humidity, or pollution sensors that are powered by ambient energy flows, send information over wireless networks, and are so cheap and small that thousands can be installed where needed. Imagine sensors scattered throughout a factory so pollutant or materials leaks can be pinpointed rapidly and precisely. Imagine sensors spread over vast areas of glacial ice, measuring motion, temperature, and ambient solar insolation at very fine geographical resolution. Imagine tiny sensors inside products that tell consumers if temperatures while in transport and storage have been within a safe range. Imagine a solar-powered outdoor trash can/compactor that notifies the dispatcher when it is full, thus saving truck trips (no need to imagine this one, it's real[81]). In short, these trends in computing will help us lower greenhouse gas emissions and allow vastly more efficient use of resources.

### It's not just about manufactured products

In a world trying to minimize climate risks, large institutions will need to modify their structures and behavior, and entrepreneurs can help them do that by creating supporting products, processes and services. To reduce emissions in an institutional context, companies will typically follow a set of steps like the ones below (it's a similar process to the one that an entrepreneur might use to develop game-changing new innovations, as I discussed earlier in this chapter):

1) Create a baseline inventory of corporate greenhouse gas emissions and track over time

2) Project greenhouse gas emissions and commit to an aggressive improvement level in a future year to which the company will work toward

3) Link greenhouse gas emissions to each business function

4) Identify opportunities for transformational environmental improvements (using whole systems integrated design) and create business plans for capturing them

5) Assign responsibility for implementation

6) Implement highest impact and most profitable changes in business processes

7) Measure impacts over time

8) Reward technical staff and managers for achieving improvement targets

9) Reevaluate opportunities each year and implement the highest impact and most profitable opportunities first

10) Lather, rinse, repeat

These "steps to sustainability" will look familiar to companies that are already taking the climate issue seriously (they apply equally well to other environmental issues).[82] Institutional processes like these hold great promise for rapid and large-scale innovation because they can be easily replicated with the help of information technology (thus taking full advantage of increasing returns to scale).[83]

Many companies use Six Sigma programs as a way to institutionalize processes like the steps above. In that case, the focus is broader than just on energy or emissions, but the idea is the same, assigning cross-departmental teams to identify opportunities, giving those teams responsibility for capturing those savings, and measuring the results. The teams are then rewarded for the real savings they produce, and in general, they find more and more (because innovation is a renewable resource, as I discuss above).

Another historical example is from Dow Chemical in the 1980s and early 1990s. Ken Nelson, an engineer with Dow USA, created a contest among lower-level employees to root out waste and save energy. The first year of the contest they found dozens of projects with a measured return on investment (ROI) of 173% per year, and over the dozen-year life of the contest, the projects saved $110 million per year for an audited average ROI of about 200%. Those savings went straight to Dow's bottom line, and never petered out. The program stopped when Nelson retired, but it is the archetypal example of how opportunities for energy savings are a renewable resource.[84]

Sometimes the way to address institutional problems is to bypass them altogether. In almost all "in house" data centers (ones run by companies whose primary business is not computing) the budget for the facilities department (which is responsible for electricity and cooling) is separate from the budget for the IT department (the folks who buy the computers). That means that the IT folks don't care one whit about buying more energy efficient servers because the savings accrue in another department's budget. The company as a whole loses in this case, because the *total cost of delivering computing services* is much higher than it needs to be.

Cloud computing providers (like Google, Microsoft, and Amazon) have fixed this problem (and others) in their own facilities, providing substantial cost savings in delivering computations for users.[85] That's why for certain kinds of computing, it no longer pays to use "in house" information technology. When people think of Lawrence Berkeley National Laboratory, where I worked for more than two decades, they often think of huge supercomputers and Nobel Prize-winning scientists, but even that pinnacle of computing excellence decided in the last few years to shift its email, calendar, and other routine computing services to the cloud. For those who wrestle with the split incentive I identify above, it's usually much easier to contract for cloud services than it is to wrestle with the difficult internal institutional problems that lead to inefficiency in many of these facilities.

Of course, that still leaves millions of dollars of wasted energy and capital on the table, so ultimately the best thing is to fix the root cause by assigning one person responsibility and authority for the whole data center, forcing the competing departments to operate under one budget, and making total cost to the company the ultimate arbiter of how things are done. This way when someone requests IT resources they understand the full cost of their actions. In the best case programmers are charged the total cost per computing cycle, which forces them to consider the cost of inefficient coding as well. That ideal is hard to achieve, but that's the only way to ensure efficient use of computing resources, because people don't think about efficient use of resources when they are ostensibly free.

One company that has developed a new way to design efficiency into new leased facilities is Vantage Data Centers, in Santa Clara, CA. I've visited their facilities twice and intensely quizzed their engineers. The key institutional innovation they've developed is what they call "collaborative design services", where they work closely with the incoming tenant to make a facility that has "cooling, airflow, and power distribution overhead" of 15 to 35% of the total electricity used to run the computers. That compares favorably to overhead of 80 to 90% for typical "in house" data centers;[86] and at the low end is similar to the overhead reported by the cloud computing companies like Google, Microsoft, Amazon, and Facebook, who lead the industry in reducing it.[87]

Vantage's collaborations with their customers are the closest thing I've seen to an integrated whole systems design process that involves two separate institutions. That's not easy to do. Typically such processes are found in product design inside companies like Apple, where the designers have complete control, but it's rare in the data center industry for separate companies to coordinate in this way in facility construction. More typically, data centers are built in a "one-size-fits-all" approach, with bad consequences for the efficiency (and cost effectiveness) of those facilities.

## CONCLUSIONS

Working forward toward a goal is helpful in identifying opportunities and barriers to the change we need. It's very much a business framing of the problem, and it's far more operational than the academic way most modelers have approached the problem of confronting the climate challenge. It also meshes nicely with the whole systems design approach, which is the ideal way to generate the game-changing innovations needed to meet the demands of the Safer Climate case. Each entrepreneur's process for finding and evaluating opportunities is a personal one, but creative applications of working forward toward a goal, whole systems integrated design, and creative use of information and communication technology can lead to a radical transformation of how we accomplish tasks while emitting vastly less pollution and saving money at the same time.

## CHAPTER 6: KEY TAKEAWAYS

• Information and communication technology (ICT) is driving rapid innovation throughout the economy that continues to accelerate. ICT is an example of what economists call a general-purpose technology, which is one that has transformational effects on the ways companies generate value and reduce costs.

• Working forward toward a goal is a business framing of the climate problem that frees you from self-imposed conceptual constraints and can help you identify what would have to happen to achieve your long-term strategic goal.

• Whole systems integrated design is a proven technique for generating game-changing innovation, but it's rarely practiced, and even more rarely done well.

• Emissions reduction opportunities start by focusing on the tasks we want to accomplish and associating those tasks with flows of energy, emissions, and costs, which you then work to minimize. This focus on tasks frees you from the constraints of how they are currently accomplished and allows you to capture compounding resource savings upstream.

• There are myriad previous studies characterizing emissions and mitigation opportunities, so start with those as you search for opportunities. You will of course need to do your own due diligence for exploring the business ideas that are most consonant with your interests and expertise.

• While carbon dioxide is the most important contributor to the climate problem, we need rapid reductions in other warming agents as well. Don't ignore those opportunities.

• Time is often the scarcest commodity for busy people, so if your product or service can reduce emissions and save people time you'll have a hit on your hands.

*(continued)*

• ICT is our ace in the hole. It speeds up data collection, helps us manage complexity, allows us to restructure our institutions more easily, and lets us rapidly learn and adapt to changing circumstances. It's also a great place to look for opportunities because it generally offers rapid speed to market and low startup costs.

• Institutional change is a powerful way to leverage low-emission innovations (and it's something largely ignored by the modeling exercises discussed in Chapter 4). It benefits strongly from increasing returns to scale and can occur rapidly, especially when facilitated by clever use of ICT.

# 7

---

## TALKING TO SKEPTICS

---

*"In order to achieve victory, you must place yourself in your oppo-
nent's skin. If you don't understand yourself, you will lose one hundred percent of the time. If you understand yourself, you will win
fifty percent of the time. If you understand yourself and your
opponent, you will win one hundred percent of the time."*

—TSUTOMU OSHIMA

In this chapter I explore some ideas that will help you respond when con-
fronted with climate "skeptics", or more precisely, "deniers" (as you undoubt-
edly will if you pitch your investment ideas to numerous investors). I'm not
going to be exhaustive in this discussion because others have already laid out
the peer-reviewed evidence in a careful and accessible way. I will point you to
the key resources, and then I'll explore some of the deeper issues about the
appropriate role of government and the nature of property rights that I see few
people actually addressing in these debates. Understanding these will allow
you to more fully address what the deniers are saying.

### THERE'S AN APP FOR THAT

The single most important web site for addressing claims of climate deniers is
*Skeptical Science*.[1] It lists every argument made by the deniers and summarizes
what the peer-reviewed scientific literature says about the topic. In fact, Skeptical Science even has apps for iOS, Android, and Nokia phones, so you can

access it while on the move. This is especially handy when you're at a party and someone makes an incorrect statement about climate—you can then quickly find the exact issue and show why their concern is unfounded. John Cook has also summarized some of the key arguments about climate science in teaching materials that are now being translated into many languages[2] and has also recently completed *The Debunking Handbook*, which is a short summary of how to most effectively respond to the denier's claims.[3]

The three other essential web resources for research on climate issues are Real Climate, Climate Progress, and Climate Science Watch, each of which has particular strengths.

*Real Climate,* run by NASA climatologist Gavin Schmidt, is the place to go for more in-depth discussions of climate science. This is where many of the real climate geeks hang out online, and it's helped me sort out many a climate science question in great depth.[4]

*Climate Progress*, run by physicist Joe Romm, is the most comprehensive source of news and research on all aspects of the climate issue, including both science and solutions. Some are put off by Joe's flamboyant language, but I find his technical analysis almost invariably on the mark, and his commentary was immensely helpful to me as I wrote this book.[5]

*Climate Science Watch*, run by long-time Washington watcher (and participant) Rick Piltz, is devoted to "holding public officials accountable for using climate research effectively and with integrity". It is the best source for learning about the insider politics in the US, and it treats issues of scientific integrity with the depth and care that they deserve.[6]

I consult each of these resources regularly, and if you're starting a climate-related business, you should too.

## THE STATE OF THE DEBATE

Because of my long tenure in the world of energy analysis, I periodically receive unsolicited missives from energy enthusiasts. Once every year or two, one of these claims to have solved the problem of perpetual motion, and I promptly throw it out. The laws of thermodynamics as well as our own common sense explicitly prohibits the existence of such a device, so I know these claims are wrong.

The science of climate change has reached a similar stage. The physical mechanisms leading to warming from greenhouse gases have been studied since the 1800s. Our knowledge and sophistication about this issue is based on well-known physical principles and many decades of study, so there's no longer doubt about these underlying mechanisms or the direction and approximate magnitude of the result if we double, triple, or quadruple the concentrations of GHGs in the atmosphere (as we're well on the path to doing).

Of course, there's some uncertainty in that result (captured by the current range of climate sensitivities of 2 to 4.5 Celsius degrees) but the direction of the effect is certain, and even at the lowest climate sensitivities the current path we're on would be disastrous for humanity and the natural world, as I show in previous chapters. It is therefore with some impatience that I read about the continuing onslaught of spurious claims by the "deniers" (the people who refuse to accept the scientific consensus on climate).

The consensus is just that: virtually all climatologists agree with the view that the earth is warming and that humans are a primary cause of that warming.[7] Unfortunately the broader public still seems to think there's some debate,[8] in large part because of the fossil fuel industry's relentless propaganda campaign.[9] There also may be a belief among some people that humans cannot affect the climate because only God is powerful enough to do that (such a belief, which is well established in certain faith traditions, makes certain groups more apt to doubt the claims of scientists about this particular issue).[10]

There are still a few honest skeptics out there (and those who doubt the climate consensus because of their religious beliefs represent a complicated case), but the vast majority of people raising questions about the science are doing so not because of any particular devotion to truth or special insight into the phenomena, but because of ideology or financial self interest. So that's why I (and others) call them deniers, which reflects a kind of willful ignorance that seems to characterize their behavior.[11] This also allows us to preserve the word skeptic for those who are skeptical in the very best sense of the term (which describes almost all scientists).

Michael Mann, a climatologist who has been attacked by the deniers but vindicated in at least nine independent reviews of those attacks,[12] has said

> ... some people who challenge global warming are not real skeptics 'because their skepticism is one-sided.'
>
> 'I would call them contrarians or, frankly in some cases, climate change deniers,' he said. 'I'm a skeptic. When I see a scientific claim being made, I want to see it subject to scrutiny and validation.'[13]

In particular, I'm focusing in this chapter on the group of people who could be considered the public face of climate denialism. This would include those responsible for impugning the integrity of Michael Mann and other climatologists, the most outspoken of the few climatologists who don't accept the scientific consensus, the corporate sponsors of the previous two groups, and the media outlets that aid and abet this behavior (many of them owned by Rupert Murdoch, but there are others).[14]

## WHO'S WHO IN THE ZOO

I crudely divide up the world into three groups:

1) people who know enough to be alarmed about climate change, which includes 97% of climatologists and the vast majority of the scientific community, plus some educated members of the public,

2) people who don't know enough to be alarmed, which is most folks, and

3) people who refuse to know enough to be alarmed, including the 2–3% of climate scientists, plus those who take seriously the climate stories run by Rupert Murdoch's media empire.

There's also a fourth category, people who say they know enough to be alarmed (or at least concerned) but propose trivial, inadequate, or ill-considered responses.[15] Joe Romm calls them "the delayers" but it's hard to know what to make of these folks, so I'll leave them out for now.

Yale University and George Mason University have conducted extensive surveys on the American public's knowledge and beliefs about climate change, and have sorted people with like beliefs into six groups (they call these the six Americas).[16] Only 12% of the US population falls into the "alarmed" category, while 10% is downright "dismissive". These two groups correspond to my categories 1 and 3 above (respectively). Some of the people in the "concerned" group (27%) probably fit in my category 1, and some of the folks in the "doubtful" group (15%) fall into my category 3, but the majority of people (including the other two Americas, the "cautious" and the "disengaged") fall into my category 2 (they just don't know enough to be alarmed).

Virtually all of the deniers share the view of William Happer, a Princeton University physics professor (but not a climatologist), who ended an essay about his extreme skepticism on climate issue by saying

> Life is about making decisions, and decisions are about trade-offs. We can choose to promote investment in technology that addresses real problems and scientific research that will let us cope with real problems more efficiently. Or we can be caught up in a crusade that seeks to suppress energy use, economic growth, and the benefits that come from the creation of national wealth.[17]

It's Happer's last sentence that is the most revealing: he believes that this "problem" of climate was invented by crusaders who want to reduce energy use and economic growth.[18] The widespread existence of this particular attitude among deniers has been extensively documented by Naomi Oreskes in her book, *Merchants of Doubt*. One of the most important of the early figures denying climate science was Fred Singer, who is quoted by Oreskes as saying (when denying the reality of the ozone hole) "that people involved in the issue 'probably [have] . . . hidden agendas of their own—not just to 'save the environment' but to change our economic system. Some of these 'coercive utopians' are socialists, some are technology hating Luddites; most have a great desire to regulate—on as large a scale as possible." Oreskes ties these beliefs at their core to a fear about government control of people's lives, and calls them a symptom of what George Soros calls "free market fundamentalism", which is the idea that unfettered markets are always the best way to organize both economic and political activity.[19]

Of course, as I discuss below, the idea that unregulated markets lead to the best outcome for society is incorrect. Markets wouldn't exist without government to define property rights and enforce contracts, so they are the product of human choices, conventions, laws, and institutions, and regulation is required to keep them functioning well (as we found out about financial markets, again, in 2008 and 2009).[20] There are better ways, worse ways, and some downright awful ways to structure markets, but just having a market is not a guarantee of even an efficient outcome, never mind a desirable outcome from society's perspective.

The deniers are hostile toward government action of any kind, but of course any externality (and especially one with big effects, like climate[21]) *requires* some kind of government action to fix it. That reality represents a threat to these people's world view, but instead of reevaluating their ideology, they twist themselves in knots to question the science, using dubious, repetitive, and tiresome arguments. It's long past time for that to stop.

## DO THE DENIERS MAKE VALID POINTS?

Once in a long while, yes, but usually not. Every concern raised by the deniers has already been analyzed, considered, and either incorporated into the climate models or dismissed as irrelevant by the scientific community. Every single one.[22] The popular arguments against climate science mimic these talking points, repeating them ad infinitum, with no acknowledgement that they have already been addressed or dismissed by the relevant expert community.

The web site Skeptical Science contains a complete list of all the various denier talking points and what the peer-reviewed scientific literature says about them.[23] The creator of that site, physicist John Cook, boils down those arguments into four convenient high-level points (under each point the site lists dozens of different ways deniers have made this particular argument):

> It's not happening
> It's not us
> It's not bad
> It's too hard [to fix]

You can find the particulars on any specific argument at Skeptical Science, but there's a higher-level approach you can take that I've found to be particularly effective. If you hear someone using such talking points, try asking the speaker these questions: "Do you feel qualified to judge the current findings of the science on combustion, or gravity, or quantum physics? No? Why then do you opine on a topic that is equally complex but upon which you have no more mastery? Why do you think your judgment on these complex issues is the equal of that of people who have studied the topic for decades?"

Typically the speaker will reply with some statement of authority, like "I've studied engineering for years", or "I'm a weather forecaster", or "my uncle Joe the physicist said so". Such responses are beside the point. Unless the speaker is an expert in the field, their opinions should be given no more weight than any other uninformed observer. Would you ask your allergist about the heart surgery your cardiologist recommends?

Credibility in scientific discussions comes not from your job or your experience (or your uncle Joe's experience), but from the real and original contributions you make to the debate. Even people who have important jobs can be wrong, and unless they back up their assertions with citations to the relevant literature and an understanding of what that literature says, their opinions should be disregarded.

That's why the carefully crafted summary documents of the IPCC should be taken so seriously. They really do represent the consensus view of scientists who have studied the topic for years and who know the scientific literature. Every line in the IPCC's technical summaries and summaries for policy makers is supposed to be supported by the science. With very few exceptions, if a claim isn't supported, it does not appear (and if a mistake is discovered, it is quickly corrected and publicly acknowledged). When skeptics make legitimate arguments, those concerns are addressed, but if they make arguments that have already been handled, they are ignored, and rightly so.

Of course, like all human institutions, the IPCC is not infallible. In 2010 it became clear that one statement about Himalayan glacial melting found in section 10.6.2 of the 2007 Working Group II report on adaptation was inaccurate. That statement read:

> Glaciers in the Himalaya are receding faster than in any other part of the world and, if the present rate continues, the likelihood of them disappearing by the year 2035 and perhaps sooner is very high if the Earth keeps

warming at the current rate. Its total area will likely shrink from the present 500,000 to 100,000 km² by the year 2035 (WWF, 2005).[24]

While the prediction of a high likelihood of the Himalayan glaciers disappearing by 2035 is incorrect and not based on peer-reviewed literature, that literature does show that these glaciers are retreating at an accelerating pace, and that roughly 500 million people depend on the annual melt from these glaciers for their water.[25]

Finding one error in a technical report of about 3000 pages is not surprising, but the basic thrust of that section of the report is consistent with the peer-reviewed literature. This particular erroneous point was not included in any of the more widely read summaries for policy makers and technical analysts, and once discovered, it was quickly corrected. It is also important to remember that the IPCC reports are summaries, they are not the peer-reviewed literature itself, so finding an error in an IPCC report is not the same thing as finding an error in the underlying science. Finally, this error was in the section of the IPCC report that focused on adaptation (Working Group II), not in the section on climate science (Working Group I), so even if this error were consequential, it would say nothing about the underlying science of climate change.

## CATEGORIES OF DENIER ARGUMENTS

Deithelm and McKee[26] identify five categories of arguments exploited by deniers on scientific topics (these are also summarized and modified a bit by Washington and Cook,[27] and I rely on their terminology in the list below):

1) Conspiracy theories

2) Fake experts

3) Cherry picking of data and results

4) Impossible expectations of what research can deliver

5) Misrepresentations and logical fallacies

This list can help you in responding to denier arguments in real time.

Putting such claims into one or more of these categories helps me organize my thoughts and yields real insights.

## ABOUT THOSE HACKED EMAILS . . .

You've probably heard something about emails from the University of East Anglia because they became part of a media circus in late 2009 and 2010.[28] Somebody hacked into the servers of the Climate Research Unit at that university, grabbed emails and documents, and then posted some out-of-context quotations online, which convinced some eager deniers that climate scientists were up to something nefarious. More of these documents were released in 2011.

The scientists who sent these emails have been vindicated in nine separate independent reviews of these documents,[29] and it's clear that the deniers have made a mountain out of a dust speck. There is no falsification of data and no secret admission that climate change really isn't an issue, just the normal back-and-forth of scientists making technical arguments for their points of view.[30] I'm not going to go into more detail because Skeptical Science lays it all out clearly, and there's no need to beat a dead horse.

## WE'VE SEEN THIS SHOW BEFORE

The supporters of the deniers follow a particular strategy, one that was well-honed by the corporate responses to various public health and environmental issues, as documented by Naomi Oreskes and others. They make excuses that parallel the high-level talking points summarized at Skeptical Science:

- It's not a problem.
- If it is a problem, we didn't cause it.
- Even if we caused it, fixing the problem would be too expensive and cost too many jobs.[31]

These are exactly the same points industries used in fighting government action on cigarettes, asbestos, seat belts, air bags, lead in paint and gasoline, catalytic converters, ozone depletion, acid rain, and any number of other related issues, and we need to start treating it as a deliberate strategy instead of just a legitimate line of argument to be analyzed and assessed in isolation. That doesn't mean industry will never raise real issues about whether and how to regulate a particular environmental problem, just that we should be more than a little skeptical whenever we hear this self-serving way of framing issues. It is especially important for members of the news media to understand this tactic, because they often unwittingly serve as megaphones for industry arguments of this form. If they realized that this strategy is a deliberate one, they might be a bit more careful in how they characterize these stories.

## FRAMING THE CONSENSUS

Former governor Arnold Schwarzenegger of California was one of the first sitting American politicians to clearly grasp the grim reality of climate change and explain what it implies. He summarized the scientific consensus about climate with the following metaphor:

> If 98 doctors say my son is ill and needs medication and two say, 'No, he doesn't, he is fine,' I will go with the ninety-eight. It's common sense — the same with global warming. We go with the majority, the large majority.[32]

Recently, Senator Sheldon Whitehouse of Rhode Island improved on that explanation in this way:

> Imagine if your child were sick and the doctor said she needed treatment, and out of prudence you went and got a second opinion. Then you went around and you actually got 99 second opinions. When you were done, you found that 97 out of 100 expert doctors agreed your child was sick and needed treatment. Imagine further that of the three who disagreed, some took money from the insurance company that would have to pay for your child's treatment. Imagine further that none of those three could say they were sure your child was OK, just that they weren't sure what her illness was or that she needed treatment, that there was some doubt.
>
> On those facts, name one decent father or mother who wouldn't start treatment for their child. No decent parent would turn away from the considered judgment of 97 percent of 100 doctors just because they weren't all absolutely certain.[33]

These two politicians are clearly masters at boiling down complex issues for lay people, and that's a skill we'll need to see a whole lot more if we're to get out of this mess.

## IS THE SCIENCE SETTLED?

The late Stephen H. Schneider gave a guest lecture in my forecasting class at Stanford in 2008, and his first slide asked a simple question: "Is the science of climate change settled?" This was, of course a trick question, because in some sense science is never settled. We are always testing our ideas against new data and theories, to see if they stand up to scrutiny.

But in another sense the answer is a resounding "Yes!" As the US National Academy of Sciences pointed out in 2010, the idea that the earth is warming and that humans are primarily responsible are "settled facts" because they have been tested using multiple independent lines of evidence and the predictions made on the basis of the science have largely been correct.[34]

I also like to think about this issue at a personal level. The science of human longevity is pretty well established (just as climate science is), and the current upper limit to human lifespan is around 120 years, give or take a few years.[35] So I'm pretty sure I'll die in the next seventy years, but exactly which year is up for grabs. I eat well, exercise, and have pretty good genes, so I'm hopeful I'll live a good long time, but you never know. I live with that inherent uncertainty, as do we all. And some miraculous medical discovery might make it possible for me to live to 200, but that remote possibility doesn't stop me from buying life insurance to protect my family in case I die, and it shouldn't stop us from acting to reduce greenhouse gas emissions as insurance against the likely effects of climate change.

## SCIENTISTS AND MONEY

One commonly expressed belief among those who deny climate change is that the scientists are "in it for the money". Texas Governor Rick Perry stated this point of view bluntly on Aug. 17, 2011:

> I do believe that the issue of global warming has been politicized. I think
> there are a substantial number of scientists who have manipulated data so
> that they will have dollars rolling into their projects. I think we're seeing it
> almost weekly or even daily, scientists who are coming forward and ques-
> tioning the original idea that man-made global warming is what is causing
> the climate to change. Yes, our climates change. They've been changing
> ever since the earth was formed. But I do not buy into, that a group of
> scientists, who in some cases were found to be manipulating this data.[36]

What's remarkable about this claim is that the climate science research
money at stake (single-digit billions, by most accounts) is surprisingly small
compared to the revenues of the global fossil fuel industry, which totaled at
least US$5 trillion in 2010 (see Appendix C). This is about ten times larger than
the revenues for the tobacco industry in that year (see Appendix D). Everyone
knows how hard the tobacco industry fought to preserve its market share in
the face of scientific evidence, funding competing and misleading research,
lying about the results, and doing everything possible to delay action on smok-
ing in the US.[37] Why should we believe that the fossil fuel companies would act
any differently to protect ten times as much annual revenue?

And the idea that scientists would lie in a coordinated way just to preserve
research funding is a ridiculous conspiracy theory, but you have to know
something about the scientific community to understand it. Scientists try to
determine truth based on the preponderance of the evidence in a process that
has open inquiry, rigorous peer review, and independent third party reproduc-
ibility of scientific claims. We also value our reputations above all else, so if we
were to accept money in exchange for "throwing" our research we would not
only be betraying the values that we hold most dear, but would be punished
for it in our expert community, and would be committing professional suicide.
Reputation is precious and perishable, and once destroyed cannot easily be
restored. In effect, taking money for altering our views is about as close as you
can get to treason in the scientific community.

So the idea that scientists are "in it for the money" is just plain silly. But I
can explain this point in a different and more personal way. I've been working
on understanding the climate issue since the mid-1980s, and I have a deep
knowledge of how economic forecasting models work. If I really wanted to
make money I could have applied my modeling smarts to working on Wall

Street, where people with quantitative modeling skills are in high demand. Why then would I have worked at a government research lab for two decades when I could have had a salary five or ten times as high? Can't think of a reason, other than that I actually care about whether human civilization survives the next century in some reasonable semblance of its current form.

## WHAT KIND OF GOVERNMENT DO WE WANT?

Imagine a company where the CEO says "We'll never raise prices, borrow money, or increase our expenses under any circumstances, nor will we act to expand existing or create new markets when we have a competitive advantage in doing so". You'd think that CEO was loony. But this is exactly what some say about government when they say that spending and taxes should never increase, that environment regulations should always be relaxed, and that government should always do less than it's doing now.

I believe that anyone who spends money should get what they pay for, and that money (particularly public funds) should be spent prudently, wisely, and carefully. But as a father, consultant, researcher, and entrepreneur, I'm also acutely aware that sometimes families, companies, governments, and societies need to invest money for the future. "You have to spend money to make money", says the old proverb. And sometimes only government can do what needs to be done.

What we need is an honest discussion about what kind of government we want and what we want it to do for us. Sometimes we'll want more government, like when we find lead in children's toys, salmonella in peanut butter, poison in medicines, an unsustainable health care system, or fraudulent assets and a lack of transparency in the financial world. We know from experience that only government can fix those things. Sometimes we'll want less government, like when old and conflicting regulations get in the way of starting innovative new companies. Only government can fix that too (although the private sector has some lessons to teach on that score). And sometimes we'll want the same government, just delivered more efficiently (like the state of California has done with the Department of Motor Vehicles in recent years, the good results of which I've experienced firsthand).

*When it comes to government, more is not better. Less is not better. Only better is better. And better is what we as a society should strive for.*

It makes no sense to oppose taxes, increased spending, or stricter regulations in every circumstance. Sometimes we need to do those things, and when we do them, we should ensure fairness, efficiency, effectiveness, accountability, and transparency so we get what we're paying for. But what we should not do is govern our actions based on ideology that is blind to fiscal, environmental, and other realities. That's neither liberal nor conservative, it's just dumb.

This brings me to the climate issue. The choice of how to fix the climate needs to be made based on facts and evidence, not on unreasoning hostility to any government action. One common theme for those opposed to action on climate is a deep concern about government. It is so deep, in fact, that these folks appear unable or unwilling to recognize the reality of the climate problem described in the earlier chapters. This is exactly backwards—once you accept that only government can do certain things about the climate problem, we move that discussion to where it should be, focusing on the question "what kind of government do we want, and how can we make it work best?" Government is us—it is not an alien force—and we will, as the old proverb says, get the government we deserve. If we don't figure out better ways to govern ourselves, we're going to be in big trouble, given the scope and nature of the climate problem.[38]

## THE CENTRAL PROBLEM OF GOVERNANCE

I've worked with my friend Stephen DeCanio, an economics professor emeritus at UC Santa Barbara, for many years. He's an economist who, like me, has a deep skepticism about the computer models used to analyze the economics of climate change. He's also a keen observer of the politics around facing the climate challenge, so I take his musings seriously.

I sent Steve an article about the failure of our elected representatives to create the fundamental reforms needed in the financial system after the market collapse of 2008, and he replied, "I'm becoming more and more convinced that the real problem doesn't have to do with economics or technology, but with governance." What he meant was that the challenges we face, whether climate change or financial meltdowns, have in common the failure of government or corporate governance to align private incentives with the public good.

What has been most disheartening to me about the debates over financial regulations, health care reform, and climate change in the US in the past few years is how obviously sensible solutions are sidelined by one side or the other based on ideology or political interest, without serious discussion of the real issues. Regulators and elected officials are "captured" by the industries they ostensibly control, and either fail or refuse to see the need for structural reform. The news industry has been reduced to entertainment, with little real analysis in all but a few news shows (some comedy shows even do better analysis than the best of the real "news" shows). And the lack of accountability for truly colossal mistakes (like the financial meltdown) breeds a depth of public cynicism that virtually ensures that further disasters lie ahead.

Yet none of this is inevitable. The Founding Fathers laid out a framework for government that stands to this day as a paragon of how to make self interest work for the common good, relying strongly on checks and balances and competing interests to prevent the accumulation of too much power by any one individual or group. The system hasn't been perfect, but it has worked remarkably well (better than all competing systems, as Winston Churchill noted). It has weathered world wars and numerous financial crises, and thus far always emerged stronger than before. But the system only works when all participants share a commitment toward working together for the common good.

Now we face new realities, with technological and financial power beyond the imagination of the people of two centuries ago, and new environmental challenges that require new ways of working together.[39] That means we must design institutions that recognize those realities, and use our new capabilities to align private interests with broader societal goals. Private enterprise is the best means yet devised for driving down costs and spreading the use of technology, but capitalism cannot survive without some check on the actions of corporations. Otherwise we end up with lead in children's toys, testing of drugs on unsuspecting patients, fraud and theft by corporate cronies, and rivers that catch on fire.

The challenge is to create the right kind of check on corporate power, keeping the spirit of innovation alive while curtailing corporate excesses. In the US, at least until recently, we seem to have been moving away from limiting corporate action in any form. Somehow the pendulum needs to swing back, but some systemic problems prevent it, including people who worry greatly about excess government power but not about excess corporate power, and vice-versa. If you worry about both, I get it, but if you only care about one or the other, I think you're missing the boat.

One important purpose of government is to promote what the US Constitution calls "the general welfare". This means designing systems that result in economic efficiency and social justice, minimizing perverse incentives. For example, one of my former neighbors is a lawyer who defends developers against environmental lawsuits. In a recent case, one of his clients bought an old railroad yard and promised significant funding to clean it up, so that housing could be built on the site. A local environmental group, sensing an opportunity to get publicity, sued anyway, even after the company met with them and promised to go beyond current requirements. The problem in this case is that the incentives for the local environmental group (to get publicity) are not aligned with the social goal of spending money on cleaning up the toxic mess left at the old industrial site, and now hundreds of thousands of dollars will be spent on legal fees that could otherwise have gone to cleaning up the site. There are many such examples where the incentives for individuals and institutions do not necessarily align with the social good. Markets are pretty good at providing the right incentives (provided certain conditions are met), but they are not infallible, and need to be designed, operated, and regulated well, otherwise we get financial crises, polluted rivers, and toxic toys.

I do wonder if all great countries reach a point where they can't reform themselves, because they are too rich, the entrenched interests are too powerful, and the people grow self-congratulatory and self-indulgent. I'm hopeful we haven't reached that point, and I don't see why it *has* to be that way. We live in a democracy, after all, and the American ability to reinvent ourselves has been proven time and time again. We just need to figure out how to get things moving in the right direction.

## PROPERTY RIGHTS AND THE CLIMATE

In discussions about the climate issue, I've often heard the argument that no one, including the government, has a right to interfere in the disposition of private property. In essence, supporters of this view believe in unrestricted property rights and place great faith in their sanctity. This position is a bit ironic, because it is precisely the lack of property rights in the global atmo-spheric commons that leads to the world's emitters using its ecological services for free and causes the problems I outline in previous chapters. The deeper issue is, however, that the most widely cited justifications for property rights contain often overlooked assumptions and cannot be used to justify their unrestricted application.

There are two fundamental justifications for property rights in Western societies: one justification is based on natural rights, the other on economic efficiency. The rights-based justification traces its roots to the writing of the English philosopher John Locke, who, in *The Second Treatise of Government,* wrote:

> Though the earth, and all inferior creatures, be common to all men, yet every man has a property in his own person; this no body has any right to but himself. The labour of his body, and the work of his hands, we may say, are properly his. Whatsoever then he removes out of the state that nature hath provided, and left it in, he hath mixed his labour with, and joined to it something that is his own, and thereby makes it his property. It being by him removed from the common state nature hath placed it in, it hath by this labour something annexed to it, that excludes the common right of other men: for this labour being the unquestionable property of the labourer, no man but he can have a right to what that is once joined to, at least where there is enough, and as good, left in common for others.

The laborer therefore deserves the fruits of his labor, as Robert Nozick and other contemporary philosophers have argued. However, the final proviso is often overlooked by advocates of unrestrained property rights, yet its effect is to limit their scope dramatically in a world dominated by tragedies of the com-mons like climate change. Determining whether a polluter is leaving "enough, and as good" for others can be difficult, but once it is determined, the "others" can act to restrict the property rights of the polluter in some undetermined way, even under the philosophy of one of the most forceful and widely-quoted advocates of natural rights to property.

The other major justification for property rights is that of economic effi-ciency. This justification has its roots in the writings of Locke and Adam Smith, but it derives the necessity for property rights by showing that property rights in a market-based economy will lead to a more efficient outcome than systems without property rights. One assumption of this justification is that consumers purchasing a good must pay the full cost of the good, including costs borne by society as a whole. If all social costs are not internalized, the production outcome will not be an efficient one. But this assumption is none other than the Lockean proviso of "enough, and as good", and the result is the same.

Both justifications for property rights therefore include the same proviso: when an individual or organization pollutes, despoils, or is generally not leaving "enough, and as good" for others, then there is justification for restricting property rights. This proviso is both efficient and just, because then manufacturers using hazardous materials have an incentive to reduce their consumption, and those consumers who use a product that requires such materials in its manufacture pay the costs of doing so.

It's also important to remember that government defines property rights and can choose how these will be structured and enforced,[40] which can strongly affect the incentives individuals and institutions have to protect the commons.[41] Many of these choices have some level of arbitrariness to them, which means we as a society can make choices that favor long-term sustainability instead of short-term profit, *and there's nothing wrong with that.*

I doubt anyone would argue nowadays that preventing people from owning others as slaves was an unwarranted abridgment of property rights, but that shift had major social and economic implications, not the least of which was living up to the promise of the Declaration of Independence, that "all men are created equal". Other examples abound, from restrictions on how companies can treat workers, to conditions on the chartering of corporations, to creation of new types of corporate entities,[42] to the penalties imposed when property rights are actually infringed by others in the society.

For many decades the property rights associated with a battery transferred fully from the manufacturer to the purchaser of that battery. In recent years, as society has become more aware of the toxic effects of chemicals in groundwater, some countries (notably those in Europe) have moved toward a modification of property rights, under the rubric of "extended producer responsibility". The manufacturer is still responsible for safely recycling that battery, even after it is sold to the customer, so in a sense the producer still owns the part of the battery's costs associated with long-term disposal. This change is not that different from property rights for land in the US, where rights for mining, water, wind generation, and air (in the sense of the right to fly through the air above some land) can be split off and sold separately, depending on the laws for the state in which the property resides.

DeCanio raises this issue clearly in the context of climate:

> Property rights begin with the government, because it is the government that defines what kinds of actions are lawful, what kinds of exchanges are permitted, and what kinds of contracts are enforceable . . .
>
> Social entitlements typically are inalienably attached to individuals. Yet the practical significance of these entitlements depends on interpretation and enforcement of laws. Ultimately it is the state that makes this determination.
>
> The reason this matters for climate policy is because the future outlines of the economy are going to be determined, to a very large degree, by the kinds of rights—in climate stability, emissions levels, or fossil fuel use—that ultimately will be policy-determined. The situation until now has been one in which users of fossil fuels have been free to dispose of the waste products of the combustion of those fuels (mainly $CO_2$) for free . . . This allocation of 'climate rights' was appropriate in the preindustrial and early industrial world, when energy demands were relatively low and human activity did not have much of an impact on the atmosphere as a whole . . .
>
> That situation no longer prevails . . . If and when governments begin to address the consequences, and assign various kinds of environmental or climate rights to people (including future potential victims of climate change), the result will be a change in the allocation of wealth.[43]

Thus, the definition of property rights depends on context, as DeCanio rightly notes, and this definition can (and should) evolve as the context changes (and boy, has it changed).

The deep insight conveyed by DeCanio is that solving the climate problem requires redefining property rights to reflect the new reality of our limited atmosphere, and no one else can do that except governments. It is therefore nonsensical for people to argue that private property rights are absolute—they are defined by government based on a certain context, and when that context changes, the way we define property rights needs to change too. The argument about climate and other environmental issues then becomes about what definition of property rights makes sense instead of focusing on the costs imposed on individuals and corporations, and that's a much more appropriate place to have the argument.

For individuals, rights come with responsibilities. That's true of people and it should also be true of companies. They are treated as persons under the law, at least from a rights perspective, but their responsibilities need to also be enumerated and enforced. If the government aggressively enforces property *rights* without also simultaneously defining and enforcing the *responsibilities* for property owners, then this imbalance will lead to outcomes that are bad for society. So we really do need a consumer products safety commission to keep lead paint out of toys, a Food and Drug Administration that aggressively enforces purity standards for consumer goods, and a government that takes a proactive role in analyzing the societal costs of private actions and takes appropriate actions when the costs of those actions are not being born by the economic actors who cause them. Even better would be giving incentives for companies to proactively behave in the most sustainable way, but that's something we're going to have to work on.

This way of looking at the problem has an additional important feature: it reveals yet another issue with economic models. These models take the current set of property rights as a given, but if these are redefined (as it is incumbent upon all market systems to do as conditions change) then the equilibrium that results may be quite different from one where property rights are kept constant. The possibility for changing property rights is therefore another important source of multiple equilibria (along with increasing returns to scale, information asymmetries, and transaction costs, to mention a few), and that means (again) that we get to *choose* the kind of society we want by our choice of property rights regimes.

## CONCLUSIONS

You can't escape addressing the deniers' arguments if you are starting a company in the climate space, so be prepared. Read the various arguments on the Skeptical Science web site, track climate news reported in other online resources so you are up to speed, and really study the summary and typology of denier arguments in Chapter 1 of *Climate Change Denial: Heads in the Sand* by Washington and Cook. Also remember to consider who else is listening to the argument (they may be more persuadable than the hard-core deniers).

Develop gentle ways to question and probe when someone asks you questions that seem to be informed by denialism. See if you can get inside your questioner's head and determine if she is driven by genuine skepticism, religious belief, an ideological antipathy toward government, a misunderstanding about the nature of property rights, or something else. You won't always be able to convince these folks, but understanding them a bit more will help you communicate better, and maybe they'll even ask you a question that will get you thinking in a new direction. You never know . . .

---

**CHAPTER 7: KEY TAKEAWAYS**

• Climate science is based on some of the most well-established principles in physical science, and all of the "issues" raised by the deniers have already been addressed by climate scientists. You can prove it by going to Skeptical Science and looking up any argument to find out what the peer-reviewed science says.

• Most deniers are motivated by antipathy toward government, but not all of them. Try to understand what motivates your questioner so you can respond appropriately. Probe their attitudes about national security, which often unexpectedly align with the need for climate action.

• Government has an essential role to play in defining property rights, enforcing contracts, and internalizing external costs. No one else can do these things, so we need to ensure that these tasks are performed in a way that leads to the kind of society we want.

• When it comes to government, more is not better. Less is not better. Only better is better. And better is what we as a society should strive for.

• Be prepared to respond gently to denier arguments, but don't worry if you can't convince a skeptical investor. Some battles aren't worth fighting, so just move on to the next investor.

---

*"It isn't what he doesn't know that bothers me, it's what he knows for sure that just ain't so."*

—VARIOUSLY ATTRIBUTED TO MARK TWAIN,
SATCHEL PAIGE, WILL ROGERS, AND OTHERS

# 8

## REASONS FOR OPTIMISM

*"Whether you think you can or think you can't,
you're right."*

—HENRY FORD

One of my students at Yale in Fall 2009 emerged from my lecture summarizing the climate problem and told me it depressed her. "It seems so hopeless," she said. I acknowledged that the problem was a daunting one, but explained again why I thought it wasn't insoluble. And the problem of assuming we can't fix the problem is that we'll stop trying things that might actually work. I call this "the pessimism trap". If we don't even try, we're ensuring the bad results we fear will actually come to pass.

In this short chapter I summarize the reasons why I think we can still address the climate issue in a way that avoids catastrophe and preserves reasonable continuity for human society. That outcome is not guaranteed, of course, but I'm still optimistic that we will, at long last, do the right thing.

By we, I mean first the United States, because most of the rest of the world already takes this issue seriously, and US leadership can transform the current stalemate into real movement.[1] To that end, the US needs to adopt a carbon price, set real emissions targets, and begin aggressive mitigation as soon as possible. It also needs to take the international relations aspect of this problem seriously, because the climate problem can't be solved without international cooperation, and the recent US public debate (such as it was) almost completely ignores this fact.[2]

As recent game theory analysis suggests, there are many degrees of freedom for reaching outcomes that preserve a livable climate, but success is by no means assured:

> The greatest reason for optimism is that science is universal; understanding the risks of climate change can eventually bring all major governments to realize that abatement is in their long-run interest. Diplomacy also can work to create incentives that will push the governments toward cooperation. Like economics more generally, game theory can offer guidance for the successful navigation of these diplomatic shoals, but is not by itself able to demonstrate the solution.[3]

Each major country or group of countries could by themselves destroy the climate, so we cannot escape the need for binding international commitments, but those cannot come about without real progress in the US, which stands today as the biggest roadblock to prompt global action. The Chinese have already indicated, by their substantial investments in renewable energy production, that they are prepared to build the technologies of the future (and to beat us in that game). If we make a real commitment to meet the constraints of the Safer Climate case, we can give the Chinese a real run for their money, and that's a race in which the whole planet wins. Once we realize that this isn't a "zero sum game", it opens up possibilities that we haven't thought of before.

There is a tendency in formal modeling assessments of the climate problem toward pessimism about the future, as I discussed in Chapters 3 and 4. Our own cognitive limitations make us unable to fully evaluate all of the options before us, and as has been shown many times before, any evaluation of options that excludes important ones will underestimate the possibilities for action and overestimate its cost.[4] But of course, we always exclude important possibilities (because we can't think of everything), so this bias is systemic. In addition, the methods used in these analyses embed structural rigidities in the forecasts that wouldn't actually be present in a world aggressively pursuing the Safer Climate case, like assuming that institutional behavior and the structure of property rights remain constant. They also ignore critical factors like increasing returns to scale, which make emissions reductions significantly easier as long as we start down a path of implementation that is a promising one. So aggressive climate action will almost certainly be easier than we think, although by no stretch of the imagination should effort at the required level be called "easy".

It is for all these reasons that I strongly advocate the "working forward toward a goal" approach to evaluating this problem, which embodies the "can do" spirit of most entrepreneurs and frees us from the mostly self-imposed constraints that prevent us from envisioning a radically different future. Humans are smart and innovative, and when challenged with a clear goal we almost invariably figure out a way to meet it. We also have at our disposal new tools that give us unprecedented power to reduce emissions and generate wealth at the same time.

For example, the renewable resource base is much larger than current human needs,[5] and the last few decades of developments in renewable energy technology can allow us to move past combustion,[6] but to do so we'll need to rethink our energy system from the ground up. We'll need to radically improve our efficiency of energy use and rely on whole system integrated design to help us get there, tapping increasing returns to scale, exploiting information and communications technology (particularly mobile ICT), and fundamentally altering our institutions. We'll also need to rethink the structure of property rights, not just related to climate risks but to broader issues of sustainability (that's one lever that is usually ignored but has great power to alter the economy's direction).

Our goal is, to paraphrase former CIA director Jim Woolsey, to turn fossil fuels into salt. In the old days, salt was an incredibly expensive strategic commodity because it was essential for preservation of meat. Now we buy a pound of it for less than a dollar in the supermarket. That's because technology has put salt in its place—refrigeration now makes salt obsolete for this previously essential application,[7] and we need to do the same thing for fossil fuels.

There's a now classic cartoon by Joel Pett, which features a scientist lecturing about climate change solutions in front of a large audience. Someone stands up in the back of the room and asks "What if it's a big hoax and we create a better world for nothing?"[8] Many of the things that would help us face the climate challenge, like reducing coal and petroleum use, stopping deforestation, and slowing population growth, are things we should be doing anyway, although the demands of the Safer Climate case make those changes more urgent than they might otherwise be. Those ancillary benefits are large, and (if properly counted) should make it easier to reach agreement on aggressive emissions reductions.

As I explained in Chapter 1, there's now no doubt that human choices can have consequences that reverberate through generations. With every action, with every day we live, we create the future. Of course, forces beyond human control also have influence, but it is how our choices relate to these external events that determine the outcome.

Of course, this realization cuts both ways. On the one hand, our current path has terrible consequences for the earth and for human society, but on the other hand, it means that there's nothing preordained about the path we're on. We have the capacity to change, learn, grow, and alter course, and now's the time to do it. Ultimately it's up to us to choose the kind of world we want for our children and grandchildren, and defeatist pessimism is in the way. I, for one, refuse to let it get the better of me.

## CHAPTER 8: KEY TAKEAWAYS

• The constraints standing between us and vastly reduced greenhouse gas emissions are mostly self-imposed—they flow from cognitive limitations that make it difficult for us to imagine a future much different from our current path.

• The technology exists for us to move past combustion in most applications, but scaling it up to meet the demands of a modern industrial society won't be easy. Of course, not doing so will be harder still, because of the damages unrestricted climate change will inflict on the earth and on human society.

• Nothing is preordained: we get to choose the kind of world we live in, so let's choose wisely.

# 9

---

## CREATING THE FUTURE

---

*"The future ain't what it used to be."*

—YOGI BERRA

When our children and grandchildren look back on our era the political squabbles of today will have been long since forgotten. What they will ask (I hope) is "How did they have the wisdom to build for the future?" That's how we need to measure our actions now. Will they thank us for acting with reason, compassion and foresight? Will they express gratitude for our wisdom? Or will they wonder what the hell we were thinking? Let's make sure we earn their gratitude, because the alternative is too unpleasant to contemplate.

In this book I've outlined the depth and breadth of the climate challenge, and summarized some insights that entrepreneurs starting new ventures in this space should find useful. That exploration began with the insight that humans are now no longer small compared to the earth. Because of our wealth, our numbers, and our technology, we can (and have) significantly altered the global life support systems upon which we all depend.

If current greenhouse gas (GHG) emissions trends continue, the earth is in for at least two doublings of greenhouse gas concentrations in the next century, which implies more than a 10-degree Fahrenheit increase in average global surface temperatures, with no end in sight. This outcome would be disastrous for humanity and for the earth's natural systems, and we should do everything in our power to avoid it. This path also opens up the real possibility of accelerated warming due to positive feedbacks (like release of carbon from rapidly melting ice, thawing permafrost, burning peat bogs, and warming methane hydrates), which in the distant past have led to even more significant changes in the earth's climate, and could do so again if we push the climate system too far.

To meet this challenge we'll need rapid GHG emission reductions in the next few decades. This conclusion is inescapable because it's *cumulative* emissions that matter, due to the long lifetime of many greenhouse gases. If we want to prevent global temperatures from increasing more than 2 Celsius degrees, we have a fixed emissions budget over the next century. If we emit more now we'll have to reduce emissions more rapidly later, so delaying action (either to gather more data or to focus on energy innovation) is foolish and irresponsible. If energy technologies improved as fast as computers there might be an argument for waiting under some circumstances, but they don't, so it's a moot point.

Of course, we need new technologies and should therefore invest heavily in research and development, but there are vast opportunities for emission reductions using current technologies, and cost reductions for these technologies are dependent on implementing them on a large scale (learning by doing only happens if we *do*). So the focus in the next few decades should be on aggressive deployment of current low-emissions technologies, bringing new technologies into the mix as they emerge.

Conventional benefit-cost analysis has often led to a different view of the problem, one that emphasizes a more cautious approach. Studies of this type attempt to balance costs and benefits using computer models, but such efforts are dependent on accurate forecasts (which are impossible for economic and social systems), and for many reasons these efforts are biased toward preserving the status quo. The models ignore important effects like increasing returns to scale, assume that structural rigidities will continue into the future, omit relevant options from consideration (thus overestimating costs), and bury ethical judgments in ostensibly technical concepts like the discount rate or the economic value of climate damages (many of which are unquantifiable in principle). These limitations make it seem like fixing the climate problem is harder and more costly than it really is, and so use of these models in this way is bound to lead us astray.

I advocate instead an evolutionary approach to this problem, implementing many different technologies, failing fast, and doing more of what works and less of what doesn't. This approach, which the National Research Council dubs "iterative risk management", recognizes the limitations of economic models and puts such analysis into an important but less grandiose role: that of comparing cost effectiveness of different mitigation options in achieving a normatively defined target (like the 2 Celsius degree warming limit).

I call this approach "working forward toward a goal" and it's a more business-oriented framing of the problem. It mirrors the way companies face big strategic challenges, because they know that forecasting the future accurately is impossible, so they set a goal and figure out what they'd have to do to meet it, then adjust course as developments dictate. It also frees you from the mostly self-imposed conceptual constraints that make it hard to envision a future much different from what exists today.

This approach is useful in identifying and evaluating opportunities both at the very highest level (like global carbon emissions) but also for analyzing component parts of possible solutions. So for example, we can consider what would have to happen to allow the utility system to use huge amounts of variable generation from renewable energy in the case where solar generated electricity becomes three times cheaper than it is today (which is a real prospect over the next decade). These kinds of thought experiments can yield real insights into where new opportunities may lie.

As I've described in the first chapter, the climate problem is big, it's urgent, and it's misunderstood, which makes it fertile ground for new business ventures. The changes we need are so large that no part of the economy will remain untouched, and that means opportunity. In fact, we'll probably need to scrap some capital in the energy sector, given the rate of emissions reductions that will be required to maintain a livable climate. Entrepreneurs can lead the way by designing new low-emission products, services, and institutional arrangements that are so much better than what they replace that people are eager to adopt them (and to scrap some of their high-emitting existing capital along the way).

Emissions reduction opportunities start by focusing on the tasks you want to accomplish and associating those tasks with flows of energy, emissions, and costs, which you then work to minimize. This focus on tasks frees you from the constraints of how they are currently accomplished and allows you to capture compounding resource savings upstream. By considering the whole system and designing to approach theoretical limits of efficiency, it is often possible to achieve drastically reduced emissions while also substantially improving other characteristics of products or services.

Information and communication technology (ICT) is accelerating the rate of innovation throughout the economy, and that development has implications for business opportunities in this space. ICT speeds up data collection, helps us manage complexity, allows us to restructure our institutions more easily, and lets us rapidly learn and adapt to changing circumstances. It also creates a continuously renewable source of emissions reductions, and is a great place to look for opportunities because it generally offers rapid speed to market and low startup costs.

When considering the climate issue, we can't avoid the issue of institutional governance. Government has an essential role to play in defining property rights, enforcing contracts, and internalizing external costs. No other institution can do these things, so we need to ensure that these tasks are performed in a way that leads to the kind of society we want. When it comes to government, more is not better. Less is not better. Only better is better. And better is what we as a society should strive for.

Surviving this stage of human development means we'll need to evolve as a species to learn how to face challenges like this one. We'll need to foster rapid innovation, fierce competition, and active coordination between businesses, all at the same time. We'll also need to change how we think about our responsibilities to each other, to the earth, and to future generations. Innovations in our values can be as powerful as those for new technologies in opening up new possibilities for the future, so we also need to explore these.

The technology now exists for us to move past combustion in most applications, but scaling it up to meet the demands of a modern industrial society won't be easy. Of course, not doing so will be harder still, because of the damages unrestricted climate change will inflict on the earth and on human society. It's long past time to get started. There's simply no more time to waste.

*"I'm skeptical that a problem as complex as climate change can be solved by any single branch of science. Technological measures and regulations are important, but equally important is support for education, ecological training and ethics — a consciousness of the commonality of all living beings and an emphasis on shared responsibility."* —VACLAV HAVEL (NY TIMES, 09/27/07)

---

## Reserves of fossil fuels

---

This Appendix estimates the lower bound estimates for carbon contained in global fossil fuel reserves and resources (which when added together make up the *resource base*) based on the 2011 Global Energy Assessment (GEA) from the International Institute for Applied Systems Analysis in Austria.* The details of how I created the calculations are explained in the footnotes to Table A-1, but they rely on the ranges reported in Table 7.1 of the GEA for conventional gas, oil and coal, and reconstruct the lower end estimates for unconventional oil and gas from the underlying data reported in Chapter 7 of the GEA. I also report lower bound estimates for methane hydrates but do not use those in the discussion in Chapter 3 above (because the quantity of carbon in just conventional and unconventional fossil fuel deposits is so much larger than those burned in the MIT policy scenarios that the exotic fuels can't enter into the picture if we are to maintain a livable climate).

*IIASA. 2011. *Global Energy Assessment*. Cambridge, UK: Cambridge University Press.

**TABLE A-1:** Lower bound estimates of energy and carbon content of fossil fuels worldwide

| | Energy content (ZJ) | | | | Carbon content (GtC) | | | |
|---|---|---|---|---|---|---|---|---|
| | Reserves | Resources | Resource base | Notes | Reserves | Resources | Resource base | Notes |
| **Conventional fuels** | | | | | | | | |
| Natural gas | 5 | 7 | 12 | 1 | 77 | 110 | 187 | 5 |
| Oil | 5 | 4 | 9 | 1 | 98 | 83 | 181 | 5 |
| Coal | 17 | 291 | 308 | 1 | 446 | 7508 | 7954 | 5 |
| Total conventional | 27 | 302 | 330 | | 621 | 7701 | 8322 | |
| **Unconventional fuels** | | | | | | | | |
| Coalbed methane | 3 | 6 | 9 | 2 | 47 | 93 | 139 | 5 |
| Shale gas | 5 | 10 | 14 | 2 | 72 | 148 | 220 | 5 |
| Deep gas | 3 | 5 | 8 | 2 | 47 | 80 | 127 | 5 |
| Tight gas | 4 | 5 | 10 | 2 | 66 | 80 | 146 | 5 |
| Oil sands | 1 | ·4 | 5 | 3 | 29 | 78 | 106 | 5 |
| Heavy oil | 6 | 1 | 7 | 3 | 123 | 26 | 149 | 5 |
| Shale oil | 1 | 2 | 3 | 3 | 22 | 43 | 66 | 5 |
| Total unconventional | 24 | 34 | 57 | | 405 | 548 | 953 | |
| **Exotic** | | | | | | | | |
| Methane hydrates | | | 65 | 4 | | | 1000 | 6 |
| Total, conv. + unconv. | 51 | 336 | 387 | | 1026 | 8249 | 9275 | |

Global notes: Resource base = reserves plus resources. Other occurrences (which are omitted from this table, but are included in GEA Table 7.1) are fossil fuel deposits that are known or suspected to exist but are so far from commercialization that they are not considered reserves or resources.

Local notes:

1) Conventional gas, oil, and coal are taken as the low end of the ranges given in Chapter 7, Table 7.1 of the IIASA. 2011. *Global Energy Assessment*. Cambridge, UK: Cambridge University Press. (hereafter GEA).

2) Mean value for energy content taken from Table 7.12 of GEA, downgraded by 25% for reserves and 35% for resources to create a lower bound. "Resources in place'" in Table 7.12 equals "resources" from the perspective of Table 7.1.

3) Mean value for energy content taken directly from Table 7.8 of GEA for reserves and calculated from Table 7.9 for resources (converted to ZJ using 42 GJ/toe), downgraded by 25% for reserves and 35% for resources to create a lower bound.

4) Energy content calculated from lower bound carbon content (from footnote 6) using gas emissions factor from footnote 5.

5) Energy statistics converted to carbon content using the IPCC conversion factors of 15.3 GtC/ZJ for gas, 20 GtC/ZJ for oil, and 25.8 GtC/ZJ for coal. Emissions are based only on the carbon content of the fuel itself. No corrections have been included for the indirect emissions associated with the extraction, processing, and transportation of the fuel to the end-user.

6) Lower bound carbon content taken from Krey, Volker, et. al. 2009. "Gas hydrates: entrance to a methane age or climate threat?" *Environmental Research Letters*. vol. 4, no. 3. pp. 034007. [http://stacks.iop.org/1748-9326/4/i=3/a=034007]. Upper bound estimates for hydrates are 4 to 40 times bigger, depending on whether the estimate is of technical or theoretical potential, according to Table 7.13 of the GEA.

## What $CO_2$ equivalent concentration corresponds to a 2 degree equilibrium warming with a climate sensitivity of 3 Celsius degrees?

Danny Cullenward, Stanford University

September 23, 2011

Assume that there is always a $\Delta T$ of 3 Celsius degrees per doubling of $CO_2$.
Therefore,

$$\Delta T = 3 \bullet \text{(the number of doublings of } CO_2) \tag{1}$$

Let "x" represent the ratio of the future concentration of $CO_2$ to the original concentration of $CO_2$. Then we can say that the number of "doublings" of $CO_2$ is $\log_2 x$, also written $\lg x$.

Substituting:

$$\Delta T = 3 \bullet \log_2 x = 3 \bullet \lg x \tag{2}$$

$$2^{\Delta T} = 2^{(3 \bullet \lg x)} = 2^{(\lg x \bullet 3)} \tag{3}$$

In general, for any exponent:

$$A^{(B*C)} = (A^B)^C \tag{4}$$

And for any exponent, where $\log X$ is in base $A$:

$$A^{(\log X)} = X \tag{5}$$

Applying equation (5) to equation (3) we see that:

$$2^{\Delta T} = (2^{\lg x})^3 = x^3 \tag{6}$$

$$x^3 = 2^{\Delta T} \tag{7}$$

$$x = 2^{(\Delta T/3)} \tag{8}$$

If we want to know by how much $CO_2$ must increase to produce a $\Delta T$ of 2 Celsius degrees, then we solve $x = 2^{2/3} = 1.58740$. We then multiply this ratio by the preindustrial concentration of 280 ppm to get 444 ppm $CO_2$ equivalent.

## Fossil fuel company revenues for 2010

Table C-1 calculates revenues for 29 of the largest oil and gas companies in the world, but does not include an estimate for the global industry because we could not find a credible source (this makes our 2010 revenue estimate for oil and gas a lower bound). The oil and gas revenues include those from upstream (exploration, production, and refining) and downstream (sales to consumers). Table C-2 calculates revenues for the global coal industry, and splits out revenues for 12 of the biggest coal producers. In both cases, revenues are taken from business data sources like Hoovers.com, Mergent.com, and company annual reports. In some cases (when these sources do not have revenue data), oil and gas revenues are estimated from annual oil and gas production and average prices for those fuels in 2010. Together, fossil fuel revenues total about $5 trillion US dollars in 2010.

## Table C-1: Oil and gas industry global revenue for top companies in 2010

| Company | Revenue Billion 2010 US $ | % of total | Notes |
|---|---|---|---|
| Exxon Mobil | 383 | 9.5% | 2 |
| Royal Dutch Shell | 378 | 9.4% | 2 |
| BP | 303 | 7.5% | 2 |
| China Petroleum & Chemical Corp. | 283 | 7.0% | 2 |
| Saudi Arabian Oil Company | 240 | 5.9% | 3 |
| Chevron | 205 | 5.1% | 2 |
| ConocoPhillips | 199 | 4.9% | 2 |
| Total | 186 | 4.6% | 2 |
| E.ON | 145 | 3.6% | 4 |
| ENI | 132 | 3.3% | 2 |
| Petroleo Brasileiro | 120 | 3.0% | 2 |
| National Iranian Oil Company | 120 | 3.0% | 5 |
| Gazprom | 119 | 2.9% | 2 |
| GDF Suez | 112 | 2.8% | 2 |
| Lukoil | 105 | 2.6% | 4 |
| Statoil | 88 | 2.2% | 2 |
| Pemex | 86 | 2.1% | 2 |
| Kuwait Petroleum Corporation | 84 | 2.1% | 6 |
| Valero Energy | 82 | 2.0% | 2 |
| Nigerian National Petroleum Corporation | 78 | 1.9% | 7 |
| Abu Dhabi National Oil Company | 77 | 1.9% | 8 |
| Repsol YPF | 74 | 1.8% | 2 |
| Marathon Oil | 74 | 1.8% | 2 |
| PDVSA | 72 | 1.8% | 9 |
| RWE AG | 68 | 1.7% | 2 |
| Petronas | 67 | 1.7% | 10 |
| OAO Rosneft | 63 | 1.6% | 11 |
| Indian Oil | 58 | 1.4% | 2 |
| Sonatrach | 39 | 1.0% | 12 |
| Total | 4,040 | 100% | 13 |

Notes:

(1) Data compiled by Zachary Schmidt [zacharys@berkeley.edu], July-November 2011.

(2) Source: Mergent Online [http://www.mergentonline.com].

(3) Oil revenues estimated using total company oil production from [http://www.saudiaramco.com/content/dam/Publications/Annual%20Review/Annual%20Review_2010_modified_080611.pdf], page 4, and the average OPEC market basket price of oil for 2010 from [http://www.opec.org/opec_web/static_files_project/media/downloads/publications/MOMR_January_2011.pdf]. Gas revenues estimated using total company gas production [http://www.saudiaramco.com/content/dam/Publications/Annual%20Review/Annual%20Review_2010_modified_080611.pdf], page 4, and the average natural gas price for 2010 from [http://www.cga.ca/publications/documents/Chart8-NaturalGasPrices.pdf].

(4) Source: Hoover's Inc. [http://www.hoovers.com].

(5) Revenues estimated using total company oil production (4.2 million barrels per day from Hoover's, [http://www.hoovers.com/company/National_Iranian_Oil_Company/hhxjhi-1.html]) and the average OPEC market basket price of oil for 2010 from [http://www.opec.org/opec_web/static_files_project/media/downloads/publications/MOMR_January_2011.pdf].

(6) Revenues in Kuwaiti dinar from p. 26 of the company's annual report for the 12 months ending 2010-03-31 [http://www.kpc.com.kw/MediaCentre/Publications/Annual%20reports/AnnualRep2010-eng.pdf], converted to US dollars using 0.2857 dinar per dollar.

(7) Oil revenues estimated using total company oil production (896,043,406 barrels produced in 2010, from NNPC 2010 Annual Statistical Bulletin, page iv. [http://www.nnpcgroup.com/Portals/0/Monthly%20Performance/2010%20ASB%201st%20edition.pdf]) and the average OPEC market basket price of oil for 2010 from [http://www.opec.org/opec_web/static_files_project/media/downloads/publications/MOMR_January_2011.pdf]. Gas revenues estimated using total company gas production (1,811.27 billion standard cu ft utilized in 2010, from NNPC 2010 Annual Statistical Bulletin, page iv. [http://www.nnpcgroup.com/Portals/0/Monthly%20Performance/2010%20ASB%201st%20edition.pdf]) and the average natural gas price for 2010 from [http://www.cga.ca/publications/documents/Chart8-NaturalGasPrices.pdf].

(8) Revenues estimated using total company oil production (2.7 million barrels/day, from [http://www.adnoc.ae/content.aspx?mid=22]) and the average OPEC market basket price of oil for 2010 from [http://www.opec.org/opec_web/static_files_project/media/downloads/publications/MOMR_January_2011.pdf].

(9) Revenues estimated using total company oil production for 2010 from [http://www.petroleumworld.com/storyt11030201.htm] and the average price of Venezuala's oil for 2010 from [http://en.mercopress.com/2011/01/22/oil-price-in-venezuela-at-two-year-high].

(10) Revenues in Malaysian ringgit from p.12 of the company's annual report [http://www.petronas.com.my/downloads/AnnualReports/AnnualReport2010.pdf], converted to US dollars using 3.221 RM per dollar.

(11) Revenues in US dollars from p.3 of the company's annual report [http://www.rosneft.com/attach/0/62/19/Rosneft_GAAP_2010_ENG.pdf].

(12) Oil revenues estimated using total company oil production (1.2 million barrels/day, from [http://www.ennaharonline.com/en/economy/5634.html]) and the average OPEC market basket price of oil for 2010 from [http://www.opec.org/opec_web/static_files_project/media/downloads/publications/MOMR_January_2011.pdf]. Gas revenues estimated using total company LNG production (31 billion cubic meters/year, from [http://uk.ibtimes.com/articles/104816/20110125/algeria-s-sonatrach-sees-steady-oil-lng-exports.htm]) and the average natural gas price for 2010 from [http://www.cga.ca/publications/documents/Chart8-NaturalGasPrices.pdf].

(13) No reliable source of total industry oil and gas revenue was available, so it was not possible to estimate the amount of revenue attributable to "other", but IBIS World contains an estimate of total revenues for the "upstream" part of the oil and gas industry, including exploration, production, and refining, and excluding downstream sales to customers. That estimate is $2,900 billion US dollars in 2010.

## Table C-2: Coal industry global revenue for 2010

| Company | Revenue Billion 2010 US $ | % of total | Notes |
|---|---|---|---|
| RWE AG | 68 | 6.3% | 2 |
| Rio Tinto | 57 | 5.3% | 2 |
| BHP Billiton | 53 | 4.9% | 2 |
| Xstrata | 30 | 2.9% | 2 |
| Anglo American | 28 | 2.6% | 2 |
| Shenhua Group | 23 | 2.1% | 2 |
| Coal India | 11 | 1.1% | 3 |
| Peabody Energy Corporation | 7 | 0.6% | 2 |
| Bumi Resources | 4 | 0.4% | 4 |
| Arch Coal | 3 | 0.3% | 2 |
| Adaro Indonesia | 3 | 0.3% | 5 |
| Banpu | 2 | 0.2% | 6 |
| Other | 782 | 73.0% | 7 |
| Total | 1070 | 100% | 7 |

(1) Data compiled by Zachary Schmidt [zacharys@berkeley.edu], July-November 2011.

(2) Source: Mergent Online [http://www.mergentonline.com].

(3) Revenues in Indian rupees from the company's annual report for 2010 [http://www.coalindia.in/Documents/Reports/Performance/Financial/200910/Page_12_17_0910.pdf], converted to US dollars using 45.7152 rupees per dollar.

(4) Revenues in US dollars from the company's annual report for 2010 [http://www.bumiresources.com/].

(5) Revenues in Indonesian rupiah from the company's annual report for 2010 [http://www.adaro.com/files/Adaro_Energy_2010_Annual_Report_English_1.pdf], converted to US dollars using 9056.73 rupiah per dollar.

(6) Revenues in Thai baht from Annual Report 2010 [http://www.banpu.com/en/05-investor-relations/investor-sec-filings.php], converted to US dollars using 31.5062 baht per dollar.

(7) Total coal industry revenues are from IBIS World. "Other" is calculated as the difference between the IBIS World total and the total revenues of the listed companies.

---

## Tobacco company revenues for 2010

---

Table D-1 calculates revenues for the global tobacco manufacturing industry, and splits out revenues for eight of the biggest tobacco producers. The tobacco industry is relatively concentrated, with the top eight firms responsible for almost 70% of total revenues. Total revenues in 2010 were about $500 billion US dollars, or about about ten times less than total fossil fuel company revenues in that year (see Appendix C).

## Table D-1: Tobacco manufacturing industry global revenue for 2010

| Company | Revenue Billion 2010 US $ | % of total |
|---|---|---|
| China National Tobacco Corp. | 82 | 17.4% |
| Philip Morris International Inc. | 68 | 14.4% |
| Japan Tobacco Inc. | 70 | 14.9% |
| Imperial Tobacco Group PLC | 44 | 9.3% |
| Altria Group (US tobacco segment) | 24 | 5.2% |
| British American Tobacco PLC | 23 | 4.9% |
| Reynolds American | 9 | 1.8% |
| Lorillard Inc. | 6 | 1.3% |
| Other | 145 | 30.9% |
| Total | 470 | 100% |

(1) Data compiled by Zachary Schmidt [zacharys@berkeley.edu], July -November 2011.
(2) Sources: IBISWorld for China National Tobacco [ http://clients.ibisworld.com], Mergent Online [http://www.mergentonline.com] for all others
(3) Total tobacco manufacturing industry revenues are from IBIS World. "Other" is calculated as the difference between the IBIS World total and the total revenues of the listed companies.

# FURTHER READING

Ackerman, Frank, and Elizabeth A. Stanton. 2011. Climate Economics: *The State of the Art*. Somerville, MA: Stockholm Environment Institute. November. [http://sei-us.org/Publications_PDF/SEI-ClimateEconomics-state-of-art-2011.pdf]. This report summarizes the latest developments in climate economics, and it's a great way to get up to speed quickly.

Archer, David. 2007. *Global Warming: Understanding the Forecast*. Malden, MA: Blackwell Publishing. [http://geoflop.uchicago.edu/forecast/docs/]. This is the best introductory book treatment I've found on the climate science. It's used at the University of Chicago for a lower level class on climate change. The web site has supplemental materials.

Allison, I., N.L. Bindoff, R.A. Bindschadler, P.M. Cox, N. de Noblet, M.H. England, J.E. Francis, N. Gruber, A.M. Haywood, D.J. Karoly, G. Kaser, C. Le Quéré, T.M. Lenton, M.E. Mann, B.I. McNeil, A.J. Pitman, S. Rahmstorf, E. Rignot, H.J. Schellnhuber, S.H. Schneider, S.C. Sherwood, R.C.J. Somerville, K. Steffen, E.J. Steig, M. Visbeck, and A.J. Weaver. 2011. *The Copenhagen Diagnosis: Updating the World on the Latest Climate Science*. Burlington, MA: Elsevier. [http://www.copenhagendiagnosis.org/]. This gives the latest concise summary of what we know about climate science, so it's a good supplement to Archer's book and the IPCC reports from 2007.

Brynjolfsson, Erik, and Andrew McAfee. 2011. *Race Against The Machine: How the Digital Revolution is Accelerating Innovation, Driving Productivity, and Irreversibly Transforming Employment and the Economy*. Digital Frontier Press. [http://raceagainstthemachine.com/]. This wonderfully concise e-book summarizes the most important research on how information technology is affecting productivity and the structure of the US economy.

Cook, John, and Stephan Lewandowsky. 2011. *The Debunking Handbook*. November. [http://sks.to/debunk]. This book is the latest from the man who created the Skeptical Science web site. No one has thought more deeply about how to address global warming denialism than Cook.

DeCanio, Stephen J. 2003. *Economic Models of Climate Change: A Critique*. Basingstoke, UK: Palgrave-Macmillan. This book contains a devastating critique from inside the economics community of the use of economic models for analyzing the climate problem.

Dumaine, Brian. 2008. *The Plot to Save the Planet: How Visionary Entrepreneurs and Corporate Titans are Creating Real Solutions to Global Warming.* New York, NY: Three Rivers Press. This book is a journalistic account of what some in the corporate world are doing to meet the climate challenge, so it's a good (but slightly dated) starting point for exploring what's happening in the marketplace.

Esty, Daniel C., and Andrew S. Winston. 2009. *Green to Gold: How Smart Companies Use Environmental Strategy to Innovate, Create Value, and Build Competitive Advantage.* Hoboken, NJ: John Wiley & Sons, Inc. [http://www.eco-advantage.com/]. This is a nice conceptual presentation of how businesses can turn ecological innovation to their advantage. It also has a lot of real-world examples, and looks at the pros and cons of hitching your star to environmental entrepreneurship.

Gore, Al. 2009. *Our Choice: A Plan to Solve the Climate Crisis.* Emmaus, PA: Rodale Books. [http://www.climatecrisis.net/]. This book is the best popular summary of climate solutions I've found, so it's an excellent place to start if you're new to the topic. The iPad version also sets a new standard for user interface design and is a real bargain.

Henson, Robert. 2011. *The Rough Guide to Climate Change.* 3rd ed. London, UK: Rough Guides, Ltd. This book is probably the most approachable guide to the climate problem, and is a good place to get started if you're new to the issue.

The IPCC reports are the comprehensive compilation of what we knew about climate circa 2007 or so, but of course we've learned a lot since then. They are still valuable resources, so I include them here:

IPCC. 2007. *Climate Change 2007: Mitigation of Climate Change—Contribution of Working Group III to the Fourth Assessment Report of the Intergovernmental Panel on Climate Change [Metz, B., O. Davidson, P. Bosch, R. Dave, and L. Meyer (eds.)].* Cambridge, United Kingdom and New York, NY, USA.: Cambridge University Press. [http://www.ipcc.ch/publications_and_data/publications_and_data_reports.shtml]

IPCC. 2007. *Climate Change 2007: The Physical Science Basis—Contribution of Working Group I to the Fourth Assessment Report of the Intergovernmental Panel on Climate Change [Solomon, S., D. Qin, M. Manning, M. Marquis, K. Averyt, M. M. B. Tignor, H. L. Miller Jr, and Z. Chen (eds.)].* Cambridge, United Kingdom and New York, NY, USA.: Cambridge University Press. [http://www.ipcc.ch/publications_and_data/publications_and_data_reports.shtml]

IPCC. 2007. *Climate Change 2007: Impacts, Adaptation, and Vulnerability—Contribution of Working Group II to the Fourth Assessment Report of the Intergovernmental Panel on Climate Change [M. Parry, O. Canziani, J. Palutikof, P. van der Linden, C. Hanson (eds.)].* Cambridge, United Kingdom and New York, NY, USA: Cambridge University Press. [http://www.ipcc.ch/publications_and_data/publications_and_data_reports.shtml]

IPCC. 2007. *Climate change 2007, Synthesis report: Summary for Policy Makers*. Geneva, Switzerland: Intergovernmental Panel on Climate Change. [http://www.ipcc.ch/pdf/assessment-report/ar4/syr/ar4_syr_spm.pdf]

Krause, Florentin, Wilfred Bach, and Jonathan G. Koomey. 1992. *Energy Policy in the Greenhouse*. NY, NY: John Wiley and Sons. This book was the first comprehensive application of the warming limit approach to the 2 Celsius degree limit, and it's still useful for those who want a deep understanding of this method. It was first published in 1989, then republished by Wiley in 1992. Email me if you want a PDF version of the 1989 edition.

Lovins, Amory B., Mathias Bell, Lionel Bony, Albert Chan, Stephen Doig, Nathan J. Glasgow, Lena Hansen, Virginia Lacy, Eric Maurer, Jesse Morris, James Newcomb, Greg Rucks, and Caroline Traube. 2011. *Reinventing Fire: Bold Business Solutions for the New Energy Era*. White River Junction, VT: Chelsea Green Publishing. This book describes a business-led transition away from fossil fuels, contains state-of-the-art thinking, illustrates how to do whole systems integrated design, and gives myriad examples of how to drastically reduce emissions and make money at the same time.

McMillan, John. 2003. *Reinventing the Bazaar: A Natural History of Markets*. New York, NY: W.W. Norton & Company, describes the socially constructed nature of different markets. It's a must-read for those thinking deeply about property rights and market structure.

Oreskes, Naomi, and Eric M. Conway. 2010. *Merchants of Doubt: How a Handful of Scientists Obscured the Truth on Issues from Tobacco Smoke to Global Warming*. New York, NY: Bloomsbury Press. This book puts the denial of climate change into a longer-term historical context, and explains how the ideology of a particular group of scientists drove them to ignore well-established facts about the way the world works.

Romm, Joseph. 2007. *Hell and High Water: Global Warming—the Solution and the Politics—and What We Should Do*. New York, NY: William Morrow, An Imprint of Harper Collins. I'm an avid reader of Romm's blog [Climate Progress, from which much of this book comes] because he has a deep understanding of what's important on climate science and solutions.

Schneider, Stephen H. 2009. *Science as a Contact Sport: Inside the Battle to Save Earth's Climate*. Washington, DC: National Geographic. Schneider's account of his personal odyssey is a fascinating read for anyone interested in the climate issue.

Sherwin Jr., Elton B. 2010. *Addicted to Energy: A Venture Capitalist's Perspective on How to Save Our Economy and our Climate*. Energy House Publishing. I'm especially fond of this book because of its no-nonsense style and wealth of practical ideas. While it's focused on advice to a hypothetical governor, business folks will find reading it an excellent way to develop new directions for their entrepreneurial energies.

Weart, Spencer R. 2008. *The Discovery of Global Warming*. Cambridge, MA: Harvard University Press. [http://www.aip.org/history/climate/] This book is a wonderful and readable exploration of the history of climate science. An expanded and updated version of the book is available for free online.

Williams, James H., Andrew DeBenedictis, Rebecca Ghanadan, Amber Mahone, Jack Moore, William R. Morrow, Snuller Price, and Margaret S. Torn. 2011. "The Technology Path to Deep Greenhouse Gas Emissions Cuts by 2050: The Pivotal Role of Electricity." *Science*. November 24. [http://www.sciencemag.org/content/early/2011/11/22/science.1208365.abstract]. This article is the best recent application of the working forward to a goal approach. It demonstrates that California (which is already relatively efficient and has low carbon emissions per kWh of electricity generated) can reduce emissions by 80% compared to 1990 levels to 2050, at modest cost.

# NOTES

## Preface

1. Kawasaki, Guy. 2004. *The Art of the Start: The Time-Tested, Battle-Hardened Guide for Anyone Starting Anything*. New York, NY: Penguin Group.
2. Laurel, Brenda. 2001. *Utopian Entrepreneur*. Cambridge, MA: MIT Press.

## Chapter 1

1. Grubler, Arnulf. 2008. "Energy transitions." In *Encyclopedia of Earth*. Edited by C. J. Cleveland. Washington, D.C.: Environmental Information Coalition, National Council for Science and the Environment. [http://www.iiasa.ac.at/~gruebler/Data/EoE_Data.html]
2. [http://www.census.gov/main/www/popclock.html]
3. Op. cit. Grubler 2008, "Energy Transitions" note 1 above.
4. [http://data.worldbank.org/indicator/NY.GDP.MKTP.CD/countries?display=default]
5. A wonderful summary of humanity's newfound powers is contained in Turner II, B. L., William C. Clark, Robert W. Kates, John F. Richards, Jessica T. Mathews, and William B. Meyer, ed. 1993. *The Earth as Transformed by Human Action: Global and Regional Changes in the Biosphere over the Past 300 Years*. Cambridge, England: Cambridge University Press. Although now almost two decades old, it still gives a wonderfully complete historical picture.

   A briefer (and very widely cited) summary is Vitousek, Peter M., Harold A. Mooney, Jane Lubchenco, and Jerry M. Melillo. 1997. "Human Domination of Earth's Ecosystems." *Science*. vol. 277, no. 5325. July 25, 1997. pp. 494-499. [http://www.sciencemag.org/content/277/5325/494.abstract]

   A more recent short review focusing on human's effect on biological diversity is here (it introduces a special issue on the topic): Magurran, Anne E., and Maria Dornelas. 2010. "Biological diversity in a changing world." *Philosophical Transactions of the Royal Society B: Biological Sciences*. vol. 365, no. 1558. November 27. pp. 3593-3597. [http://rstb.royalsocietypublishing.org/content/365/1558/3593.abstract]
6. Myers, Ransom A., and Boris Worm. 2003. "Rapid worldwide depletion of predatory fish communities." *Nature*. vol. 423, no. 6937. May 15. pp. 280-283. [http://dx.doi.org/10.1038/nature01610]
7. Op. cit. Magurran and Dornelas 2010, note 5 above.
8. Boyce, Daniel G., Marlon R. Lewis, and Boris Worm. 2010. "Global phytoplankton decline over the past century." *Nature*. vol. 466, no. 7306. July 29. pp. 591-596. [http://dx.doi.org/10.1038/nature09268]. The 40% decline figure comes from the following online news article: Connor, Steve. 2010. "The dead sea: Global warming blamed for 40 per cent decline in the ocean's phytoplankton." *The Independent*. London, UK. [http://

www.independent.co.uk/environment/climate-change/the-dead-sea-global-warming-blamed-for-40-per-cent-decline-in-the-oceans-phytoplankton-2038074.html].

9. Lindberg, Steve, Russell Bullock, Ralf Ebinghaus, Daniel Engstrom, Xinbin Feng, William Fitzgerald, Nicola Pirrone, Eric Prestbo, and Christian Seigneur. 2007. "A Synthesis of Progress and Uncertainties in Attributing the Sources of Mercury in Deposition." *Ambio*. vol. 36, no. 1. pp. 19-32. [http://www.jstor.org/stable/4315781]

10. Swain, Edward B., Paul M. Jakus, Glenn Rice, Frank Lupi, Peter A. Maxson, Jozef M. Pacyna, Alan Penn, Samuel J. Spiegel, and Marcello M. Veiga. 2007. "Socioeconomic Consequences of Mercury Use and Pollution." *Ambio*. vol. 36, no. 1. pp. 45-61. [http://www.jstor.org/stable/4315783]

11. Mergler, Donna, Henry A. Anderson, Laurie Hing Man Chan, Kathryn R. Mahaffey, Michael Murray, Mineshi Sakamoto, and Alan H. Stern. 2007. "Methylmercury Exposure and Health Effects in Humans: A Worldwide Concern." *Ambio*. vol. 36, no. 1. pp. 3-11. [http://www.jstor.org/stable/4315779]

12. Anton, M. Scheuhammer, Michael W. Meyer, Mark B. Sandheinrich, and Michael W. Murray. 2007. "Effects of Environmental Methylmercury on the Health of Wild Birds, Mammals, and Fish." *Ambio*. vol. 36, no. 1. pp. 12-18. [http://www.jstor.org/stable/4315780]

13. Colborn, Theo, Dianne Dumanoski, and John Peterson Myers. 1997. *Our Stolen Future: Are We Threatening our Fertility, Intelligence, and Survival? A Scientific Detective Story*. New York, NY: Plume, an imprint of the Penguin Group.

14. Freinkel, Susan. 2011. *Plastic: A Toxic Love Story*. New York, NY: Houghton Mifflin Harcourt. Susan Freinkel was on Public Radio's Fresh Air program on April 19, 2011—she talked about how drug companies are required to do significant testing before allowing new drugs on the market, but we require virtually no testing for plastics, many of which are ingested by humans inadvertently as part of the food chain.

15. Steffen, Will, Regina Angelina Sanderson, Peter D. Tyson, Jill Jäger, Pamela A. Matson, Berrien Moore III, Frank Oldfield, Katherine Richardson, Hans-Joachim Schellnhuber, Billie L. Turner, and Robert J. Wasson. 2004. *Global Change and the Earth System: A Planet Under Pressure (Global Change- The IGBP Series)*. Berlin: Springer-Verlag.

16. See the summary of humanity's effects on the global environment on pages 6 and 7 of Turner II et al. (1993). *The Earth as Transformed by Human Action*. Op. cit. note 5. Population data from Grubler 2008, "Energy Transitions" Op. cit. note 1 above.

17. The most complete and up-to-date summary of what the peer-reviewed literature says is on the web at [http://www.skepticalscience.com/]. That site characterizes "skeptic" arguments in an easy-to-understand way and then cites the arguments and literature needed to understand what we really know about each topic.

    The best introductory book treatment I've found is one used at the University of Chicago for a lower level class on climate change: Archer, David. 2007. *Global Warming: Understanding the Forecast*. Malden, MA: Blackwell Publishing. [http://geoflop.uchicago.edu/forecast/docs/]. The web site has supplemental materials.

    A summary that gives more recent developments on climate science is Allison, I., N.L. Bindoff, R.A. Bindschadler, P.M. Cox, N. de Noblet, M.H. England, J.E. Francis, N. Gruber, A.M. Haywood, D.J. Karoly, G. Kaser, C. Le Quéré, T.M. Lenton, M.E. Mann, B.I. McNeil, A.J. Pitman, S. Rahmstorf, E. Rignot, H.J. Schellnhuber, S.H. Schneider, S.C. Sherwood, R.C.J. Somerville, K. Steffen, E.J. Steig, M. Visbeck, and A.J. Weaver. 2009. *The Copenhagen Diagnosis, 2009: Updating the World on the Latest Climate Science*.

Sydney, Australia: The University of New South Wales Climate Change Research Centre (CCRC). [http://www.copenhagendiagnosis.org/]. There's an updated 2011 version published by Elsevier.

18. Now to be clear, I don't think all regulations fall into the "overly restrictive" category. Those banning lead in children's toys, for example, are perfectly appropriate. And as long as the criteria used to design the regulations are based on performance rather than being overly prescriptive, then they are probably OK. An efficiency regulation for refrigerators that mandates a certain efficiency level would pass this test, but one that mandated a certain model of fridge compressor probably wouldn't.

19. I'd like to distinguish here between the responsible advocates of white roofs and pavements (like Art Rosenfeld), which almost always make sense, and of modest geoengineering to buy time (like Tom Wigley and Paul Crutzen), which could under very restrictive conditions make sense, from the claims of ill-informed people like Steven Levitt, Stephen Dubner, and Bjorn Lomborg, who somehow think that creating an uncontrolled experiment with the global environment is the way to counter the uncontrolled experiment on the global environment that we are now running with climate change. The latter view is simply and dangerously wrong, as Martin Bunzi points out in a post on Climate Progress: [http://climateprogress.org/2010/09/27/martin-bunzl-geoengineering-fix-solar-radiation-management-aerosols-volcanoes/]. That same post quotes Stanford scientist Ken Caldeira, someone who advocates studying geoengineering, as saying "Thinking of geoengineering as a substitute for emissions reduction is analogous to saying, 'Now that I've got the seatbelts on, I can just take my hands off the wheel and turn around and talk to people in the back seat.' It's crazy . . . ."

20. The first use of the Sputnik analogy for the climate issue of which I'm aware was my testimony before the Joint Economic Committee of the US Congress in July 2008 (*Testimony of Jonathan Koomey, Ph.D. for a hearing on "Efficiency: The Hidden Secret to Solving Our Energy Crisis"*. Joint Economic Committee of the U.S. Congress. U.S. Congress. Washington, DC: US Congress. July 30, 2008.). Tom Friedman of the *New York Times* started using this analogy independently in September 2009. For an historical treatment of developments after the Sputnik launch, see Dickson, Paul. 2003. *Sputnik: The Shock of the Century*. New York, NY: Berkley Books.

21. See chapter 19 of my 2008 book, *Turning Numbers into Knowledge: Mastering the Art of Problem Solving*. 2nd ed. Oakland, CA: Analytics Press. [http://www.analyticspress.com]. You can download that chapter and read a short blog post on the topic at [http://www.koomey.com/post/3704280038].

22. IEA. 2009. *World Energy Outlook 2009*. Paris, France: International Energy Agency, Organization for Economic Cooperation and Development (OECD). November. p. 52 [http://www.worldenergyoutlook.org/]. In the very next version of this report, the IEA estimated that the costs had increased by $1 trillion over the 2009 estimates. IEA. 2010. *World Energy Outlook 2010*. Paris, France: International Energy Agency, Organization for Economic Cooperation and Development (OECD). November 9. pp. 404-405 [http://www.worldenergyoutlook.org/]

23. One example is that of wind power, where China installed half of all new wind installations in 2010, and in that year surpassed the US in total installed wind capacity. GWEC. 2011. *Global Wind Report: Annual Market Update 2010*. Global Wind Energy Council. [http://www.gwec.net]. China also spent almost three times as much as the US did on

energy RD&D in the 2004 to 2008 period: See Chapter 24 in IIASA. 2011. *Global Energy Assessment*. Cambridge, UK: Cambridge University Press.

24. Oreskes, Naomi, and Eric M. Conway. 2010. *Merchants of Doubt: How a Handful of Scientists Obscured the Truth on Issues from Tobacco Smoke to Global Warming*. New York, NY: Bloomsbury Press.

   The way industry uses uncertainty in science to argue against regulations is also explored in Freudenburg, William R., Robert Gramling, and Debra J. Davidson. 2008. "Scientific Certainty Argumentation Methods (SCAMs): Science and the Politics of Doubt." *Sociological Inquiry*. vol. 78, no. 1. February. pp. 2–38.

   Dunlap, Riley E., and Aaron McCright. 2011. "Chapter 10: Organized Climate Change Denial." In *The Oxford Handbook of Climate Change and Society*. Edited by J. S. Dryzek, R. B. Norgaard and D. Schlosberg. Oxford, UK: Oxford University Press. pp. 144-160.

25. Isaacson, Walter. 2011. *Steve Jobs*. New York, NY: Simon & Schuster. p. 154.

## Chapter 2

1. 97% of climate scientists are convinced by the evidence that humans are causing climate change: [http://www.skepticalscience.com/global-warming-scientific-consensus.htm]. Oreskes, Naomi, and Eric M. Conway. 2010. *Merchants of Doubt: How a Handful of Scientists Obscured the Truth on Issues from Tobacco Smoke to Global Warming*. New York, NY: Bloomsbury Press.

   Also see Anderegg, William R. L., James W. Prall, Jacob Harold, and Stephen H. Schneider. 2010. "Expert credibility in climate change." *Proceedings of the National Academy of Sciences*. June 21. [http://www.pnas.org/content/early/2010/06/04/1003187107.abstract]

2. NAS. 2010. *Advancing the Science of Climate Change*. Washington, DC: National Academy of Sciences. [http://www.nap.edu/catalog.php?record_id=12782].

3. [http://www.skepticalscience.com/global-warming-scientific-consensus-intermediate.htm]

4. IPCC. 2007. *Climate change 2007, Synthesis report: Summary for Policy Makers*. Geneva, Switzerland: Intergovernmental Panel on Climate Change. [http://www.ipcc.ch/pdf/assessment-report/ar4/syr/ar4_syr_spm.pdf]

5. [http://data.giss.nasa.gov/gistemp/graphs/]

6. For a clear and comprehensive summary of the sources and emissions of all the various warming agents in the US, see US EPA. 2011. *Inventory Of US Greenhouse Gas Emissions And Sinks: 1990 – 2009*. Washington, DC: US Environmental Protection Agency. April 15. [http://www.epa.gov/climatechange/emissions/usinventoryreport.html]

7. A "concentration" describes how much of a certain gas is in a cubic meter of atmosphere (it's typically measured in parts per million, which is similar to a fraction of the total).

8. Siegenthaler, Urs, Thomas F. Stocker, Eric Monnin, Dieter Luthi, Jakob Schwander, Bernhard Stauffer, Dominique Raynaud, Jean-Marc Barnola, Hubertus Fischer, Valerie Masson-Delmotte, and Jean Jouzel. 2005. "Stable Carbon Cycle—Climate Relationship During the Late Pleistocene." *Science*. vol. 310, no. 5752. November 25. pp. 1313-1317. [http://www.ncdc.noaa.gov/paleo/pubs/siegenthaler2005/siegenthaler2005.html]

9. Data taken from Petit, J. R., J. Jouzel, D. Raynaud, N. I. Barkov, J. M. Barnola, I. Basile, M. Bender, J. Chappellaz, M. Davis, G. Delaygue, M. Delmotte, V. M. Kotlyakov, M. Legrand, V. Y. Lipenkov, C. Lorius, L. Pepin, C. Ritz, E. Saltzman, and M. Stievenard. 1999. "Climate and atmospheric history of the past 420,000 years from the Vostok ice

core, Antarctica." *Nature*. vol. 399, no. 6735. pp. 429-436. [http://dx.doi.
org/10.1038/20859, http://www.nature.com/nature/journal/v399/n6735/
suppinfo/399429a0_S1.html]

10. [http://www.realclimate.org/index.php/archives/2004/12/how-do-we-know-that-recent-cosub2sub-increases-are-due-to-human-activities-updated/]

11. IPCC. 2007. *Climate Change 2007: The Physical Science Basis—Contribution of Working Group I to the Fourth Assessment Report of the Intergovernmental Panel on Climate Change* [Solomon, S., D. Qin, M. Manning, M. Marquis, K. Averyt, M. M. B. Tignor, H. L. Miller Jr, and Z. Chen (eds.)]. Cambridge, United Kingdom and New York, NY, USA: Cambridge University Press. [http://www.ipcc.ch/publications_and_data/publications_and_data_reports.shtml]

12. Broecker, Wallace S. 1975. "Climatic Change: Are We on the Brink of a Pronounced Global Warming?" *Science*. vol. 189, no. 4201. August 8, 1975. pp. 460-463. [http://www.sciencemag.org/content/189/4201/460.abstract]

13. See Figure SPM.5, p.14 in the IPCC 2007 Working Group I report, *Climate Change 2007: The Physical Science Basis,* and the detailed review in National Research Council. 2006. *Surface Temperature Reconstructions for the Last 2,000 Years*. Washington, DC: National Academies Press. [http://www.nap.edu]. As I discuss later, the embodied warming commitment is even larger than this, because some of this effect is being masked by the cooling effect of sulfate aerosols emitted from coal combustion, but these emissions will be eliminated in scenarios where fossil fuel consumption is rapidly reduced.

14. Weart, Spencer R. 2008. *The Discovery of Global Warming*. Cambridge, MA: Harvard University Press. [http://www.aip.org/history/climate/]

15. Skeptical Science has a summary of these measurements here: [http://www.skepti-calscience.com/Quantifying-the-human-contribution-to-global-warming.html]. Also see Rahmstorf, Stefan, Anny Cazenave, John A. Church, James E. Hansen, Ralph F. Keeling, David E. Parker, and Richard C. J. Somerville. 2007. "Recent Climate Observations Compared to Projections." *Science*. vol. 316, no. 5825. May 4, 2007. pp. 709. [http://www.sciencemag.org/content/316/5825/709.abstract]

    See also Hansen, James, Larissa Nazarenko, Reto Ruedy, Makiko Sato, Josh Willis, Anthony Del Genio, Dorothy Koch, Andrew Lacis, Ken Lo, Surabi Menon, Tica Novakov, Judith Perlwitz, Gary Russell, Gavin A. Schmidt, and Nicholas Tausnev. 2005. "Earth's Energy Imbalance: Confirmation and Implications." *Science*. vol. 308, no. 5727. June 3, 2005. pp. 1431-1435. [http://www.sciencemag.org/content/308/5727/1431.abstract]

16. Harries, John E., Helen E. Brindley, Pretty J. Sagoo, and Richard J. Bantges. 2001. "Increases in greenhouse forcing inferred from the outgoing longwave radiation spectra of the Earth in 1970 and 1997." *Nature*. vol. 410, no. 6826. March 15. pp. 355-357.

17. Philipona, Rolf, Bruno Dürr, Christoph Marty, Atsumu Ohmura, and Martin Wild. 2004. "Radiative forcing - measured at Earth's surface - corroborate the increasing greenhouse effect." *Geophys. Res. Lett.* vol. 31, no. 3. pp. L03202. [http://dx.doi.org/10.1029/2003GL018765]

    Also see Evans, W., & Puckrin, E. (2006, January). Measurements of the radiative surface forcing of climate, Retrieved from 18th Conference on Climate Variability and Change Web site: [http://ams.confex.com/ams/Annual2006/techprogram/paper_100737.htm]

18. John Cook at Skeptical Science made a graph showing ocean heat building up substan-tially over time (http://www.skepticalscience.com/graphics.php?g=4) based on data from

Murphy, D. M., S. Solomon, R. W. Portmann, K. H. Rosenlof, P. M. Forster, and T. Wong. 2009. "An observationally based energy balance for the Earth since 1950." *Journal of Geophysical Research*. vol. 114, no. D17107. September 9. [http://www.agu.org/journals/jd/jd0917/2009JD012105/2009JD012105.pdf] and Domingues, Catia M., John A. Church, Neil J. White, Peter J. Gleckler, Susan E. Wijffels, Paul M. Barker, and Jeff R. Dunn. 2008. "Improved estimates of upper-ocean warming and multi-decadal sea-level rise." *Nature*. vol. 453, no. 7198. June 19. pp. 1090-1093. [http://www.nature.com/nature/journal/v453/n7198/abs/nature07080.html]

19. Strong, Aaron, Kelly Levin, and Dennis Tirpak. 2011. *Climate Science: Major New Discoveries*. Washington, DC: World Resources Institute. October. [http://www.wri.org/publication/climate-science]

20. IPCC Working Group I report (2007). *Climate Change 2007: The Physical Science Basis—Contribution of Working Group I to the Fourth Assessment Report of the Intergovernmental Panel on Climate Change* [Solomon, S., D. Qin, M. Manning, M. Marquis, K. Averyt, M. M. B. Tignor, H. L. Miller Jr, and Z. Chen (eds.)]. Cambridge, United Kingdom and New York, NY, USA: Cambridge University Press. [http://www.ipcc.ch/publications_and_data/publications_and_data_reports.shtml]

21. Schweiger, Axel, Ron Lindsay, Jinlun Zhang, Mike Steele, Harry Stern and Ron Kwok. 2011. "Uncertainty in Modeled Arctic Sea Ice Volume." *In Press at JGR Oceans*. June 2. [http://psc.apl.washington.edu/wordpress/schweiger-2011/]

22. [http://psc.apl.washington.edu/wordpress/research/projects/arctic-sea-ice-volume-anomaly/]

23. Domingues, Catia M., John A. Church, Neil J. White, Peter J. Gleckler, Susan E. Wijffels, Paul M. Barker, and Jeff R. Dunn. 2008. "Improved estimates of upper-ocean warming and multi-decadal sea-level rise." *Nature*. vol. 453, no. 7198. June 19. pp. 1090-1093. [http://www.nature.com/nature/journal/v453/n7198/abs/nature07080.html]

   Murphy, D. M., S. Solomon, R. W. Portmann, K. H. Rosenlof, P. M. Forster, and T. Wong. 2009. "An observationally based energy balance for the Earth since 1950." *Journal of Geophysical Research*. vol. 114, no. D17107. September 9. [http://www.agu.org/journals/jd/jd0917/2009JD012105/2009JD012105.pdf]

24. Min, Seung-Ki, Xuebin Zhang, Francis W. Zwiers, and Gabriele C. Hegerl. 2011. "Human contribution to more-intense precipitation extremes." *Nature*. vol. 470, no. 7334. pp. 378-381. [http://dx.doi.org/10.1038/nature09763]

25. IPCC. 2007. *Climate change 2007, Synthesis report: Summary for Policy Makers*. Geneva, Switzerland: Intergovernmental Panel on Climate Change. [http://www.ipcc.ch/pdf/assessment-report/ar4/syr/ar4_syr_spm.pdf]

26. The most comprehensive summary of observable scientific evidence for climate change is IPCC. 2007. *Climate Change 2007: The Physical Science Basis—Contribution of Working Group I to the Fourth Assessment Report of the Intergovernmental Panel on Climate Change* [Solomon, S., D. Qin, M. Manning, M. Marquis, K. Averyt, M. M. B. Tignor, H. L. Miller Jr, and Z. Chen (eds.)]. Cambridge, United Kingdom and New York, NY, USA: Cambridge University Press. [http://www.ipcc.ch/publications_and_data/publications_and_data_reports.shtml]

   The synthesis report for the IPCC Fourth Assessment report [http://www.ipcc.ch/pdf/assessment-report/ar4/syr/ar4_syr.pdf] is a compact summary of the scientific evidence and its implications. Figure 1.2 in that document summarizes the number and type of biological and physical data series assessing climate impacts reviewed for that report, and of the hundreds of data series reviewed, more than 90% are consistent with the observed warming trends.

Also see John Cook's excellent summary of the big picture on climate at [http://www.skepticalscience.com/big-picture.html].

27. Henson, Robert. 2011. *The Rough Guide to Climate Change*. 3rd edition. London, UK: Rough Guides, Ltd. pp. 4-5.

28. To learn more about how well climate models are validated, see [http://www.skepticalscience.com/climate-models.htm].

29. For example, see [http://www.skepticalscience.com/climate-sensitivity-advanced.htm] and Knutti, Reto, and Gabriele C. Hegerl. 2008. "The equilibrium sensitivity of the Earth's temperature to radiation changes." *Nature Geoscience*. vol. 1, no. 11. October 26. pp. 735 - 743.

30. Roe, Gerard H., and Marcia B. Baker. 2007. "Why Is Climate Sensitivity So Unpredictable?" *Science*. vol. 318, no. 5850. October 26. pp. 629-632 [http://www.sciencemag.org/content/318/5850/629.abstract]. By unpredictable, the authors mean "why is there such a large uncertainty range for climate sensitivity?".

31. Kiehl, Jeffrey. 2011. "Lessons from Earth's Past." *Science*. vol. 331, no. 6014. January 14. pp. 158-159. [http://www.sciencemag.org/content/331/6014/158.short]

32. Paleoclimate data yield global temperatures and greenhouse gas concentrations going back for millions of years.

33. Rignot, E., I. Velicogna, M. R. van den Broeke, A. Monaghan, and J. T. M. Lenaerts. 2011. "Acceleration of the contribution of the Greenland and Antarctic ice sheets to sea level rise." *Geophysical Research Letters*. vol. 38, no. L05503. March 4.

34. Schaefer, Kevin, Tingjun Zhang, Lori Bruhwiler, and Andrew P. Barrett. 2011. "Amount and timing of permafrost carbon release in response to climate warming." *Tellus B*. vol. 63, no. 2. April. pp. 165-180. [http://dx.doi.org/10.1111/j.1600-0889.2011.00527.x]

35. Turetsky, M. R., W. F. Donahue, and B. W. Benscoter. 2011. "Experimental drying intensifies burning and carbon losses in a northern peatland." *Nat Commun*. vol. 2, November 1. pp. 514. [http://dx.doi.org/10.1038/ncomms1523]

Ise, Takeshi, Allison L. Dunn, Steven C. Wofsy, and Paul R. Moorcroft. 2008. "High sensitivity of peat decomposition to climate change through water-table feedback." *Nature Geosci*. vol. 1, no. 11. pp. 763-766. [http://dx.doi.org/10.1038/ngeo331] and [http://www.nature.com/ngeo/journal/v1/n11/suppinfo/ngeo331_S1.html]

36. Shakhova, Natalia, Igor Semiletov, Anatoly Salyuk, Vladimir Yusupov, Denis Kosmach, and Örjan Gustafsson. "Extensive Methane Venting to the Atmosphere from Sediments of the East Siberian Arctic Shelf." *Science*. vol. 327, no. 5970. March 5, 2010. pp. 1246-1250. [http://www.sciencemag.org/content/327/5970/1246.abstract]

37. Hansen, James, Makiko Sato, Pushker Kharecha, David Beerling, Robert Berner, Valerie Masson-Delmotte, Mark Pagani, Maureen Raymo, Dana L. Royer, and James C. Zachos. 2008. "Target Atmospheric $CO_2$ : Where Should Humanity Aim?" *The Open Atmospheric Science Journal*. vol. 2, pp. 217-231.

38. [http://www.nasa.gov/topics/earth/features/20100108_Is_Antarctica_Melting.html]

39. See Weitzman, Martin L. 2011. *Fat-Tailed Uncertainty in the Economics of Catastrophic Climate Change*. February 23. [http://www.economics.harvard.edu/faculty/weitzman/papers_weitzman].

40. Grubler, Arnulf. 2008. "Energy transitions." In *Encyclopedia of Earth*. Edited by C. J. Cleveland. Washington, D.C.: Environmental Information Coalition, National Council

for Science and the Environment. [http://www.iiasa.ac.at/~gruebler/Data/EoE_Data.html]. Real GDP growth from 1900 to 2000 was about 2.9%/year, and from 1950 to 2000 was 3.8%/year, so the MIT no-policy case represents slower economic growth than historical trends might indicate.

41. ibid.

42. Lee, Ronald. 2011. "The Outlook for Population Growth." *Science*. vol. 333, no. 6042. July 29. pp. 569-573. [http://www.sciencemag.org/content/333/6042/569.abstract]

43. Source: Bandivadekar, Anup, et al. *On the Road in 2035: Reducing Transportation's Petroleum Consumption and GHG Emissions*. Cambridge: Massachusetts Institute of Technology, 2008. Electric Power Research Institute. *Environmental Assessment of Plug-In Hybrid Electric Vehicles*. Palo Alto: National Resource Defense Council, 2007. Summary graph at [http://www.pewclimate.org/blog/nigron/understanding-ghg-emis-sions-plug-electric-vehicles].

44. US DOE. 2010. *International Energy Outlook 2010*. Washington, DC: Energy Information Administration, US Department of Energy. DOE/EIA-0484(2010). July. [http://eia.doe.gov/oiaf/ieo/]

 IEA. 2010. *World Energy Outlook 2010*. Paris, France: International Energy Agency, Organization for Economic Cooperation and Development (OECD). November 9. [http://www.worldenergyoutlook.org/]

45. As with all such estimates, data and assumptions need to be constantly updated as new information is developed. For example, in May 2011, the UN updated its population predictions to reflect new data, particularly about population growth in Africa [http://esa.un.org/unpd/wpp/]. The new estimates raised expected world population in 2050 to 2100 by 3 to 4% compared to the assumptions in the MIT scenarios.

46. The MIT no-policy case assumes increases in cement emissions and substantial reductions in net land-use emissions of $CO_2$ compared to current levels of about 1.5 GtC per year in 2005 (taken from Houghton, R.A. 2008. Carbon Flux to the Atmosphere from Land-Use Changes: 1850-2005. In TRENDS: A Compendium of Data on Global Change. Carbon Dioxide Information Analysis Center, Oak Ridge National Laboratory, US Department of Energy, Oak Ridge, Tenn., USA [http://cdiac.ornl.gov/]). Land-use emissions ramp down in the MIT case to 10% of current levels by 2060, which means that most deforestation will have stopped by that point (or will be offset by reforestation activities).

47. Jackson, Stacy C. 2009. "Parallel Pursuit of Near-Term and Long-Term Climate Mitigation." *Science*. vol. 326, no. 5952. October 23. pp. 526-7. [http://www.sciencemag.org/content/326/5952/526.short]

48. 1350 ppm /280 ppm = 4.8. One doubling is 2.0, two doublings is 4.0.

49. The median climate sensitivity for the MIT model is 2.9 Celsius degrees.

50. Personal Communication (email) from Professor Michael Oppenheimer, Climatologist at Princeton University, March 5, 2010.

51. Koomey, Jonathan, and Florentin Krause. 2009. *Why 2 degrees really matters*. [http://thinkprogress.org/romm/2009/12/06/205058/copenhagen-two-degrees-warming-target/]

52. The physicist Joe Romm gives a useful and comprehensive summary of the effects of continuing current emissions trends here: [http://thinkprogress.org/romm/2011/09/28/330109/science-of-global-warming-impacts/]

53. See Section 3.8 of the IPCC Working Group I report (2007), *Climate Change 2007: The Physical Science Basis* for a discussion of "Changes in Extreme Events" due to climate change.

54. US Climate Change Science Program. 2008. *Weather and Climate Extremes in a Changing Climate—Regions of Focus: North America, Hawaii, Caribbean, and U.S. Pacific Islands*. Washington, DC: US Climate Change Science Program and the Subcommittee on Global Change Research. Synthesis and Assessment Product 3.3. June. [http://downloads.climatescience.gov/sap/sap3-3/sap3-3-final-all.pdf]

    Dai, Aiguo. 2010. "Drought under global warming: a review." *Wiley Interdisciplinary Reviews: Climate Change*. vol. 2, no. 1. October 19. pp. 45-65. [http://dx.doi.org/10.1002/wcc.81]

    Rahmstorf, Stefan, and Dim Coumou. 2011. "Increase of extreme events in a warming world." *Proceedings of the National Academy of Sciences*. October 24. [http://www.pnas.org/content/early/2011/10/18/1101766108.abstract]

    Romm, Joseph. 2011. "Desertification: The next dust bowl." *Nature*. vol. 478, no. 7370. October 27. pp. 450-451. [http://dx.doi.org/10.1038/478450a]

55. IPCC. 2007. *Climate change 2007, Synthesis report: Summary for Policy Makers*. Geneva, Switzerland: Intergovernmental Panel on Climate Change. [http://www.ipcc.ch/pdf/assessment-report/ar4/syr/ar4_syr_spm.pdf]

56. Balint, M., S. Domisch, C. H. M. Engelhardt, P. Haase, S. Lehrian, J. Sauer, K. Theissinger, S. U. Pauls, and C. Nowak. 2011. "Cryptic biodiversity loss linked to global climate change." *Nature Clim. Change*. vol. 1, no. 6. August 21. pp. 313-318. [http://dx.doi.org/10.1038/nclimate1191].

    Barnosky, Anthony D., Nicholas Matzke, Susumu Tomiya, Guinevere O. U. Wogan, Brian Swartz, Tiago B. Quental, Charles Marshall, Jenny L. McGuire, Emily L. Lindsey, Kaitlin C. Maguire, Ben Mersey, and Elizabeth A. Ferrer. 2011. "Has the Earth's sixth mass extinction already arrived?" *Nature*. vol. 471, no. 7336. March 3. pp. 51-57. [http://dx.doi.org/10.1038/nature09678]

57. Hayhoe, Katharine, Cameron Wake, Bruce Anderson, Xin-Zhong Liang, Edwin Maurer, Jinhong Zhu, James Bradbury, Art DeGaetano, Anne Marie Stoner, and Donald Wuebbles. 2008. "Regional climate change projections for the Northeast USA." *Mitigation and Adaptation Strategies for Global Change*. vol. 13, no. 5-6. June. pp. 425-436.

58. Vermeer, Martin, and Stefan Rahmstorf. 2009. "Global sea level linked to global temperature." *Proceedings of the National Academy of Sciences*. December 7, 2009. [http://www.pnas.org/content/early/2009/12/04/0907765106.abstract]

59. Ridgwell, Andy, and Daniela N. Schmidt. 2010. "Past constraints on the vulnerability of marine calcifiers to massive carbon dioxide release." *Nature Geosci*. vol. 3, no. 3. March. pp. 196-200. [http://dx.doi.org/10.1038/ngeo755]

60. Sale, Peter. 2011. *Our Dying Planet: An Ecologist's View of the Crisis We Face*. Berkeley, CA: University of California Press.

    Also see the case study documented here for real data on what acidification does to marine life: Dias, B.B., M.B. Hart, C.W. Smart, and J.M. Hall-Spencer. 2010. "Modern seawater acidification: the response of foraminifera to high-$CO_2$ conditions in the Mediterranean Sea." *Journal of the Geological Society*. vol. 167, no. 5. September 1. pp. 843-846. [http://jgs.lyellcollection.org/cgi/content/abstract/167/5/843]

61. Of course, there are also other good reasons for avoiding such geo-engineering shenanigans. Our power to change the natural environment far exceeds our ability to predict the effects of those changes, and always will, as David Bella pointed out in the late 1970s:

Bella, David A. 1979. "Technological Constraints on Technological Optimism." *Technological Forecasting and Social Change.* vol. 14, June. pp. 15-26.

62. Archer, D., and V. Brovkin. 2008. "The millennial atmospheric lifetime of anthropogenic $CO_2$." *Climatic Change.* vol. 90, pp. 283–297

63. Solomon, Susan, Gian-Kasper Plattner, Reto Knutti, and Pierre Friedlingstein. 2009. "Irreversible climate change due to carbon dioxide emissions." *Proceedings of the National Academy of Sciences.* January 28, 2009. [http://www.pnas.org/content/early/2009/01/28/0812721106.abstract]

   Matthews, H. Damon, and Ken Caldeira. 2008. "Stabilizing climate requires near-zero emissions." *Geophys. Res. Lett.* vol. 35, no. 4. pp. L04705. [http://dx.doi.org/10.1029/2007GL032388]

64. Table 2.14 in the 2007 IPCC Working Group I report, *Climate Change 2007: The Physical Science Basis,* p.212.

## Chapter 3

1. For discussion of historical temperatures and the 2-degree limit see Chapter 1 in Krause, Florentin, Wilfred Bach, and Jonathan G. Koomey. 1992. *Energy Policy in the Greenhouse.* NY, NY: John Wiley and Sons. For more recent assessments of predicted impacts see the Working Group I and II reports from the IPCC's Fourth Assessment Report, posted at [http://www.ipcc.ch/publications_and_data/publications_ipcc_fourth_assessment_report_wg1_report_the_physical_science_basis.htm] and [http://www.ipcc.ch/publications_and_data/publications_ipcc_fourth_assessment_report_wg2_report_impacts_adaptation_and_vulnerability.htm]

2. See the interview at [http://www.learner.org/courses/envsci/scientist/transcripts/holdren.html] and this summary [http://belfercenter.ksg.harvard.edu/publication/18022/global_warning.html].

3. Pacala, S., and Rob Socolow. 2004. "Stabilization Wedges: Solving the Climate Problem for the Next 50 Years with Current Technologies" *Science.* vol. 305, no. 5686. August 13. pp. 968-972. [http://www.sciencemag.org/cgi/content/abstract/305/5686/968]

4. [http://cmi.princeton.edu/wedges/] has this graph available for download, as well as course materials and other helpful resources.

5. Laitner, John A. "Skip", Stephen J. DeCanio, Jonathan G. Koomey, and Alan H. Sanstad. 2003. "Room for Improvement: Increasing the Value of Energy Modeling for Policy Analysis." *Utilities Policy (also LBNL-50627).* vol. 11, no. 2. June. pp. 87-94. Krause, Florentin, Paul Baer, and Stephen DeCanio. 2001. *Cutting Carbon Emissions at a Profit: Opportunities for the U.S.* El Cerrito, CA: International Project for Sustainable Energy Paths. April. [http://www.mediafire.com/file/wwz2jnjexr5h6wn/ipsepcutcarbon_us.pdf]

6. This error of omission also affects estimates of the potential damages from climate change, with researchers unable to put dollar values on important effects (like species extinction) or deal properly with risk and uncertainty, but still reporting their results in a framework that claims to yield an assessment of our optimal choices. A 2009 conference explored some of the issues in making such assessments: Gulledge, Jay, L. J. Richardson, L. Adkins, and S. Seidel, eds. 2009. *Assessing the Benefits of Avoided Climate Change: Cost Benefit Analysis and Beyond.* Proceedings of the Workshop on Assessing the Benefits of Avoided Climate Change. Washington, DC: Pew Center on Global Climate Change. March 16–17.

7. Interlaboratory Working Group on Energy-Efficient and Clean-Energy Technologies.

2000. *Scenarios for a Clean Energy Future*. Oak Ridge, TN and Berkeley, CA: Oak Ridge National Laboratory and Lawrence Berkeley National Laboratory. ORNL/CON-476 and LBNL-44029. November. [http://www.ornl.gov/sci/eere/cef/]

　　Brown, Marilyn A., Mark D. Levine, Walter Short, and Jonathan G. Koomey. 2001. "Scenarios for a Clean Energy Future." *Energy Policy (Also LBNL-48031)*. vol. 29, no. 14. November. pp. 1179-1196.

8.　Koomey, Jonathan. 2002. "From My Perspective: Avoiding "The Big Mistake" in Forecasting Technology Adoption." *Technological Forecasting and Social Change*. vol. 69, no. 5. June. pp. 511-518.

9.　Struck, Doug. 2011. "Climate Scientist Fears His 'Wedges' Made It Seem Too Easy." In *National Geographic*. May 17. [Read online at http://news.nationalgeographic.com/news/energy/2011/05/110517-global-warming-scientist-concern/]

10.　See the recently commissioned Gemasolar plant in Spain for one way to address the storage issue, using molten salt heat storage [http://www.nrel.gov/csp/solarpaces/project_detail.cfm?projectID=40]. There are many other ways, some based on long proven technologies (like pumped storage, flywheels, compressed air, or batteries) and others that are more exotic, like molten salts.

11.　See the IPCC WG III report (2007), p. 149-150, and Gritsevskyi, Andrii, and Nebojsa Nakicenovic. 2000. "Modeling uncertainty of induced technological change." *Energy Policy*. vol. 28, no. 13. November. pp. 907-921.

12.　The best summary critique of these models from inside the economics community is in DeCanio, Stephen J. 2003. *Economic Models of Climate Change: A Critique*. Basingstoke, UK: Palgrave-Macmillan.

13.　To be clear, I think retrospective benefit-cost analysis is very much worth doing (to inform our future choices based on history), but it's the prospective use of it to estimate benefits and costs far into the future that is doomed to failure. For a broad treatment of the limitations of benefit-cost analysis, see Ackerman, Frank, and Lisa Heinzerling. 2004. *Priceless: On Knowing the Price of Everything and the Value of Nothing*. New York, NY: The New Press. For a more philosophical treatment see Kysar, Douglas A. 2010. *Regulating from Nowhere: Environmental Law and the Search for Objectivity*. New Haven, CT: Yale University Press.

14.　Ackerman, Frank, Stephen DeCanio, Richard Howarth, and Kristen Sheeran. 2009. "Limitations of integrated assessment models of climate change." *Climatic Change*. vol. 95, no. 3. pp. 297-315. [http://dx.doi.org/10.1007/s10584-009-9570-x].

15.　O'Neill, Brian C., Paul Crutzen, Arnulf Grübler, Minh Ha Duong, Klaus Keller, Charles Kolstad, Jonathan Koomey, Andreas Lange, Michael Obersteiner, Michael Oppenheimer, William Pepper, Warren Sanderson, Michael Schlesinger, Nicolas Treich, Alistair Ulph, Mort Webster, and Chris Wilson. 2006. "Commentary: Learning and Climate Change." *Climate Policy*. vol. 6, no. 5. pp. 585-589.

16.　Personal Communication (email) to Jonathan Koomey from Professor Michael Oppenheimer, Climatologist at Princeton University, March 5, 2010.

17.　Koomey, Jonathan, and Florentin Krause. 2009. *Why 2 degrees really matters*. [http://thinkprogress.org/romm/2009/12/06/205058/copenhagen-two-degrees-warming-target/]

18.　Oppenheimer, Michael, and Annie Petsonk. 2005. "Article 2 of the UNFCCC: Historical Origins, Recent Interpretations." *Climatic Change*. vol. 73, no. 3. pp. 195-226. [http://dx.doi.org/10.1007/s10584-005-0434-8]

　　Randalls, Samuel. 2010. "History of the 2°C climate target." *Wiley Interdisciplinary*

*Reviews: Climate Change*. vol. 1, no. 4. July/August. pp. 598-605. [http://dx.doi.
org/10.1002/wcc.62]

19. For the first comprehensive analysis of the warming limit approach in the context of a 2
    degree warming limit, see Krause, Florentin, Wilfred Bach, and Jonathan G. Koomey.
    1989. *From Warming Fate to Warming Limit: Benchmarks to a Global Climate
    Convention*. El Cerrito, CA: International Project for Sustainable Energy Paths, which
    was republished as Krause, Florentin, Wilfred Bach, and Jonathan G. Koomey. 1992.
    *Energy Policy in the Greenhouse*. NY, NY: John Wiley and Sons.

20. IEA. 2009. *World Energy Outlook 2009*. Paris, France: International Energy Agency,
    Organization for Economic Cooperation and Development (OECD). November. [http://
    www.worldenergyoutlook.org/]

21. This result, which I derived using the concentrations from the MIT no-policy case, a 3
    Celsius degree climate sensitivity, and some math in Appendix B, is related to the compli-
    cated concept of warming commitments. Real climate also has a helpful discussion of
    these issues in a blog post and related comments here: [http://www.realclimate.org/index.
    php/archives/2010/03/climate-change-commitments/].

      Matthews, H. Damon, and Andrew J. Weaver. 2010. "Committed climate warming."
    *Nature Geosci*. vol. 3, no. 3. pp. 142-143. [http://dx.doi.org/10.1038/ngeo813]

      Ramanathan, V., and Y. Feng. 2008. "On avoiding dangerous anthropogenic interfer-
    ence with the climate system: Formidable challenges ahead." *Proceedings of the National
    Academy of Sciences*. vol. 105, no. 38. September 23, 2008. pp. 14245-14250. [http://
    www.pnas.org/content/105/38/14245.abstract]

      Schellnhuber, Hans Joachim. 2008. "Global warming: Stop worrying, start panick-
    ing?" *Proceedings of the National Academy of Sciences*. vol. 105, no. 38. September 23,
    2008. pp. 14239-14240. [http://www.pnas.org/content/105/38/14239.short]

      Solomon, Susan, Gian-Kasper Plattner, Reto Knutti, and Pierre Friedlingstein. 2009.
    "Irreversible climate change due to carbon dioxide emissions." *Proceedings of the
    National Academy of Sciences*. January 28, 2009. [http://www.pnas.org/content/
    early/2009/01/28/0812721106.abstract]

      Wigley, T. M. L. 2005. "The Climate Change Commitment." *Science*. vol. 307, no.
    5716. March 18, 2005. pp. 1766-1769. [http://www.sciencemag.org/content/307/5716/
    1766.abstract]

22. Nusbaumer, Jesse, and Katsumi Matsumoto. 2008. "Climate and carbon cycle changes
    under the overshoot scenario." *Global and Planetary Change*. vol. 62, no. 1-2. pp.
    164-172. [http://www.sciencedirect.com/science/article/pii/S092181810800012X]

23. Hurteau, Matthew, Bruce Hungate, and George Koch. 2009. "Accounting for risk in
    valuing forest carbon offsets." *Carbon Balance and Management*. vol. 4, no. 1. pp. 1.
    [http://www.cbmjournal.com/content/4/1/1]

      Hurteau, Matthew D., and Matthew L. Brooks. 2011. "Short- and Long-Term Effects
    of Fire on Carbon in US Dry Temperate Forest Systems." *BioScience*. vol. 61, no. 2.
    October 12. pp. 139-146. [http://www.bioone.org/doi/abs/10.1525/bio.2011.61.2.9]

      Girod, C. M., G. C. Hurtt, S. Frolking, J. D. Aber, and A. W. King. 2007. "The Tension
    between Fire Risk and Carbon Storage: Evaluating U.S. Carbon and Fire Management
    Strategies through Ecosystem Models." *Earth Interactions*. vol. 11, no. 2. 2011/10/12. pp.
    1-33. [http://dx.doi.org/10.1175/EI188.1]

      Bowman, David M. J. S., Jennifer K. Balch, Paulo Artaxo, William J. Bond, Jean M.
    Carlson, Mark A. Cochrane, Carla M. D,ÄôAntonio, Ruth S. DeFries, John C. Doyle,

Sandy P. Harrison, Fay H. Johnston, Jon E. Keeley, Meg A. Krawchuk, Christian A. Kull, J. Brad Marston, Max A. Moritz, I. Colin Prentice, Christopher I. Roos, Andrew C. Scott, Thomas W. Swetnam, Guido R. van der Werf, and Stephen J. Pyne. 2009. "Fire in the Earth System." *Science*. vol. 324, no. 5926. April 24. pp. 481-484. [http://www.sciencemag.org/content/324/5926/481.abstract]

24. [http://www.skepticalscience.com/Carbon-dioxide-equivalents.html]

25. [http://www.realclimate.org/index.php/archives/2007/10/co2-equivalents/]

26. The kind of analysis needed is similar to that described in Wigley, Tom. 2011. "Coal to gas: the influence of methane leakage." *Climatic Change*. vol. 108, no. 3. pp. 601-608. [http://dx.doi.org/10.1007/s10584-011-0217-3]. That study showed that the net warming impact of switching from coal to gas was strongly affected by the decline of aerosols in the first few decades after the shift toward natural gas, and affected in later decades by the amount of leakage in methane associated with increased natural gas use. Eventually the long-term effect of reduced carbon emissions can exceed the relatively short-term warming effects from the first two issues, but for gas leakage rates of greater than 2%, the net warming effect of switching to gas is neutral to positive over the time scales of interest to us here (i.e., the next century or so). The aerosol effect is generic to any technology switch that reduces coal use, so it needs to be counted in assessing the near-term warming effects of reducing coal use. That's why combining reductions in coal use with rapid reductions in short-lived warming agents like soot, methane, and tropospheric ozone is a good idea.

27. IPCC. 2007. *Climate Change 2007: Mitigation of Climate Change—Contribution of Working Group III to the Fourth Assessment Report of the Intergovernmental Panel on Climate Change* [Metz, B., O. Davidson, P. Bosch, R. Dave, and L. Meyer (eds.)]. Cambridge, United Kingdom and New York, NY, USA: Cambridge University Press. [http://www.ipcc.ch/publications_and_data/publications_and_data_reports.shtml], p.151.

28. Meinshausen, Malte, Nicolai Meinshausen, William Hare, Sarah C. B. Raper, Katja Frieler, Reto Knutti, David J. Frame, and Myles R. Allen. 2009. "Greenhouse-gas emission targets for limiting global warming to 2 degrees C." *Nature*. vol. 458, April 30. pp. 1158-1162. [http://www.nature.com/nature/journal/v458/n7242/full/nature08017.html]. These authors created an Excel tool, supplied in the online supplemental information, to allow scenario analysts to use estimates of cumulative emissions from different scenarios to assess the probability of each scenario exceeding 2 Celsius degrees.

29. Because of differences in the way the MIT folks conducted their analysis, they estimate a much higher probability of exceeding 2 Celsius degrees for the Level 1 case (80%), but I'm relying on the Meinshausen et al. analysis for these probabilities because it is based on a more comprehensive set of scenario analyses. I used Meinshausen's calculator based on carbon emissions from 2000 to 2049–using $CO_2$ equivalent emissions would give a higher chance (about 50%) of exceeding 2 Celsius degrees for the Level 1 case. Both of these analyses also focused on the period up until 2100, so they don't account for the possibility of briefly exceeding 2 Celsius degrees before 2100 but dipping back down again as the effect of emissions reductions take hold.

30. MIT's Level 1 case almost completely eliminates emissions of the other gases by 2100.

31. Knutti, Reto, and Gabriele C. Hegerl. 2008. "The equilibrium sensitivity of the Earth's temperature to radiation changes." *Nature Geoscience*. vol. 1, no. 11. October 26. pp. 735 - 743.

32. Krause, Florentin, Wilfred Bach, and Jon Koomey. 1989. *From Warming Fate to Warming*

*Limit: Benchmarks to a Global Climate Convention*. El Cerrito, CA: International Project for Sustainable Energy Paths. This book was republished as Krause, Florentin, Wilfred Bach, and Jonathan G. Koomey. 1992. *Energy Policy in the Greenhouse*. NY, NY: John Wiley and Sons.

33. Caldeira, Ken, Atul K. Jain, and Martin I. Hoffert. 2003. "Climate Sensitivity Uncertainty and the Need for Energy Without $CO_2$ Emission" *Science*. vol. 299, no. 5615. pp. 2052-2054. [http://www.sciencemag.org/cgi/content/abstract/299/5615/2052]

34. Hansen, James. 2009. *Storms of my Grandchildren: The Truth about the Coming Climate Catastrophe and our Last Chance to Save Humanity*. New York, NY: Bloomsbury USA.

35. Some economic analyses also show that achieving such levels would not be ruinously expensive, even given the demonstrated tendency of such analyses to overestimate costs. Ackerman, Frank, Elizabeth A. Stanton, Stephen J. DeCanio, Eban Goodstein, Richard B. Howarth, Richard B. Norgaard, Catherine S. Norman, and Kristen A. Sheeran. 2009. *The Economics of 350: The Benefits and Costs of Climate Stabilization*. Portland, OR: Economics for Equity and Environment. October. [http://www.e3network.org/papers/Economics_of_350.pdf]

36. See Appendix A for detailed lower bound estimates on the fossil fuel resource base.

37. For example, see the reports of the Externe project of the European Commission: [http://www.externe.info/], Muller, Nicholas Z., Robert Mendelsohn, and William Nordhaus. 2011. "Environmental Accounting for Pollution in the United States Economy." *American Economic Review* vol. 101, no. 5. August. pp. 1649–1675, and Epstein, Paul R., Jonathan J. Buonocore, Kevin Eckerle, Michael Hendryx, Benjamin M. Stout Iii, Richard Heinberg, Richard W. Clapp, Beverly May, Nancy L. Reinhart, Melissa M. Ahern, Samir K. Doshi, and Leslie Glustrom. 2011. "Full cost accounting for the life cycle of coal." *Annals of the New York Academy of Sciences*. vol. 1219, no. 1. February 17. pp. 73-98. [http://dx.doi.org/10.1111/j.1749-6632.2010.05890.x].

## Chapter 4

1. Ackerman, Frank, Stephen DeCanio, Richard Howarth, and Kristen Sheeran. 2009. "Limitations of integrated assessment models of climate change." *Climatic Change*. vol. 95, no. 3. pp. 297-315. [http://dx.doi.org/10.1007/s10584-009-9570-x]. A more popular treatment of some of these issues is Ackerman, Frank. 2009. *Can We Afford the Future?: The Economics of a Warming World (The New Economics)*. London, UK: Zed Books.

2. Winger, John G. and Carolyn A. Nielsen, "Energy, The Economy and Jobs," *Energy Report from Chase* (New York: Energy Economics Division, Chase Manhattan Bank, Sept. 1976).

3. Ascher, William. 1978. *Forecasting: An Appraisal for Policy Makers and Planners*. Baltimore, MD: Johns Hopkins University Press.

4. Craig, Paul, Ashok Gadgil, and Jonathan Koomey. 2002. "What Can History Teach Us?: A Retrospective Analysis of Long-term Energy Forecasts for the U.S." In *Annual Review of Energy and the Environment 2002*. Edited by R. H. Socolow, D. Anderson and J. Harte. Palo Alto, CA: Annual Reviews, Inc. (also LBNL-50498). pp. 83-118.

5. DeCanio, Stephen J. 2003. *Economic Models of Climate Change: A Critique*. Basingstoke, UK: Palgrave-Macmillan.

6. Koomey, Jonathan. 2002. "From My Perspective: Avoiding "The Big Mistake" in Forecasting Technology Adoption." *Technological Forecasting and Social Change*. vol. 69, no. 5. June. pp. 511-518.

7. Howarth, Richard B. 2011. "Chapter 23: Intergenerational Justice." In *The Oxford Handbook of Climate Change and Society*. Edited by J. S. Dryzek, R. B. Norgaard and D. Schlosberg. Oxford, UK: Oxford University Press. pp. 338-352.
8. Arthur, W. Brian. 1990. "Positive Feedbacks in the Economy." In *Scientific American*. February. pp. 92-99.
9. DeCanio, Stephen J. 2003. *Economic Models of Climate Change: A Critique*. Basingstoke, UK: Palgrave-Macmillan. pp. 11-13.
10. One of the best concise summaries of these issues is Ackerman, Frank, Stephen DeCanio, Richard Howarth, and Kristen Sheeran. 2009. "Limitations of integrated assessment models of climate change." *Climatic Change*. vol. 95, no. 3. pp. 297-315. [http://dx.doi.org/10.1007/s10584-009-9570-x]

## Chapter 5

1. My use of this quote does not imply that I'm cavalier about economics, simply that when the alternative is catastrophe, the way we respond should be quite different from normal times, and these are clearly not normal times.
2. [http://jpetrie.myweb.uga.edu/bulldog.html]
3. Lovins, Amory B., E. Kyle Datta, Odd-Even Bustnes, Jonathan G. Koomey, and Nathan J. Glasgow. 2004. *Winning the Oil Endgame: Innovation for Profits, Jobs, and Security*. Old Snowmass, Colorado: Rocky Mountain Institute. September. [http://www.oilendgame.com]. p. 1.
4. See the discussion of the continuity rate in Chapter 6 of Krause, Florentin, Wilfred Bach, and Jonathan G. Koomey. 1992. *Energy Policy in the Greenhouse*. NY, NY: John Wiley and Sons.
5. The 6% is the sum of 3%/year retirements and about 3% per year growth in emissions, all expressed as a percentage of year 2012 emissions.
6. The most comprehensive recent analysis of a case that is roughly comparable to the Safer Climate case is this one: IEA. 2010. *World Energy Outlook 2010*. Paris, France: International Energy Agency, Organization for Economic Cooperation and Development (OECD). November 9. [http://www.worldenergyoutlook.org/]. pp. 403 has the macroeconomic cost estimates for that scenario, which is 3.2% in 2035. That estimate ignores the value of energy savings from efficiency investments (it is not clear if it also ignores the co-benefits from reduced air pollution). Costs of a few percent of GDP represent large numbers in absolute terms but are the equivalent of delaying reaching a given level of GDP by a year or two at typical GDP growth rates.
7. Celebi, Metin, Frank C. Graves, Gunjan Bathla, and Lucas Bressan. 2010. *Potential Coal Plant Retirements Under Emerging Environmental Regulations*. The Brattle Group, Inc. December 8. [http://www.brattle.com/documents/uploadlibrary/upload898.pdf]
8. See Figure 5-6 in Lovins, Amory B., Mathias Bell, Lionel Bony, Albert Chan, Stephen Doig, Nathan J. Glasgow, Lena Hansen, Virginia Lacy, Eric Maurer, Jesse Morris, James Newcomb, Greg Rucks, and Caroline Traube. 2011. *Reinventing Fire: Bold Business Solutions for the New Energy Era*. White River Junction, VT: Chelsea Green Publishing, p. 175.
9. For details, see Muller, Nicholas Z., Robert Mendelsohn, and William Nordhaus. 2011. "Environmental Accounting for Pollution in the United States Economy." *American Economic Review* vol. 101, no. 5. August. pp. 1649–1675, and Epstein, Paul R., Jonathan J. Buonocore, Kevin Eckerle, Michael Hendryx, Benjamin M. Stout III, Richard Heinberg,

Richard W. Clapp, Beverly May, Nancy L. Reinhart, Melissa M. Ahern, Samir K. Doshi, and Leslie Glustrom. 2011. "Full cost accounting for the life cycle of coal." *Annals of the New York Academy of Sciences.* vol. 1219, no. 1. February 17. pp. 73-98. [http://dx.doi.org/10.1111/j.1749-6632.2010.05890.x].

10. For a wonderful example of a state-of-the-art retrofit of an iconic existing building (and an example of whole systems integrated design as well), see the Empire State Building example in Chapter 3 of Lovins, Amory B., Mathias Bell, Lionel Bony, Albert Chan, Stephen Doig, Nathan J. Glasgow, Lena Hansen, Virginia Lacy, Eric Maurer, Jesse Morris, James Newcomb, Greg Rucks, and Caroline Traube. 2011. *Reinventing Fire: Bold Business Solutions for the New Energy Era.* White River Junction, VT: Chelsea Green Publishing.

11. Mills, Evan. 2009. *Building Commissioning: A Golden Opportunity for Reducing Energy Costs and Greenhouse Gas Emissions.* Berkeley, CA: Prepared by Lawrence Berkeley National Laboratory for the California Energy Commission Public Interest Energy Research (PIER). July 21. [http://cx.lbl.gov/2009-assessment.html]

12. I describe our personal experiences here: [http://www.koomey.com/post/8765851978].

13. IEA. 2009. *World Energy Outlook 2009.* Paris, France: International Energy Agency, Organization for Economic Cooperation and Development (OECD). November. [http://www.worldenergyoutlook.org/].

    IEA. 2010. *World Energy Outlook 2010.* Paris, France: International Energy Agency, Organization for Economic Cooperation and Development (OECD). November 9. [http://www.worldenergyoutlook.org/]

14. See p. 403 of the *World Energy Outlook 2010.* Recall that macroeconomic cost estimates are typically overestimates of the true costs, for all the reasons I lay out in Chapter 4. For the investment calculations in Figure 2-3 I used world GDP figures based on market exchange rates from US DOE. 2011. *International Energy Outlook 2011.* Washington, DC: Energy Information Administration, U.S. Department of Energy. DOE/EIA-0484(2011). April 26. [http://eia.doe.gov/oiaf/ieo/]

15. Ackerman, Frank, Elizabeth A. Stanton, Stephen J. DeCanio, Eban Goodstein, Richard B. Howarth, Richard B. Norgaard, Catherine S. Norman, and Kristen A. Sheeran. 2009. *The Economics of 350: The Benefits and Costs of Climate Stabilization.* Portland, OR: Economics for Equity and Environment. October. [http://www.e3network.org/papers/Economics_of_350.pdf].

    Ackerman, Frank, Stephen DeCanio, Richard Howarth, and Kristen Sheeran. 2009. "Limitations of integrated assessment models of climate change." *Climatic Change.* vol. 95, no. 3. pp. 297-315. [http://dx.doi.org/10.1007/s10584-009-9570-x]

    IPCC. 2007. *Climate Change 2007: Mitigation of Climate Change—Contribution of Working Group III to the Fourth Assessment Report of the Intergovernmental Panel on Climate Change* [Metz, B., O. Davidson, P. Bosch, R. Dave, and L. Meyer (eds.)]. Cambridge, United Kingdom and New York, NY, USA: Cambridge University Press. [http://www.ipcc.ch/publications_and_data/publications_and_data_reports.shtml], Table SPM.4, p. 12. See also p.151, which states clearly that incorporating technology learning effects in the models can drastically reduce the costs from a few percent of GDP to approximately zero (or even negative).

16. Worrell, Ernst, Lynn Price, Nathan Martin, Chris Hendriks, and Leticia Ozawa Meida. 2001. "Carbon Dioxide Emissions From The Global Cement Industry." *Annual Review of*

*Energy and the Environment*. vol. 26, no. 1. pp. 303-329. [http://www.annualreviews.org/doi/abs/10.1146/annurev.energy.26.1.303]

17. Tilman, David, Kenneth G. Cassman, Pamela A. Matson, Rosamond Naylor, and Stephen Polasky. 2002. "Agricultural sustainability and intensive production practices." *Nature*. vol. 418, no. 6898. pp. 671-677. [http://dx.doi.org/10.1038/nature01014]

18. Black, Tim. 1999. "Impediments to effective fertility reduction: Contraception should be moved out of the hands of doctors." *British Medical Journal*. vol. 319, no. 7215. October 9. pp. 932–933.

19. This area has been less well studied than some others. Some examples include shifting toward more service- and information-based economies or using zoning policies to affect land-use patterns.

20. Weber, Christopher L., and H. Scott Matthews. 2008. "Food-Miles and the Relative Climate Impacts of Food Choices in the United States." *Environmental Science & Technology*. vol. 42, no. 10. 2011/10/26. pp. 3508-3513. [http://dx.doi.org/10.1021/es702969f]

    Carlsson-Kanyama, Annika, and Alejandro D González. 2009. "Potential contributions of food consumption patterns to climate change." *The American Journal of Clinical Nutrition*. vol. 89, no. 5. May 1, 2009. pp. 1704S-1709S. [http://www.ajcn.org/content/89/5/1704S.abstract]

21. Hummel, Holmes. 2006. *Interpreting Global Energy and Emission Scenarios: Methods for Understanding and Communicating Policy Insights*. Thesis, Interdisciplinary Program on Environment and Resources, Stanford University. [http://www.holmeshummel.net/Dissertation.htm].

22. For example, GDP is an imperfect measure of human welfare that varies country by country. There is some dependence of each parameter on the other parameters (e.g., population growth depends in part on economic activity). Using the Kaya identity for large regions can also mask regional and sectoral changes that are important. If there is significant carbon sequestration (capturing the carbon from fuel combustion) the carbon per unit energy term can be affected by that technology in ways that can be misleading. Also, some sources of GHGs don't fit neatly into the Kaya equation, like emissions from cement production, changes in land use, and emissions of methane, nitrous oxides, and other GHGs. In spite of these complexities, even the simple version of the identity shown in the text can help us think more rigorously about climate solutions.

23. Grubler, Arnulf. 2008. "Energy transitions." In *Encyclopedia of Earth*. Edited by C. J. Cleveland. Washington, D.C.: Environmental Information Coalition, National Council for Science and the Environment. [http://www.iiasa.ac.at/~gruebler/Data/EoE_Data.html]

24. The approach I advocate is what the National Research Council calls "iterative risk management." NRC. 2011. *America's Climate Choices*. Washington, DC: National Research Council of the National Academies. The National Academies Press. p.1.

    For a treatment of climate risk issues from the national security perspective, see Mabey, Nick, Jay Gulledge, Bernard Finel, and Katherine Silverthorne. 2011. *Degrees of Risk: Defining a Risk Management Framework for Climate Security*. Washington, DC: Third Generation Environmentalism. February. [http://www.pewclimate.org/publications/degrees-risk-defining-risk-management-framework-climate-security]

## Chapter 6

1. Lovins, Amory B. 2005. *Energy End-Use Efficiency*. Rocky Mountain Institute for

InterAcademy Council (Amsterdam). September 19. [http://www.rmi.org/images/other/ Energy/E05-16_EnergyEndUseEff.pdf]

2. One of my students at UC Berkeley in Fall 2011 described how Germany is exploring the use of old mine shafts to create pumped storage so they can phase out nuclear power using renewable energy. In this case, you'd need to build a reservoir at the top of the mine, run water into the mine when power is needed, then pump it back up to the reservoir when power is available. There are technical issues to work out, but I thought it was an interesting example of applying a tried-and-true technology (pumped storage) in a new and innovative way.

3. Bresnahan, Timothy F., and M. Trajtenberg. 1995. "General purpose technologies: 'Engines of growth'?" *Journal of Econometrics*. vol. 65, no. 1. pp. 83-108. [http://ideas. repec.org/a/eee/econom/v65y1995i1p83-108.html]

4. Brynjolfsson, Erik, and Andrew McAfee. 2011. *Race Against The Machine: How the Digital Revolution is Accelerating Innovation, Driving Productivity, and Irreversibly Transforming Employment and the Economy*. Digital Frontier Press. [http://raceagainst-themachine.com/]

5. Schwartz, Peter. 1996. *The Art of the Long View: Planning for the Future in an Uncertain World*. New York, NY: Doubleday.
    Koomey, Jonathan. 2008. *Turning Numbers into Knowledge: Mastering the Art of Problem Solving*. 2nd ed. Oakland, CA: Analytics Press. [http://www.analyticspress.com] (see Chapter 26: Tell a Good Story)
    Ghanadan, Rebecca, and Jonathan Koomey. 2005. "Using Energy Scenarios to Explore Alternative Energy Pathways in California." *Energy Policy*. vol. 33, no. 9. June. pp. 1117-1142.

6. [http://www.gbn.com/]

7. Randall, Doug, and Chris Ertel. 2005. "Moving beyond the official future." *Financial Times*. September 15. [http://www.ft.com/intl/cms/s/1/b20ef12e-25eb-11da-a4a7-00000e2511c8.html]

8. Gigaton Throwdown. 2009. *Redefining What's Possible for Clean Energy by 2020: Job Growth, Energy Security, and Climate Change Solutions*. San Francisco, CA: Gigaton Throwdown. June. [http://www.gigatonthrowdown.org/]

9. The latest data on installed costs for PV systems in the US is in Barbose, Galen, Naïm Darghouth, Ryan Wiser, and Joachim Seel. 2011. *Tracking the Sun IV: An Historical Summary of the Installed Cost of Photovoltaics in the United States from 1998 to 2010*. Berkeley, CA: Lawrence Berkeley National Laboratory. LBNL-5047E. September. [http:// eetd.lbl.gov/ea/ems/reports/lbnl-5047e.pdf]

10. [http://www.nytimes.com/2010/07/18/business/18novel.html], [http://www.economist. com/node/16295708]

11. Isaacson, Walter. 2011. *Steve Jobs*. New York, NY: Simon & Schuster. pp. 471-2.

12. Lovins, Amory, Michael Bendewald, Michael Kinsley, Lionel Bony, Hutch Hutchinson, Alok Pradhan, Imran Sheikh, and Zoe Acher. 2010. *Factor Ten Engineering Design Principles*. Old Snowmass, CO: Rocky Mountain Institute (RMI). X10-10. [http://www. rmi.org/rmi/Library/2010-10_10xEPrinciples]

13. You can read the full list of whole systems design principles at RMI's Factor Ten Engineering page: [http://www.rmi.org/rmi/10xE]

14. This way of looking at energy problems began to take root in the 1970s as it became clear that the efficiency of energy use, as compared to the theoretical minimum energy

needed to accomplish certain tasks, was appallingly low (on the order of 10 to 15% for the entire economy). For details see Lovins, Amory B. 1979. *Soft Energy Paths: Toward a Durable Peace*. New York, NY: Harper Colophon Books and AIP. 1975. *Efficient Use of Energy: The American Physical Society Studies on the Technical Aspects of the More Efficient Use of Energy* (AIP Conference Proceedings No. 25). New York, NY: American Institute of Physics.

15. AIP. 1975. *Efficient Use of Energy: The American Physical Society Studies on the Technical Aspects of the More Efficient Use of Energy* (AIP Conference Proceedings No. 25). New York, NY: American Institute of Physics.

16. [http://en.wikipedia.org/wiki/Aseptic_processing]

17. AIP. 1975. *Efficient Use of Energy: The American Physical Society Studies on the Technical Aspects of the More Efficient Use of Energy* (AIP Conference Proceedings No. 25). New York, NY: American Institute of Physics.

18. Hawken, Paul, Amory Lovins, and L. Hunter Lovins. 2008. *Natural Capitalism: Creating the Next Industrial Revolution*. New York, NY: Back Bay Books. [http://www.natcap. org/]. p. 70.

19. Lovins, Amory B., E. Kyle Datta, Odd-Even Bustnes, Jonathan G. Koomey, and Nathan J. Glasgow. 2004. *Winning the Oil Endgame: Innovation for Profits, Jobs, and Security*. Old Snowmass, Colorado: Rocky Mountain Institute. September. [http://www.oilendgame. com]. p. 87.

20. Lovins, Amory B., Mathias Bell, Lionel Bony, Albert Chan, Stephen Doig, Nathan J. Glasgow, Lena Hansen, Virginia Lacy, Eric Maurer, Jesse Morris, James Newcomb, Greg Rucks, and Caroline Traube. 2011. *Reinventing Fire: Bold Business Solutions for the New Energy Era*. White River Junction, VT: Chelsea Green Publishing, p. 60.

21. Mills, Evan. 2005. "The Specter of Fuel-Based Lighting." *Science*. vol. 308, no. 5726. May 27, 2005. pp. 1263-1264. [http://www.sciencemag.org/content/308/5726/1263.short]
    Apple, J., R. Vicente, A. Yarberry, N. Lohse, E. Mills, A. Jacobson, and D. Poppendieck. 2010. "Characterization of particulate matter size distributions and indoor concentrations from kerosene and diesel lamps." *Indoor Air*. vol. 20, no. 5. October. pp. 399-411. [http://dx.doi.org/10.1111/j.1600-0668.2010.00664.x]

22. Ibid, Mills. 2005.

23. Lovins, Amory B. 1992. *Energy-Efficient Buildings: Institutional Barriers and Opportunities*. E-Source/RMI. Strategic Issues Paper. December. [http://www.rmi.org/rmi/ Library/1992-02_EnergyEfficientBuildingsBarriersOpportunities]
    Koomey, Jonathan G. 1990. *Energy Efficiency Choices in New Office Buildings: An Investigation of Market Failures and Corrective Policies*. PhD Thesis, Energy and Resources Group, University of California, Berkeley. [Download from http://enduse.lbl. gov/Projects/EfficiencyGap.html]

24. Isaacson, Walter. 2011. *Steve Jobs*. New York, NY: Simon & Schuster. pp. 472-3.

25. Table 2.14, 2007 IPCC Working Group I report, *Climate Change 2007: The Physical Science Basis,* p.212.

26. [http://emf.stanford.edu/publications/emf_21_multigreenhouse_gas_mitigation_and_ climate_policy/]

27. [http://epa.gov/climatechange/]

28. The International Standards Organization has a set of well defined procedures for conducting such analyses, which you can find here: [http://www.iso.org/iso/catalogue_ detail?csnumber=38498].

29. The latest version of the EDGAR database is [http://edgar.jrc.ec.europa.eu/index.php], while older versions are here: [http://themasites.pbl.nl/en/themasites/edgar/index.html]. EDGAR. 2011. *Long-Term Trend In Global CO2 Emissions, 2011 Report*. Ispra, Italy: European Commission, Emission Database for Global Atmospheric Research (EDGAR). [http://edgar.jrc.ec.europa.eu/i]

30. [http://cdiac.ornl.gov]

31. [http://carma.org/]

32. IEA. 2010. *World Energy Outlook 2010*. Paris, France: International Energy Agency, Organization for Economic Cooperation and Development (OECD). November 9. [http://www.worldenergyoutlook.org/]

33. US DOE. 2010. *International Energy Outlook 2010*. Washington, DC: Energy Information Administration, US Department of Energy. DOE/EIA-0484(2010). July. [http://eia.doe.gov/oiaf/ieo/]

34. US DOE. 2009. *Emissions of Greenhouse Gases in the United States 2008*. Washington, DC: Energy Information Administration, US Department of Energy. DOE/EIA-0573 (2008). December 8.

35. US EPA. 2011. *Inventory of US Greenhouse Gas Emissions and Sinks: 1990-2009*. Washington, DC: US Environmental Protection Agency. 430-R-11-005. April. [http://www.epa.gov/climatechange/emissions/usinventoryreport.html]

36. [http://www.arb.ca.gov/ei/ei.htm]

37. US DOE. 2011. *Annual Energy Outlook 2011, with Projections to 2035*. Washington, DC: Energy Information Administration, US Department of Energy. DOE/EIA-0383(2011). April. [http://eia.doe.gov/oiaf/aeo/ ]

38. [http://www.eia.gov/consumption/residential/]

39. [http://www.eia.gov/emeu/cbecs/]

40. [http://www.eia.gov/emeu/mecs/]

41. [http://www.eia.gov/emeu/rtecs/contents.html]

42. [http://cta.ornl.gov/data/]

43. [http://www.eia.gov/consumption/residential/]

44. For the AHS, see [http://www.census.gov/prod/www/abs/h150.html]. For the latest decennial census, see [http://2010.census.gov/2010census/].

45. Gore, Al. 2009. *Our Choice: A Plan to Solve the Climate Crisis*. Emmaus, PA: Rodale Books. [http://www.climatecrisis.net/]

46. Their US study is this one: Creyts, Jon, Anton Derkach, Scott Nyquist, Ken Ostrowski, and Jack Stephenson. 2007. *Reducing US Greenhouse Gas Emissions: How Much at What Cost?* US Greenhouse Gas Abatement Mapping Initiative, McKinsey & Company and the Conference Board. December. The complete set of country studies is online at [http://www.mckinsey.com/en/Client_Service/Sustainability/Latest_thinking/Costcurves.aspx]

47. All of these groups fall under the Environmental Energy Technologies Division: [http://eetd.lbl.gov/]

48. Interlaboratory Working Group on Energy-Efficient and Clean-Energy Technologies. 2000. *Scenarios for a Clean Energy Future*. Oak Ridge, TN and Berkeley, CA: Oak Ridge National Laboratory and Lawrence Berkeley National Laboratory. ORNL/CON-476 and LBNL-44029. November. [http://www.ornl.gov/sci/eere/cef/]

49. GGI scenario database: [http://www.iiasa.ac.at/Research/GGI/DB/index.html/?sb=10]

50. MacKay, David JC. 2009. *Sustainable Energy—Without the Hot Air*. Cambridge, UK: UIT. [http://www.withouthotair.com]

51. Harvey, L. D. Danny. 2010. *Energy and the New Reality 1: Energy Efficiency and the Demand for Energy Services*. London, UK: Earthscan.
Harvey, L. D. Danny. 2010. *Energy and the New Reality 2: Carbon-Free Energy Supply*. London, UK: Earthscan.
52. Sherwin Jr., Elton B. 2010. *Addicted to Energy: A Venture Capitalist's Perspective on How to Save Our Economy and our Climate*. Energy House Publishing.
53. CCST. 2011. *California's Energy Future: The View to 2050 (Summary Report)*. Sacramento, CA: California Council on Science and Technology. May. [http://www.ccst.us/publications/2011/2011energy.pdf]
54. Lovins, Amory B., E. Kyle Datta, Thomas Feiler, Karl R. Rábago, Joel N. Swisher, Andrew Lehmann, and Ken Wicker. 2002. *Small is Profitable: The Hidden Economic Benefits of Making Electrical Resources the Right Size*. Old Snowmass, CO: Rocky Mountain Institute. [http://www.smallisprofitable.org/]
55. Lovins, Amory B., E. Kyle Datta, Odd-Even Bustnes, Jonathan G. Koomey, and Nathan J. Glasgow. 2004. *Winning the Oil Endgame: Innovation for Profits, Jobs, and Security*. Old Snowmass, Colorado: Rocky Mountain Institute. September. [http://www.oilendgame.com]
56. Lovins, Amory B., Mathias Bell, Lionel Bony, Albert Chan, Stephen Doig, Nathan J. Glasgow, Lena Hansen, Virginia Lacy, Eric Maurer, Jesse Morris, James Newcomb, Greg Rucks, and Caroline Traube. 2011. *Reinventing Fire: Bold Business Solutions for the New Energy Era*. White River Junction, VT: Chelsea Green Publishing.
57. Lovins, Amory B. 2005. *Energy End-Use Efficiency*. Rocky Mountain Institute for InterAcademy Council (Amsterdam). September 19. [http://www.rmi.org/images/other/Energy/E05-16_EnergyEndUseEff.pdf]
58. Goldstein, David B. 2010. *Invisible Energy: Strategies to Rescue the Economy and Save the Planet*. Pt. Richmond, CA: Bay Tree Publishing.
59. Thorpe, Ann. 2007. *The Designer's Atlas of Sustainability: Charting the Conceptual Landscape through Economy, Ecology, and Culture*. Washington, DC: Island Press.
60. Wigley, Tom. 2011. "Coal to gas: the influence of methane leakage." *Climatic Change*. vol. 108, no. 3. pp. 601-608. [http://dx.doi.org/10.1007/s10584-011-0217-3], p. 607.
61. De La Chesnaye, Francisco C., and John P. Weyant. 2006. "Special issue: EMF 21 Multi-Greenhouse Gas Mitigation and Climate Policy." *Energy Journal*. vol. 27. Special issue #3. December. [http://emf.stanford.edu/files/pubs/22519/SpecialIssueEMF21.pdf]
62. On landfill methane, see [http://www.epa.gov/lmop/publications-tools/]. On coal bed methane see [http://www.epa.gov/cmop/docs/2008_mine_vent_symp.pdf], [http://www.unece.org/energy/se/cmm.html] and [http://www.epa.gov/cmop/resources/technical_options.html]. For methane emissions reductions from oil and gas systems, see [http://www.epa.gov/gasstar/tools/recommended.html].
63. See [http://www.iiasa.ac.at/Admin/INF/feature_articles/Options/2010/November/short_lived_pollutants.html], [http://www.beyondhfcs.org/files/studies/iiasa-hfcs-eu-27.pdf], [http://www.iiasa.ac.at/rains/reports/IR-07-nonCO2-final_27May2008.pdf], and [http://www.iiasa.ac.at/Research/GGI/publications/Rao_Riahi2005/index.html]
64. [http://globalchange.mit.edu/files/document/MITJPSPGC_Reprint06-10.pdf]
65. [http://www.globalchange.umd.edu/publications/?search=methane]
66. [http://www.catf.us/resources/whitepapers/files/Methane-Tapping_the_Untapped_Potential.pdf]
67. Osterwalder, Alexander, and Yves Pigneur. 2010. *Business Model Generation: A*

*Handbook for Visionaries, Game Changers, and Challengers*. Hoboken, NJ: John Wiley and Sons.

68. See chapter 38 of Koomey, Jonathan. 2008. *Turning Numbers into Knowledge: Mastering the Art of Problem Solving*. 2nd ed. Oakland, CA: Analytics Press. [http://www.analytics-press.com].

69. [http://HomeEnergySaver.lbl.gov]

70. [http://hes.lbl.gov/consumer/licensing]

71. Atkyns, Robert, Michele Blazek, and Joseph Roitz. 2002. "Measurement of environmental impacts of telework adoption amidst change in complex organizations: AT&T survey methodology and results." *Resources, Conservation, and Recycling*. vol. 36, no. 3. October. pp. 267-285.

72. Weber, Christopher, Jonathan G. Koomey, and Scott Matthews. 2010. "The Energy and Climate Change Impacts of Different Music Delivery Methods." *The Journal of Industrial Ecology*. vol. 14, no. 5. October. pp. 754–769. [http://dx.doi.org/10.1111/j.1530-9290.2010.00269.x]

73. The Climate Group. 2008. *SMART 2020: Enabling the low carbon economy in the information age*. London, UK: The Climate Group. [http://www.smart2020.org/]

74. Brynjolfsson, Erik, and Lorin M. Hitt. 1996. "Paradox Lost?: Firm-level Evidence on the Returns to Information Systems Spending." *Management Science*. vol. 42, no. 4. April. pp. 541-558.

75. Brynjolfsson, Erik, and Lorin M. Hitt. 2000. "Beyond Computation: Information Technology, Organizational Transformation and Business Performance." *Journal of Economic Perspectives*. vol. 14, no. 4. Fall. pp. 23-48.

76. Brynjolfsson, Erik, and Andrew McAfee. 2011. *Race Against The Machine: How the Digital Revolution is Accelerating Innovation, Driving Productivity, and Irreversibly Transforming Employment and the Economy*. Digital Frontier Press. [http://raceagainst-themachine.com/]

77. Brynjolfsson, Erik, and Lorin M. Hitt. 2000. "Beyond Computation: Information Technology, Organizational Transformation and Business Performance." *Journal of Economic Perspectives*. vol. 14, no. 4. Fall. pp. 23-48.

78. Koomey, Jonathan G., Stephen Berard, Marla Sanchez, and Henry Wong. 2011. "Implications of Historical Trends in the Electrical Efficiency of Computing." *IEEE Annals of the History of Computing*. vol. 33, no. 3. July-September. pp. 46-54. [http://doi.ieeecomputersociety.org/10.1109/MAHC.2010.28]

79. Greene, Kate. 2011. "A New and Improved Moore's Law." In *Technology Review*. September 12. [http://www.technologyreview.com/computing/38548/?p1=A1]
   "A deeper law than Moore's?" In *The Economist*. October 10, 2011. [http://www.economist.com/blogs/dailychart/2011/10/computing-power]

80. Eisenberg, Anne. 2010. "Bye-Bye Batteries: Radio Waves as a Low-Power Source." *The New York Times*. New York, NY. July 18. p. BU3. [http://www.nytimes.com/2010/07/18/business/18novel.html]

81. [http://bigbellysolar.com/]

82. For a brief CEO-level treatment of the response of how businesses should respond to the climate issue see Hoffman, Andrew J., and John G. Woody. 2008. *Climate Change: What's Your Business Strategy?* Boston, MA: Harvard Business Press.
   For a more detailed treatment that discusses both opportunities and downside risks of integrating environmental concerns with business operations, see Esty, Daniel C., and

Andrew S. Winston. 2009. *Green to Gold: How Smart Companies Use Environmental Strategy to Innovate, Create Value, and Build Competitive Advantage*. Hoboken, NJ: John Wiley & Sons, Inc. [http://www.eco-advantage.com/]

83. Consider the example of CVS Pharmacies, which distributes innovations in ordering and other processes to thousands of stores worldwide once they've been tested in a few stores: McAfee, Andrew, and Erik Brynjolfsson. 2008. "Investing in the IT that Makes a Competitive Difference." *Harvard Business Review*. July-August. pp. 98-108.

84. Lovins, Amory B., Mathias Bell, Lionel Bony, Albert Chan, Stephen Doig, Nathan J. Glasgow, Lena Hansen, Virginia Lacy, Eric Maurer, Jesse Morris, James Newcomb, Greg Rucks, and Caroline Traube. 2011. *Reinventing Fire: Bold Business Solutions for the New Energy Era*. White River Junction, VT: Chelsea Green Publishing, p. 157.

85. For a description of four ways cloud computing providers have become more efficient, see [http://www.koomey.com/post/8014999803].

86. Koomey, Jonathan. 2011. *Growth in data center electricity use 2005 to 2010*. Oakland, CA: Analytics Press. August 1. [http://www.analyticspress.com/datacenters.html]

87. See, for example [http://www.google.com/about/datacenters/], [http://opencompute.org/], and [http://www.datacenterknowledge.com/archives/2008/10/20/microsoft-pue-of-122-for-data-center-containers/]

## Chapter 7

1. [http://www.skepticalscience.com]

2. Cook, John. 2010. *A Scientific Guide to Global Warming Skepticism*. Warner, Australia: University of Queensland. December 8. [http://sks.to/guide]

3. Cook, John, and Stephan Lewandowsky. 2011. *The Debunking Handbook*. November. [http://sks.to/debunk]

4. [http://www.realclimate.org/]

5. [http://thinkprogress.org/romm/issue/]

6. [http://www.climatesciencewatch.org/]

7. Doran, Peter T., and Maggie Kendall Zimmerman. 2009. "Examining the Scientific Consensus on Climate Change." *Eos Trans. AGU*. vol. 90, no. 3. [http://dx.doi.org/10.1029/2009EO030002]

   Oreskes, Naomi. 2004. "The Scientific Consensus on Climate Change." *Science*. vol. 306, no. 5702. December 3, 2004. pp. 1686. [http://www.sciencemag.org/content/306/5702/1686.short]

   Anderegg, William R. L., James W. Prall, Jacob Harold, and Stephen H. Schneider. 2010. "Expert credibility in climate change." *Proceedings of the National Academy of Sciences*. June 21. [http://www.pnas.org/content/early/2010/06/04/1003187107.abstract]

8. One recent study found that only 39% of the US public correctly knows that most scientists are convinced that global warming is happening, while 3% believe that scientists don't think global warming is happening, and 40% state that there is still a lot of disagreement in the scientific community about this question. Leiserowitz, Anthony, Edward Malbach, Connie Roser-Renouf, and Nicholas Smith. 2011. *Global Warming's Six Americas in May 2011*. New Haven, CT: Yale University and George Mason University, Yale Project on Climate Change Communications. May. [http://environment.yale.edu/climate/files/SixAmericasMay2011.pdf]

9. Oreskes, Naomi, and Eric M. Conway. 2010. *Merchants of Doubt: How a Handful of Scientists Obscured the Truth on Issues from Tobacco Smoke to Global Warming*. New

York, NY: Bloomsbury Press.

    Hoggan, James, and Richard Littlemore. 2009. *Climate Cover-Up: The Crusade to Deny Global Warming*. Vancouver BC, Canada: Greystone Books.

    Hanley, Charles J. 2011. "The American 'allergy' to global warming: Why?" *The Associated Press*. September 25. [http://www.google.com/hostednews/ap/article/ALeqM5h chUFDTcFVXkIzVWWH9iYGIXmCtw?docId=d837de45d0f44d3e8d178949d13b180c]

10. Donner, Simon D. 2011. "Making the climate a part of the human world." *In press at the Bulletin of the American Meteorological Society*. October. [http://journals.ametsoc.org/doi/pdf/10.1175/2011BAMS3219.1]

11. Washington, Haydn, and John Cook. 2011. *Climate Change Denial: Heads in the Sand*. London, UK: Routledge.

12. ibid.

13. Associated Press Writer. 2010. "Pennsylvania global warming researcher calls self 'skeptic'." *Associated Press*. March 29. [http://adstest.climate.weather.com/articles/ap-global-warming-researcher-calls-self-skeptic.html]

14. For a comprehensive investigation of all of the bad actors and their antics, see Powell, James Lawrence. 2011. *The Inquisition of Climate Science*. New York, NY: Columbia University Press.

15. In this category I place Bjorn Lomborg, a man whom I debated in April 2010. He's a very nice fellow, and I would enjoy chatting (and sparring) with him again, but that doesn't make his arguments any more correct.

16. Leiserowitz, Anthony, Edward Malbach, Connie Roser-Renouf, and Nicholas Smith. 2011. *Global Warming's Six Americas in May 2011*. New Haven, CT: Yale University and George Mason University, Yale Project on Climate Change Communications. May. [http://environment.yale.edu/climate/files/SixAmericasMay2011.pdf]

17. Happer, William. 2011. "The Truth About Greenhouse Gases: The dubious science of the climate crusaders." In *First Things*. June/July. pp. [http://www.firstthings.com/article/2011/05/the-truth-about-greenhouse-gases]

18. This view also implicitly reflects the incorrect belief that reducing energy use must therefore reduce economic activity, but that's not the main point here.

19. Oreskes, Naomi, and Eric M. Conway. 2010. *Merchants of Doubt: How a Handful of Scientists Obscured the Truth on Issues from Tobacco Smoke to Global Warming*. New York, NY: Bloomsbury Press. p. 249.

20. McMillan, John. 2003. *Reinventing the Bazaar: A Natural History of Markets*. New York, NY: W.W. Norton & Company, describes the socially constructed nature of different markets. It's a must-read for those thinking deeply about property rights and market structure.

21. Sagoff has argued that climate is not a market failure in a formal sense because there are no markets that would allow exchanges between the present and the future. His article is worth a read if you are a connoisseur of these issues. Sagoff, Mark. 2011. "Chapter 4: The Poverty of Climate Economics." In *The Oxford Handbook of Climate Change and Society*. Edited by J. S. Dryzek, R. B. Norgaard and D. Schlosberg. Oxford, UK: Oxford University Press. pp. 55-66.

22. [http://www.skepticalscience.com/] has the complete list.

23. [http://www.skepticalscience.com/]

24. IPCC. 2007. *Climate Change 2007: Impacts, Adaptation, and Vulnerability— Contribution of Working Group II to the Fourth Assessment Report of the Intergovernmental Panel on Climate Change* [M. Parry, O. Canziani, J. Palutikof, P. van

der Linden, C. Hanson (eds.)]. Cambridge, United Kingdom and New York, NY, USA: Cambridge University Press. [http://www.ipcc.ch/publications_and_data/publications_and_data_reports.shtml], p.493.

25. [http://www.skepticalscience.com/IPCC-Himalayan-glacier-2035-prediction-intermediate.htm]

26. Diethelm, Pascal, and Martin McKee. 2009. "Denialism: what is it and how should scientists respond?" *The European Journal of Public Health*. vol. 19, no. 1. January 1, 2009. pp. 2-4. [http://eurpub.oxfordjournals.org/content/19/1/2.short]

27. Washington, Haydn, and John Cook. 2011. *Climate Change Denial: Heads in the Sand*. London, UK: Routledge.

28. [http://www.skepticalscience.com/Climategate-CRU-emails-hacked-intermediate.htm]

29. ibid.

30. For example, see [http://skepticalscience.com/Kevin-Trenberth-travesty-cant-account-for-the-lack-of-warming.htm].

31. The definitive debunking of this particular widely used canard is Goodstein, Eban. 1999. *The Trade-Off Myth: Fact and Fiction About Jobs and the Environment*. Washington, DC: Island Press. This book also gives examples of the persistent tendency for forecasts of the costs of meeting regulations to overstate actual costs substantially.

32. Quoted by Tom Friedman of the New York Times: [http://www.nytimes.com/2007/04/15/opinion/15iht-web-0415edgreen-full.5291830.html]

33. [http://thinkprogress.org/romm/2011/10/19/347768/senator-whitehouses-climate-speech/]

34. NAS. 2010. *Advancing the Science of Climate Change*. Washington, DC: National Academy of Sciences. [http://www.nap.edu/catalog.php?record_id=12782].

35. [http://en.wikipedia.org/wiki/Oldest_people]

36. Kessler, Glenn. 2011. "Rick Perry's made-up 'facts' about climate change." *The Washington Post*. Washington, DC. August 18. p. [http://www.washingtonpost.com/blogs/fact-checker/post/rick-perrys-made-up-facts-about-climate-change/2011/08/17/gIQApV-F5LJ_blog.html]

37. Brandt, Allan M. 2007. *The Cigarette Century: The Rise, Fall, and Deadly Persistence of the Product that Defined America*. New York, NY: Basic Books.

38. The late Stephen Schneider asked "can democracy survive complexity?", which is exactly the right question. We'd better hope the answer is yes. Schneider, Stephen H. 2009. *Science as a Contact Sport: Inside the Battle to Save Earth's Climate*. Washington, DC: National Geographic. pp. 259-260.

39. This line of argument is eloquently developed in the first few chapters of Orr, David W. 2009. *Down to the Wire: Confronting Climate Collapse*. Oxford, UK: Oxford University Press.

40. de Soto, Hernando. 2003. *The Mystery of Capital: Why Capitalism Triumphs in the West and Fails Everywhere Else*. New York, NY: Basic Books.
    McMillan, John. 2003. *Reinventing the Bazaar: A Natural History of Markets*. New York, NY: W.W. Norton & Company.

41. The structure of government itself can affect the incentives of those in government to protect the environment, as Tom Friedman explains using the example of Costa Rica: [http://www.nytimes.com/2009/04/12/opinion/12friedman.html].

42. Marquis, Christopher, Andrew Klaber, and Bobbi Thomason. 2010. *HBS Case Study: B Lab—Building a New Sector of the Economy*. Cambridge, MA: Harvard Business School.

9-411-047. September 27. [http://hbr.org/product/b-lab-building-a-new-sector-of-the-economy/an/411047-PDF-ENG]

43. DeCanio, Stephen J. 2003. *Economic Models of Climate Change: A Critique*. Basingstoke, UK: Palgrave-Macmillan. pp. 11-12

## Chapter 8

1. I'm hopeful that Winston Churchill's reading of the American character was correct when he said "You can always count on Americans to do the right thing—after they've tried everything else."

2. I'm indebted to Stephen J. DeCanio for this insight.

3. DeCanio, Stephen J., and Anders Fremstad. 2011. "Game theory and climate diplomacy." *Ecological Economics (in press)*. [http://www.sciencedirect.com/science/article/pii/S0921800911001698]

4. Laitner, John A. "Skip", Stephen J. DeCanio, Jonathan G. Koomey, and Alan H. Sanstad. 2003. "Room for Improvement: Increasing the Value of Energy Modeling for Policy Analysis." *Utilities Policy (also LBNL-50627)*. vol. 11, no. 2. June. pp. 87-94.

5. For example, the total solar radiation reaching the earth's surface is 89,000 terawatts, compared to total human energy consumption (expressed as power) of around 14 terawatts in 2000. Incoming solar radiation from [http://en.wikipedia.org/wiki/File:Breakdown_of_the_incoming_solar_energy.svg]. Total world energy consumption from Grubler, Arnulf. 2008. "Energy transitions." In *Encyclopedia of Earth*. Edited by C. J. Cleveland. Washington, D.C.: Environmental Information Coalition, National Council for Science and the Environment. [http://www.iiasa.ac.at/~gruebler/Data/EoE_Data.html]. There is also a significant heat flow from the earth's core that can be tapped as geothermal energy, and that source is one that is only now beginning to be explored in a serious way [http://blog.smu.edu/research/2011/10/25/vast-coast-to-coast-clean-energy-source-confirmed-by-first-google-org-funded-geothermal-mapping-report/].

6. For one view of how to use renewables to phase out fossil fuels and power the global economy, see Lovins, Amory B., Mathias Bell, Lionel Bony, Albert Chan, Stephen Doig, Nathan J. Glasgow, Lena Hansen, Virginia Lacy, Eric Maurer, Jesse Morris, James Newcomb, Greg Rucks, and Caroline Traube. 2011. *Reinventing Fire: Bold Business Solutions for the New Energy Era*. White River Junction, VT: Chelsea Green Publishing.
    Also see Jacobson, Mark Z., and Mark A. Delucchi. 2011. "Providing all global energy with wind, water, and solar power, Part I: Technologies, energy resources, quantities and areas of infrastructure, and materials." *Energy Policy*. vol. 39, no. 3. March. pp. 1154-1169. [http://www.sciencedirect.com/science/article/pii/S0301421510008645]
    Delucchi, Mark A., and Mark Z. Jacobson. 2011. "Providing all global energy with wind, water, and solar power, Part II: Reliability, system and transmission costs, and policies." *Energy Policy*. vol. 39, no. 3. March. pp. 1170-1190. [http://www.sciencedirect.com/science/article/pii/S0301421510008694]

7. Woolsey, R. James, and Anne Korin. 2007. "Turning Oil into Salt." In *National Review*. September 25. [http://www.nationalreview.com/articles/222256/turning-oil-salt/r-james-woolsey]

8. [http://i.usatoday.net/news/opinion/cartoons/2009/December/e091207_pett.jpg]

# INDEX

academia, 3
Adams, John, 11
Arrhenius, Svante, 15, 17

Brynjolfsson, Erik, 92
business-as-usual (BAU) case, 41–43, 106

capital stocks, turnover of, xviii, 50–51,
    52f, 74-80, 76f
carbon dioxide ($CO_2$) emissions. *See* green-
    house gas (GHG) emissions
carbon dioxide ($CO_2$)-equivalent concen-
    trations
    calculating, 31, 54
    *See also* greenhouse gas (GHG)-
        equivalent concentrations
carbon emissions. *See* greenhouse gas
    (GHG) emissions
carbon sequestration, 54, 60, 183
China, 12, 85, 107, 146
choices, value, 48, 152
choices, values, and path dependence, 6
Churchill, Winston, 73
Clean Energies Futures study, 107
climate change
    factors contributing to, 11–15, 13f,
        31–33, 32f
    future, 21–23, 33–35
    impact on human and natural systems,
        35–37
    initial discovery of, 15, 17
    misunderstandings regarding, 7
    public knowledge and beliefs about, 127
    scientific evidence for, 11–20
    standard application of benefit-cost anal-
        ysis to, 63–64, 64f, 68–70, 150 (*see
        also* cost-benefit analysis)

*See also specific topics*
climate change debate
    state of the, 124–26
    who's who in the, 126–28
    *See also specific topics*
Climate Progress, 124
Climate Science Watch, 124
climate sensitivity to changes in GHG con-
    centrations, 17, 21–23, 33–34
climate stabilization, importance and
    urgency of, 7, 37
coal companies, revenues of, 157, 160t
coal plants, 1, 26–27, 45, 78
collaborative design services, 120
"commissioning," 79
computing, 119–20
    historical trends in the efficiency of, 114–
        15, 116f
computing services, cost of delivering, 119
Cook, John, 128
cooling, power required for, xii
Corning Glass, 97–98
cost effectiveness, xvi, 49, 70
cost-benefit analysis, 49, 63–64, 64f, 71, 150
Crane, Peter, 3

*Debunking Handbook, The* (Cook), 124
Decanio, Stephen, 70, 136–37, 141
"delayers," 126
denier arguments, categories of, 126–27,
    130–32
deniers, climate change, 123–26
    strategy used by supporters of, 131–32
    validity of points made by, 128–30
    *See also* climate change debate
*Designer's Atlas of Sustainability* (Thorpe),
    109

## ABOUT THE AUTHOR

Credit: Grigorieff Photography

**Jonathan Koomey** understands the climate issue as only an entrepreneurial scientist can. He's been part of the climate debate for more than two decades, as a scientist at one of the nation's foremost research labs, as a Consulting Professor at Stanford University, and as a visiting professor at Stanford University (2004–5 and 2008), Yale University (2009), and most recently at the University of California at Berkeley (2011). He is the author or coauthor of more than 150 articles and reports, as well as ten books, including the first comprehensive analysis of the implications of a 2-degree warming limit in 1989 (twenty years before the G8 nations accepted this normative target). He has been a technical advisor to half a dozen startup companies, and was a judge and advisor for the 2005 California Clean Tech Open.

## ABOUT ANALYTICS PRESS

**Analytics Press** teaches critical thinking skills and business analytics by publishing books, course materials, and software, and by organizing seminars and workshops. For more details, contact us at http://www.analyticspress.com or Analytics Press, P.O. Box 1545, Burlingame, CA 94011-1545.

***Show Me the Numbers: Designing Tables and Graphs to Enlighten***, by Stephen Few, is the first practical and comprehensive guide to table and graph design written specifically for the needs of business. If you create tables and graphs or manage those who do, this book will alleviate countless hours of confusion and frustration.

***Now You See It, by Stephen Few,*** does for visual data analysis what Few did for data presentation in *Show Me the Numbers*. It teaches practical techniques that anyone can use—only this time they're for making sense of information, not presenting it.

***Turning Numbers into Knowledge: Mastering the Art of Problem Solving***, by Jonathan G. Koomey, Ph.D., is a lively and entertaining guide to making informed professional and personal choices. Its insights help people beat information overload, hone their decision-making skills, and achieve success in this information-glutted world.